The Civilization of the American Indian Series

(Complete list on page 239)

Peter Pitchlynn: Chief of the Choctaws

"The Snapping Turtle–Choctaw," George Catlin's portrait of Peter Pitchlynn, chief and delegate of the Choctaw Nation, 1806–1881. (Courtesy National Collection of Fine Arts, Smithsonian Institution)

Peter Pitchlynn:
CHIEF OF THE CHOCTAWS

by W. David Baird

University of Oklahoma Press

Norman

International Standard Book Number: 0–8061–0991–2

Library of Congress Catalog Card Number: 72–177331

Peter Pitchlynn: Chief of the Choctaws is Volume 116 in *The Civilization of the American Indian Series.*

For my mother and father,
Faye and Everette Baird

Preface

The Thomas Gilcrease Institute of American History and Art in Tulsa, Oklahoma, is noted for its exceptional collection of western American art. Almost as impressive though not as well known are its manuscript holdings. This pleasant fact became apparent to me some years ago when I was doing research on the educational development of the Choctaw Indians, one of the Five Civilized Tribes. The collection of most assistance to me contained the papers of Peter Pitchlynn and comprised some twenty-one feet of manuscript resources. For a historian to locate such a wealth of untapped materials was analogous to Patrick McLaughlin and Peter O'Riley's discovery of the Comstock Lode. With my interest in the Choctaws and my general acquaintance with Pitchlynn's historical contributions, I made a resolution then to do a biographical study of the man. Fortunately other documents recording his career had also been preserved. Excellent manuscript and archival materials are available at the Oklahoma Historical Society, Oklahoma City; the Western History Collection of the University of Oklahoma Library, Norman; and the National Archives, Washington, D.C. These, along with the Gilcrease materials, have made it possible to reconstruct Pitchlynn's life with reasonable accuracy, something that the lack of documents makes impossible for most of the tribal leaders of the era.

Peter Pitchlynn deserves a biography. Born in 1806, he was an intrinsically interesting man. With a European father and a half-blood Choctaw mother, he was genetically and environmentally more white than red. In many ways the circumstances of his birth denied him total admission into traditional Indian society, but it also gave him advantages that enabled him to assume a position of leadership in the tribe. Identifying with the Indians, he played an important part in Choctaw affairs prior to, during, and after removal to Oklahoma. In the West, he either wrote or influenced the several tribal constitutions adopted during the nineteenth century and then participated in the governments created by them. Pitchlynn was architect of the educational system and the principal Choctaw spokesman during diplomatic negotiations with other Indians and the United States. He represented the tribe's financial interests in Washington from 1853 until 1881 except for the Civil War years when he returned to Indian Territory. During the critical months of 1864, the Choctaws overlooked his white blood and elected him chief of the tribe, an accomplishment that highlighted a remarkable career.

As an individual Pitchlynn was at the same time the product of his era and of two cultures, exhibiting the strengths and weaknesses of both. The nineteenth century brought a period of phenomenal economic growth to the United States. The market place and industrial expansion provided exciting and unprecedented opportunities for financial gain. First an observer, Pitchlynn soon became a participant in the economic system and, like other Americans of the era, sought his fortune in speculation and occasionally even peculation instead of agricultural toil. Culturally, his life also reflected both white and Indian characteristics. In addition to the economic system, he embraced the white man's religion, his method of education, and his social accouterments. Yet, at the same time, he retained the Indian's sense of oneness with nature, his pride in his heritage, and his insistence upon common ownership of tribal properties. Adopting such diverse cultural attributes and affected by the times in which he lived, Pitchlynn could not help developing an extremely complex personality and life style.

But the real significance of Pitchlynn's life is not that he was influenced by the era or the clash of two cultures, but that his story is to a large extent also the story of the Choctaws. His life coincided with the most dramatic alterations in the tribal society, geographic location, economic development, and political evolution. What is more, at every critical stage of tribal history during the nineteenth century, he either observed the events or played a crucial role. Consequently, any student of the Choctaws is obliged to consider the career of Peter Pitchlynn, and any biographer of Pitchlynn must relate at least in part the story of the tribe. It is wholly impossible to present one without the other.

The primary objective of this book is to tell a story that deserves to be told. Peter Pitchlynn was an important Indian personality and the Choctaws a major Indian tribe. It is rare that historians have the chance to observe tribal reaction to government policy and white social contact from the Indian point of view; Pitchlynn's life, despite his white blood, permits just such an opportunity. It also provides other insights—this man who was the product of two cultures was never fully accepted by either. Also, implicit in the chronicling of Pitchlynn's all-consuming interest, the so-called net proceeds claim, is the chaos that can result when a well-developed society imposes its standards and mores upon a less sophisticated one. Finally, this volume examines aspects of Choctaw history that a general survey cannot possibly consider.

If the book meets its objectives, it is due in no small measure to the generous assistance of friends and family. Very special thanks go to my mentor, Professor A. M. Gibson, University of Oklahoma, who patiently directed and gently corrected every aspect of the manuscript. Professors Donald J. Berthrong, Purdue University, Gilbert C. Fite, Eastern Illinois University, and Walter Rundell, Jr., Iowa State University, all took time from their busy schedules to read the biography and offer helpful suggestions for its improvement. Numerous discussions with my colleagues, Professors James J. Hudson and Walter L. Brown, have materially aided the completion of this study. Also, I am especially indebted to Professor Orland Maxfield, University of Arkansas, for preparing the maps and to the University of Arkansas Research Committee for its generous financial assistance.

I would be remiss not to extend my appreciation to Mrs. Rella Looney at the Oklahoma Historical Society, to Mr. Pat Edwards and Mrs. Marie Keen at the Gilcrease Institute, to Mr. Jack Haley at the University of Oklahoma Library, and to Mrs. Laura D. S. Harrell at the Department of Archives and History, Jackson, Mississippi. Furthermore, the research could not have been completed without the hospitality of Mr. and Mrs. Dale Tacker and Mr. and Mrs. Mike Hornsby, all of Tulsa, Oklahoma. Nor could this work have been accomplished without the special interest of my brother, Marvin Baird, McLean, Virginia. I thank them all for their support and confidence. Finally, to my wife, Jane, who cheerfully typed the manuscript in its early stages and also assumed my responsibilities at home, I express my gratitude, my admiration, and my love.

W. DAVID BAIRD

Fayetteville, Arkansas
August 11, 1971

Contents

Illustrations

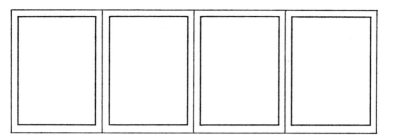

Maps

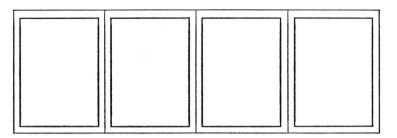

List of Abbreviations

The following abbreviations are used in the footnotes:

G.M.	Gilcrease (Museum)
N.A.	National Archives
O.H.S.	Oklahoma Historical Society
O.I.A.	Office of Indian Affairs
U.O.L.	University of Oklahoma Library
U.T.L.	University of Texas Library

Peter Pitchlynn: Chief of the Choctaws

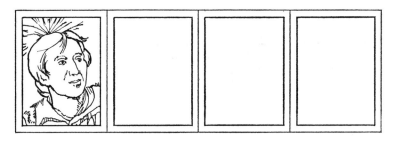

CHAPTER I

The Pitchlynn Heritage

The first Europeans to encounter the Choctaw Indians found them in what is now central and southern Mississippi. Proud and practical, the Choctaws were excellent agriculturalists, raising large quantities of corn as well as beans, pumpkins, and melons. They were more patient and calculating than warlike or religious, and placed great stock in their governmental system. The nation was divided into three politically independent districts—the Northeastern, the Southern, and the Northwestern—over each of which presided a chief who with his two counterparts and other regional leaders met periodically in a national council. Everything considered, the Choctaws were little distinguished from other Muskhogean tribes except for their tendency to imitate and adopt "the customs of the more advanced and more numerous race with which they came in contact."[1]

The Choctaws first met the "more numerous race" in 1540 when Hernando de Soto made his way from the Gulf of Mex-

[1] Angie Debo, *The Rise and Fall of the Choctaw Republic*, 10, 11, 23; John R. Swanton, *Source Material for the Social and Ceremonial Life of the Choctaw Indians*.

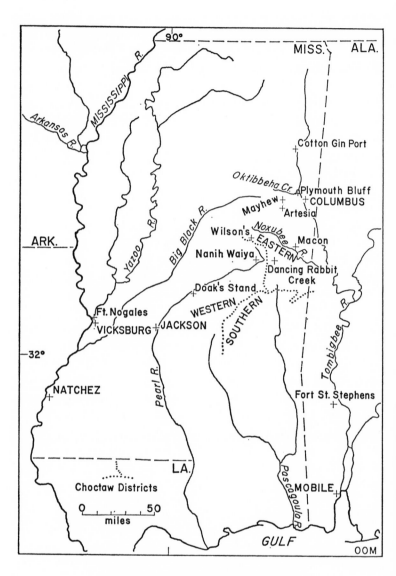

CHOCTAW NATION BEFORE REMOVAL

ico to the Mississippi River. This expedition represented the initial interest of Spain in what is now the southeastern United States, an interest that was soon contested by other international powers. In the late seventeenth century first French and then British nationals also appeared among the Choctaws and, like their Spanish rivals, sought either to trade with the Indians or make military allies of them. The sons of France, one of whom was the progenitor of the famous LeFlore family, successfully dominated the tribe throughout the first half of the eighteenth century. But the Peace of Paris in 1763 which terminated the French and Indian War forced France to abandon her favored position among the Choctaws and to withdraw entirely from the vast American West. That treaty left only the Spaniards and the British to contest for the allegiance of the Choctaws.

Among the many British traders and agents who traveled to the interior was Isaac Pitchlynn, the grandfather of Peter Perkins Pitchlynn.[2] Isaac's genesis and exact mission unfortunately were not recorded. A contemporary wrote that he was a British officer on his way from the East Coast to the Natchez settlements, while a more recent authority has asserted that he was a Tory merchant. Despite this confusion, Isaac Pitchlynn's importance lay not in his profession but in his symbolization of British interest in the contested region. Destiny limited his role, however, for on his initial journey into the Choctaw country in late 1774 he died from some unknown affliction, leaving to the care of the tribe his son, John.[3]

[2] Apparently the Pitchlynn name originated with a resident of King's *Lynn*, England who worked with *pitch*. The information comes from the great-grandson of Peter Perkins Pitchlynn, Peter Paul Pitchlynn, now a resident of Tulsa, Oklahoma, who researched the name at Somerset House, London.

[3] Compare the letter fragment by William S. Halbert, Box 31, Vol. LX, 413, Foreman Collection, Gilcrease Museum (hereinafter G.M.), with Mary Elizabeth Young, *Redskins, Ruffleshirts, and Rednecks*, 25; John Pitchlynn,

Little was recorded about the childhood of John Pitchlynn prior to his arrival among the Indians. Authorities agree that he was born on a ship lying off the Caribbean island of St. Thomas during the 1750's, probably about 1756. Of his mother we know only that she had relatives in Georgia, and of his childhood only that he had the advantage of some education. He must have arrived in the Choctaw Nation when he was eighteen. Settling within the eastern part of the tribal lands after the death of his father, Pitchlynn found already resident the three Folsom brothers, Nathaniel, Ebenezer, and Edmund. Tribal members quickly accepted him as a friend, adviser, and trader, and though the dates are extremely imprecise, early in the 1780's he took as his first wife Rhoda Folsom, the half-blood daughter of Ebenezer. They had three sons who reached maturity, James, John, Jr., and Joseph C.[4]

At least until 1806, John resided in the vicinity of present-day Macon, Mississippi, on the Noxubee River, a tributary of the Tombigbee. The year before, his first wife having died, he had married for a second time, choosing as his wife Sophia Folsom, one of Nathaniel's twenty-five half-blood children.[5] Before 1825, the second Mrs. John Pitchlynn gave birth to eight children who later reached maturity—Peter Perkins, Silas, Mary, Rhoda, Thomas, Eliza, Elizabeth, and Kiziah. Thus, like others of his time, John Pitchlynn fathered a large family, at least eleven of whom reached adulthood.

By 1810, John had moved from Noxubee River and had re-

Subject File, Mississippi Department of Archives and History (hereinafter Miss. Archives). The British Public Record Office could find no record of the service of Isaac Pitchlynn.

[4] William A. Love, "Lowndes County, Its Antiquities and Pioneer Settlers," *Publications of the Mississippi Historical Society*, Vol. VII 363–65; Gideon Lincecum, "Autobiography," *Publications of the Mississippi Historical Society*, Vol. VIII, 472.

[5] H. B. Cushman, *History of the Choctaw, Chickasaw, and Natchez Indians*, 332 (hereinafter *History of the Indians*).

settled on the west bank of the Tombigbee River near its junction with Oktibbeha Creek, a point about five miles north of present Columbus, Mississippi. Located in the Northeastern District and known locally as Plymouth Bluff, his trading post became an important crossroads and trading center on the famous Gaines' Trace. George S. Gaines, a transplanted Virginian, in 1807 headed the United States trading post at Fort St. Stevens on the lower Tombigbee. To get supplies to that frontier outpost, after 1810 the government freighted goods down the Ohio and up the Tennessee River to Colbert's Ferry in northwestern Alabama. From that point Gaines transported the provisions overland in a southwesterly direction to Pitchlynn's post at Plymouth Bluff, where boats were constructed and from which merchandise was floated down the Tombigbee to Fort St. Stevens.[6] For the Pitchlynns, Gaines' Trace reduced their isolation, re-emphasized the non-Indian aspects of their home environment, and alienated them somewhat from traditional Choctaw society.

A resourceful man, John Pitchlynn was soon engaged in economic activities other than trading. He owned large herds of cattle which he grazed on the nearby prairies, and, when cotton culture became profitable, he invested sizable sums in slaves, equipment, and improved lands. Cotton was his principal agricultural interest, but corn was also important. Joint owner of a stage line that connected Columbus with Jackson, Mississippi, on occasion he also acted as banker, frequently lending money in amounts of more than a thousand dollars.[7]

While John Pitchlynn grew in prestige and wealth, the final phases of the international struggle for Choctaw allegiance

[6] *Mobile Daily Tribune*, Gaines MSS, Vol. E, Miss. Archives; George J. Leftwich, "Cotton Gin Port and Gaines' Trace," *Publications of the Mississippi Historical Society*, Vol. VII, 266.

[7] Probate Records of John Pitchlynn, Estate Docket 92, Records of the Chancery Courts, Lowndes County; John Pitchlynn to Peter Pitchlynn, March 14, 1824, Pitchlynn MSS, G.M.

commenced. After the American Revolution and by the terms of the second Treaty of Paris in 1783, Britain divided her interest south of Canada between the United States and the Spanish Empire, the latter regaining control of East and West Florida. Whether Spain retained her presence on the Gulf Coast and especially her claim to lands north of the thirty-first parallel depended in large measure upon her success in winning the support of the southeastern Indians. At the same time, foreign influence along the lower Mississippi Valley seemed to endanger the continuation of the American confederated government. The ensuing contest between the Old and the New World powers for domination of the Indian tribes lasted until the Adams-Onís Treaty of 1819.

In the early approaches to the Choctaws, the Americans won the first round. In December, 1785, after a fatiguing journey of seventy-seven days and constant harassment by Spanish-inspired Creek Indians, tribal representatives arrived at Hopewell on the Keowee River in South Carolina. There they acknowledged United States sovereignty and the right of that government to control their trade and establish three trading posts within their borders. John Pitchlynn served as an interpreter during the negotiations and, at the request of the Choctaws, received from the American commissioners a permanent appointment to that post. The commissioners acceded to the tribe's request because they observed in Pitchlynn, described as "a very honest, sober young man," a means of securing greater influence with the Indians.[8]

Yet Spanish intrigue among the Choctaws continued. In early 1787 the governor of West Florida, Esteban Miró, ar-

[8] Charles Kappler, ed., *Indian Affairs: Laws and Treaties*, II, 11–14; Benjamin Hawkins, Indian Agent South of the Ohio, to Secretary of War James J. Henry, April 24, 1797, and statement of James A. Robertson, Nashville, August 28, 1795, HR 10A–F2.1, Committee on Claims, Records of the House of Representatives, National Archives (hereinafter N.A.); *American State Papers: Indian Affairs*, I, 49–50.

ranged to provide the tribe with better trading goods and to send French traders, always welcome among the Choctaws, to counteract the growing influence of Americans such as John Pitchlynn. Miró's successor, Hector, Baron de Carondelet, constructed Fort Nogales near the mouth of the Yazoo River, having received permission to do so from the Choctaws at Natchez in 1792. Later the Spaniards signed a treaty of friendship with the Choctaws and secured the site on the lower Tombigbee where Fort Confederation would ultimately be located.[9]

To counter this growing Spanish influence but also to recruit allies for Anthony Wayne's army in the old Northwest, William Blount, governor of the newly created Territory South of the Ohio River, called Pitchlynn and other tribal leaders to Nashville in August, 1792. To accomplish his ends, the governor needed a large delegation, but at the appointed time only 110 Choctaws appeared. He learned regretfully that Spanish agents had intervened to limit the size of the party. Blount, consequently, could do little more than reaffirm the Hopewell Treaty. He also took the occasion to reappoint John Pitchlynn, whom he described as "a warm active man, and friend to the United States," as interpreter, allowing him a salary of $300 a year.[10]

Although the Nashville conference accomplished little, employing John proved judicious. The Choctaws returned to their homes and drove the Spanish agents from their midst, an action facilitated by the Treaty of San Lorenzo, which was signed by the United States and Spain in 1796. Then, beginning in 1801, the tribe agreed to a series of treaties that delineated their boundaries and made them virtually dependent upon the United States government. John Pitchlynn signed all these compacts

[9] Jack D. L. Holmes, *Gayoso: The Life of a Spanish Governor in the Mississippi Valley, 1789–1799*, 150.

[10] W. C. C. Claiborne, near Natchez, to Secretary of War Henry Dearborn, August 22, 1802, in Dunbar Rowland, ed., *Official Letter Books of W. C. C. Claiborne*, I, 166; *American State Papers: Indian Affairs*, I, 283–88.

except that of 1801 in his official capacity as interpreter to the
Choctaws. The Treaty of 1805 even provided him with a payment of $2,500 "to compensate him for certain losses sustained
in the Choctaw country, and as a grateful testimonial of the
nation's esteem." Doubtless he encouraged the adoption of the
various treaties and concurred in the land-cession provisions.
"He is zealous for the interest of the United States," wrote one
American official. "I do not believe that he has been or can be
corrupted by any man acting against the government."[11]

But the United States neglected to recognize John Pitchlynn's contribution in a tangible way. He received no pay for
his critical service between 1786 and 1792. In 1802, William
C. C. Claiborne, governor of Mississippi Territory, interceded
in his behalf and urged Washington officials to allow Pitchlynn's claim for compensation. The government denied Claiborne's request, and the petition remained unpaid until 1814.[12]
Despite this breach of faith, Pitchlynn continued to act in behalf of the United States, frequently implementing governmental policy in the eastern part of the Choctaw Nation as
temporary Indian agent.[13]

But John Pitchlynn made an even greater contribution to
the United States. In the spring of 1811 the great Shawnee
orator Tecumseh met the Choctaws in council near the Pitchlynn home. He called upon the chiefs to join him in opposition
to the Americans and, as evidence of the righteousness of his
course, referred to the prophecies of the white man's Bible. But
the Choctaws were not impressed. The great chief Pushmataha
spoke so forcefully in behalf of the United States, and John
Pitchlynn, using his own biblical knowledge, proved so effec-

[11] *American State Papers: Indian Affairs*, I, 327; Samuel Mitchell, Choctaw
Agent, to Col. Henley, February 9, 1798, Folder 1798–1, Pitchlynn MSS, G.M.
[12] William C. C. Claiborne, near Natchez, to Secretary of War Henry
Dearborn, August 22, 1802, in Rowland, *Official Letter Books*, I, 166; 12 Cong.,
2 sess., *House Report 32*, 1.
[13] *Executive Journal*, W. C. C. Claiborne, 1801–1803, 204, Miss. Archives.

tively "that the day of prophecy had passed" that Tecumseh and his party retired in disgrace.[14] The Choctaw alliance with the United States remained unbroken.

That the tribe continued its allegiance proved fortunate for the Americans, especially during the War of 1812. When the Creeks, on August 30, 1813, attacked Fort Mims and massacred some five hundred men, women, and children, the United States looked to the Choctaws for military assistance. A latter-day Paul Revere carried news of the uprising north to General Andrew Jackson in Nashville, pausing for a fresh horse at John Pitchlynn's. In the meantime, Choctaw agent George S. Gaines and Pushmataha hastened to Mobile to inform General Thomas Flournoy of the massacre and to offer their military services. After some hesitation Flournoy accepted and sent Gaines back to recruit Choctaw troops. The agent went directly to the home of John Pitchlynn, where he met John McKee, a courier with orders from Jackson to promote a combined Choctaw-Chickasaw attack on a Creek village at the falls of Black Warrior River. Pitchlynn exerted all of his great influence to enlist warriors for the expedition, advised Nashville authorities about the movements of Creek war parties, urged the governor of Mississippi Territory to provide the Choctaws with ammunition and clothing, and dispensed hospitality to the forces congregating in his area. Having enlisted nearly six hundred Choctaws, the Indian allies, with Pitchlynn as interpreter, set out for the Creek Nation on January 1, 1814. They reached the Creek village on the seventh but, finding it deserted, burned it and returned home without casualties or glory.[15]

---

[14] Love, "Lowndes County," 363; Cushman, *History of the Indians*, 242–60; J. F. H. Claiborne, *Mississippi, as a Province, Territory and State*, 328.

[15] R. S. Cotterill, *The Southern Indians*, 183; John Pitchlynn, Choctaw Nation, to Willie Blount, September, 1813, Andrew Jackson MSS (microfilm), Tennessee State Library and Archives; *Mobile Daily Tribune*, Vol. E, Claiborne MSS, and John Pitchlynn, Choctaw Nation, to Governor David

The Choctaws and John Pitchlynn made other contributions to the United States war effort. By order of Jackson, John served as interpreter and adjutant in the command of General Uriah Blue during the Pensacola campaign and at a later date as "first sergeant in the Pushmataha Company"; at least two of Pitchlynn's sons by his first wife, James and John, Jr., enlisted in the American forces. He provided hospitality to Tennessee volunteers on their way to New Orleans and throughout the war reported constantly on conditions among the Indians. As for the Choctaws, their most important contribution to the American war effort aside from their military assistance was essentially indirect: they had not supported Britain or Spain. That the tribe remained faithful to the American alliance was as much John Pitchlynn's doing as that of anyone else.[16]

The Treaty of Ghent that ended the War of 1812 signaled the beginning of a new era for the United States and the Choctaws. Americans were overcome by a sense of national pride, stemming in part from Jackson's great victory over the British at New Orleans. Surely their government, they felt, was destined to rule over much of the North American continent. When focused upon the Gulf Coast such sentiment augured ill for Spain's continued control. Finally, in 1819, Spanish officials accepted the inevitable and by terms of the Adams-Onís Treaty terminated their 234-year occupation of Florida. For the Choctaws the withdrawal of Spain meant that the in-

---

Holmes, September 30, 1813, Series A, Vol. XIII, Box 2, Governor MSS, Miss. Archives; George Smith, "Pitchlands," to Andrew Jackson, November 22, 1813, in John S. Bassett, *Correspondence of Andrew Jackson*, I, 358; Payroll Records, John McKee MSS, Manuscript Division, University of Alabama Library.

16 Uriah Blue, Baldwin County, Alabama, to the Secretary of War, April 23, 1824, N.A., Office of Indian Affairs (hereinafter O.I.A.), Choctaw Agency, Letters Received, Microcopy 234, Roll 169; John Pitchlynn, Subject File, Miss. Archives; John Coffee, Pitchlynn, to Andrew Jackson, October 14, 1814, in Bassett, *Correspondence of Andrew Jackson*, II, 74.

ternational contest for their allegiance was at an end and that they must now look entirely to the United States.

The postwar era was also a period of vigorous economic expansion. Increasing western settlement, improved transportation facilities, and a thriving commercial agriculture accounted for much of the growth. Cotton, for example, now grown in areas west of the Tidewater and marketed in Europe, had a production increase of 150 per cent between 1815 and 1819. To the Choctaws such an invigorated cotton culture meant that vast numbers of Americans, no longer restrained by the prospects of Spanish retaliation, looked to their fertile acres as possible cotton fields. Tribal cessions to the United States heretofore had largely been hunting grounds and of little consequence. But now white men coveted the very homes of the Choctaws.

The cry of the western settlers for more land carried all the way to Washington. Since the purchase of Louisiana, the presidential administrations of Thomas Jefferson and James Madison had encouraged eastern tribes to give up their ancestral lands and move west of the Mississippi River. Through 1816 only a few Indians, some of them Choctaws, had availed themselves of the opportunity. The following year, President James Monroe's secretary of war, John C. Calhoun, determined to push the same general policy but only as a measure of preserving and civilizing the Indians rather than as a means of dispossessing them. In applying his program to the Choctaws, he sent a three-member commission to meet with the tribal leaders in October, 1818. When the chiefs learned the purpose of the talks, however, they terminated the negotiations. The tribal agent, John McKee, who had participated in the discussions, reported that removal opposition "originated entirely with the half-breeds and white men residing in the country." Precisely whom he had in mind the record does not reflect, but it was surely not John Pitchlynn or his family. As a matter of fact, James Pitchlynn, John's oldest son, wrote Andrew Jackson in December, 1818, and March, 1819, that with a suitable treaty and compensation for his personal efforts he could get from one-third to one-half of the Choctaws in Mississippi to move west. Prematurely styling himself "Chief of the Choctaw Nation West," he wrote again in June, 1819, that most of the leading men were favorable to a land cession, including his father and Pushmataha.[17]

On the strength of this intelligence and the public's disappointment with the previous unsuccessful discussion, Secretary Calhoun decided to try again for Choctaw removal. Substituting Jackson for one of the original members, he sent the commission back to meet with the Choctaws in August. The response of the tribe proved that James Pitchlynn had either underestimated sentiment against removal or overestimated mixed-blood influence, and also proved that his father's "zeal and industry" in behalf of the United States had been in vain. Both Pushmataha and Moshulatubbee, the Northeastern District chief, spoke against ceding the ancestral domain in exchange for lands west of the Mississippi. "I am well acquainted with the country contemplated for us," declared Pushmataha, "I have often had my feet sorely bruised there by the roughness of its surface." As that observation represented the dominant view of the tribe, all hope for a removal treaty vanished.[18]

With the failure of the negotiations in 1819, Calhoun's inclination was to postpone other attempts until he could be sure of securing a land cession. But public opinion would not wait. Choctaw landholding in Mississippi was considered a great detriment to the state. This pressure plus additional optimistic

17 James Pitchlynn, Nashville, to Andrew Jackson, December, 1818, in Bassett, *Correspondence of Andrew Jackson*, II, 405; Pitchlynn, Choctaw Nation, to Andrew Jackson, March 18, 1819, and June 22, 1819, in *American State Papers: Indian Affairs*, II, 229, 231.

18 Arthur H. DeRosier, Jr., *The Removal of the Choctaw Indians*, 46–47 (hereinafter *Choctaw Removal*).

messages from James Pitchlynn that, despite the implications of the August conference, many full bloods did desire to move west, encouraged the Secretary to request immediate negotiations with the tribe. In the spring of 1820 he appointed Jackson and General Thomas Hinds of Mississippi to a special commission with authority to secure a land cession from the Choctaws, who reluctantly agreed to meet the new team at Doak's Stand, a post on the Natchez road.

In late September Jackson and Hinds reached Doak's Stand, where they were welcomed by John and James Pitchlynn. Beginning on October 3, Jackson, with John interpreting, explained to the assembled tribe that the President wanted the Choctaws to move beyond the Mississippi River to lands purchased for them from the Quapaws, fertile lands that would be permanently retained by the Indians. He did not propose that the tribe cede all of its ancestral domain or that everyone agree to move. Those who wished to stay and farm ought to be permitted to do so, but those who emigrated would preserve themselves from the corrupt influence of the white man. When the Choctaws remained reluctant, Jackson responded with threats, informing the tribe that he had saved their country by victories over Britain and Spain and that he wanted to save them a third time by arranging for their removal. No attempt would ever be made, he said, to treat again with the Choctaws east of the Mississippi River. The tribe must negotiate while it could. Such vigorous language, along with judicious distribution of presents and $4,600 in cash, of which $500 went to John Pitchlynn and $75 to James, achieved the General's purpose. The tribe signed the Treaty of Doak's Stand on October 18, 1820.[19]

The treaty provided for the cession of a sizable tract of land in what is now west-central Mississippi. "For and in consideration of" this cession, the United States gave to the Choctaws an area bounded on the north by the Arkansas and Canadian

[19] *American State Papers: Indian Affairs*, II, 230, 235-37, 244.

rivers, on the west by a line from the source of the Canadian due south to the Red River, on the south by the Red River, and on the east by a line from a point three miles below the mouth of the Little River to the southeastern corner of the Cherokee lands. Thus for part of their lands in the East (5,000,-ooo acres), the Choctaws received permanent title to a vast domain in the West (13,000,000 acres). Educational benefits, a resident agent, emigration assistance, and an annual appropriation of $600 for the purpose of organizing and maintaining a corps of lighthorse were additional compensations.[20]

The Pitchlynns had played a significant role in the negotiations for the treaty, James in a preliminary capacity, and John as interpreter at the treaty grounds. Both upheld the stated policy of the government for removal. Though such a course placed them at cross-purposes with other important mixed-blood families, particularly their relatives the Folsoms, among the full bloods John Pitchlynn suffered little in stature for his support of Jackson. James, on the other hand, dropped entirely from the historical record, neither condemned nor remembered by the tribe.

Soon after the Doak's Stand negotiations a clamor of protest arose from the western domain ceded to the Choctaws. The land reserved to the tribe fell within the borders of Arkansas Territory as the eastern limit followed a northeasterly line from present Fulton, Arkansas, to a point on the Arkansas River in Perry County. The area just west of that boundary had been surveyed into seventeen townships and offered for sale well before the Doak's Stand treaty. Now several thousand settlers faced dispossession upon the arrival of the Choctaws. To accommodate those who lived west of the line, Secretary Calhoun decided to negotiate with the tribe once more and called tribal leaders and their interpreter, John Pitchlynn, to Washington in early November, 1824.

[20] Kappler, *Indian Affairs: Laws and Treaties*, II, 191–95.

To secure the desired border change, the government exerted every effort to make the Choctaw stay in the national capital a happy one. In ninety days it supplied the delegates with liquor valued at $2,500, clothing worth $1,000, and jewelry costing $400.[21] The living was so riotous and the dissipation so extreme that the old war chief Pushmataha, a member of the delegation, contracted croup from overexposure and died on December 24, 1824. Appearances to the contrary, it would be unfair to say that the government planned to buy a treaty. The Choctaws, under the leadership of young J. L. McDonald (once a resident in the home of Commissioner of Indian Affairs Thomas McKenney) drove a hard bargain. But without question the entertainment weakened the resistance of the delegation, and they ultimately agreed to cede back to the United States that area east of a line running directly south to the Red River from a point on the Arkansas River one hundred paces east of Fort Smith. For this concession the Choctaws received $6,000 annually forever for the purposes of education.[22] John Pitchlynn supported the Treaty of 1825 and again demonstrated his great value to the United States.

The Pitchlynn family exerted influence in tribal activities other than diplomatic. No one, for example, contributed more than John to early Indian education. In 1820 he helped the Reverend Mr. Cyrus Kingsbury select the site, a few miles west of his home, for Mayhew, a mission school directed by the American Board of Commissioners for Foreign Missions. Through the influence of John and his son Joseph, in March, 1820, the Southern District of the Choctaw Nation agreed to contribute a part of its annuities to the mission school. Two years later, Pitchlynn himself contributed $1,000 to the institution. To be

21 Debts Contracted by the Choctaw Delegation, 1824, N.A., O.I.A., Choctaw Agency, Letters Received, Microcopy 234, Roll 169.
22 *American State Papers: Indian Affairs*, II, 547-58; Kappler, *Indian Affairs: Laws and Treaties*, II, 211-14.

sure, he received personal benefits from his donation, as his children attended the school. Yet, in helping himself, John also contributed significantly to the educational development of the tribe as a whole.[23]

The elder Pitchlynn knew the value of religion in his own life and saw to it that his family received training in spiritual values common to his own white culture. He opened his home to visiting preachers, who usually repaid his hospitality by special worship services for the family and biblical exhortation. When the Presbyterian Cyrus Kingsbury, for example, visited Pitchlynn's home in the interest of Mayhew Mission in early 1820, he learned that a Methodist minister had been holding regular services there for the past year. John was a charter member of the Masonic Lodge in Columbus, Mississippi. He seems also to have been a student of the scriptures in his own right, for he successfully refuted Tecumseh's appeal to supernatural prophecy by his own biblical knowledge and late in life found real solace in the Christian promises. With such habits and faith, his family was influenced, not to a life of religious fervor but to one distinctly different from that of Indians who adhered to the old religion.

But John Pitchlynn was more than a government interpreter and public benefactor. He had deep affection for his large family, over which he ruled as patriarch. As his children married, he gave them generous gifts of money and property and encouraged them to settle near him. When his older sons died before he did, their families were incorporated into his household, as on occasion were non-related orphans. He was genuinely heartbroken when the removal treaty in 1830 dispersed his family. Deep affection prompted him to implore Peter to return and comfort him in old age. He was a man of integrity,

---

[23] *Missionary Herald*, Vol. XVI, 365–68 and Vol. XVIII, 373; Cyrus Kingsbury to E. Brashares, May 10, 1820, II, Folder 134, John McKee MSS, Library of Congress; Reminiscences, George S. Gaines MSS, Miss. Archives.

honor, sobriety, and tenderness; in a different society John would have been a leader of note rather than a little-remembered trader.

If a father ever elevated one son above others, John so lifted the eldest child of his second wife—her first born and his fondest hope. Born on January 30, 1806, in the Indian town of Hush-ook-wa on the Noxubee River, an early site of his father's trading post, Peter Perkins Pitchlynn was one-quarter Choctaw. His half-blood mother, Sophia Folsom, was an exceptional woman in every way. Although Peter remained her favorite, she gave birth to at least seven other children, cared for them during the prolonged absences of her husband, and after his death emigrated with them to Indian Territory, where she died in 1870. Young Pitchlynn, christened *Ha-tchoc-tuck-nee* ("Snapping Turtle") by his fullblood friends, spent his first years where his father initially settled. By 1810 he had moved with his parents to Plymouth Bluff. While his father and older half-brothers were involved in tribal and international affairs, Peter's early life remained uncomplicated. His first real duties consisted of watching his father's cattle herds that grazed the intermittent prairies. He also remembered wading the streams and roaming the foothills trapping beaver and hunting. As a youngster he enjoyed all kinds of social activities and athletics, especially the Choctaw ball play; his early life was not unlike that of the average young Choctaw.[24]

Yet young Pitchlynn did not grow up in an Indian environment. Instead, his family's financial status and the visits of traders, travelers, and ministers made his father's home an outpost of "civilization." This, plus the growing frequency of contact with white settlers on the very frontiers of the tribal do-

[24] Charles Lanman, "Peter Pitchlynn, Chief of the Choctaws," *Atlantic Monthly* (April, 1870), 486. This article was based upon an interview with Pitchlynn in 1870. All subsequent works have used it in part or in whole. See also Memo Book, Folder 79–39, Pitchlynn MSS, G.M.; George Catlin, *Letters and Notes on . . . the North American Indian*, II, 140.

main, meant that Peter was less a Choctaw than he thought he was, then and particularly later. Still, the advantages of his "position" as the son of a wealthy white trader were not always realized, a fact that became painfully apparent to him with increasing outside contacts. For example, two incidents illustrated to him his need of a formal education. The first was observing a fellow Choctaw who was partly educated in New England write a letter to President James Monroe; the other was engaging in long conversations with his white friend, Gideon Lincecum, a frontier physician and later a noted naturalist. "We dwelt in a remote wilderness," Peter once wrote to Lincecum, "where the light of Science and civilization had never shot a single ray. Twas then you came and took me by the hand and led me by your council to the source of knowledge."[25]

So, in 1820, young Pitchlynn resolved to obtain more than a rudimentary education. At the age of fourteen, he left his parents and entered the school nearest his father's home, which he remembered later was some "200 miles" away among the hills of Tennessee. Peter may have confused this educational experience with his enrollment in the Chickasaw mission school, Charity Hall, established in 1820 near Cotton Gin Port, Mississippi. In any event, by October he had completed an academic quarter at some institution north of his home, after which he returned to Mississippi in time to observe the negotiations at Doak's Stand.[26]

After at least one more year of academic training at a school in Columbia, Tennessee, Peter completed the first stage of his education. He had attended at least two institutions, Charity Hall and Columbia Academy, and may very well have entered

[25] Lanman, "Peter Pitchlynn," *Atlantic Monthly* (April, 1870), 486; Letter Fragment, Folder Un–125, Pitchlynn MSS, G.M.

[26] Lanman, "Peter Pitchlynn," *Atlantic Monthly* (April, 1870), 486; Carolyn Foreman, "Charity Hall, An Early Chickasaw School," *The Chronicles of Oklahoma*, Vol. XI (September, 1933), 912–23.

a third, but under no circumstances was he in school more than two years. Yet it would be unfair to conclude that his educational experience lacked substance or breadth. It built upon his early training, improved his natural abilities, and whetted his appetite for additional knowledge. He acquired a limited but select library, and he discovered that his favorite subjects were moral philosophy, poetry (especially Shakespeare), history, biography, Choctaw mythology, medicine, and natural philosophy. Altogether his training reinforced his white background and separated him even farther from the traditional Indian pattern.[27]

Like his father and brothers before him, young Pitchlynn was also ambitious for public office. When the treaty of 1820 (the Treaty of Doak's Stand) provided for a police unit known locally as the lighthorse, he spared no effort until he obtained a position of leadership. Just when the group organized in Peter's Northeastern District is in question. He recalled late in life that it was formed in 1824 upon the occasion of his election as captain, but Cyrus Kingsbury, writing contemporaneously, placed the date as 1821, making no mention of Pitchlynn's contribution at all. This slight discrepancy illustrates Pitchlynn's habit of forgetting events which occurred before he assumed command of the situation. The lighthorse under him, whatever its date of origin, effectively curtailed the liquor traffic and in other matters of law acted as police, judge, and jury. He remembered his service in that picturesque force with fondness and pride and answered to the title "Colonel" the rest of his life.[28]

By 1824 matters other than education and tribal affairs were

[27] Lanman, "Peter Pitchlynn," *Atlantic Monthly* (April, 1870), 486; Notebook, Folder 79–39, Pitchlynn MSS, G.M.; James L. McDonald, Choctaw Agency, to Thomas L. McKenney, September 29, 1826, N.A., O.I.A., Schools, Letters Received, Microcopy 234, Roll 773.

[28] *Missionary Herald*, Vol. XIX, 8; Lanman, "Peter Pitchlynn," *Atlantic Monthly* (April, 1870), 486; Cushman, *History of the Indians*, 157.

interesting Peter. He selected as his wife Rhoda Folsom, a half-blood daughter of Nathaniel and a half-sister of his mother. The Reverend Cyrus Kingsbury performed the Christian ceremony for the monogamous marriage which Peter characteristically later asserted killed the practice of polygamy among the Indians. He exaggerated his contribution, however; the institution still existed some fifty years later.[29] For his home young Pitchlynn chose a site southwest of his father's place, two miles south of present Artesia, Mississippi, on the edge of a large prairie near the Mayhew Mission settlement. His father provided slaves to assist in constructing a home and cutting fence rails. Peter soon had a small crop planted, was raising hogs and cattle, and had ambitions of slave ownership. Some time later in 1825, Rhoda gave birth to his daughter, Lavina.[30]

The appearance of the fourth generation within the Pitchlynn family in North America marked a milestone in its evolution. Arriving in the middle of an international contest for Choctaw allegiance, John Pitchlynn had acquired the respect of the tribe even while he served the interests of the United States. His position enabled him to acquire wealth and provide benefits for his family not available to members of the tribe. From this vantage point, young Peter Pitchlynn lived a life different from that of the average Choctaw. Yet despite his white blood and background, he frequently identified with the Indians; consequently his role in tribal affairs tended to be different from that of his father. Unlike John, Peter's primary loyalty was to the Choctaws, and with them his fortunes and those of his family would rise and fall.

29 Lanman, "Peter Pitchlynn," *Atlantic Monthly* (April, 1870), 487.

30 John Pitchlynn, Oktibbeha, to Peter Pitchlynn, March 14, 1824, July 19, 1824, and December 11, 1825, Pitchlynn MSS, G.M.; Folsom Family File, Grant Foreman Collection, Indian Archives, Oklahoma Historical Society (hereinafter O.H.S.).

CHAPTER II

The Struggle for Power

Elevation of mixed-bloods to positions of prominence in tribal affairs occurred with some frequency during the nineteenth century. The southeastern Indians sanctioned such advancement especially if the mixed-bloods identified with and paid homage to the hopes and aspirations of the more numerous full bloods.[1] Peter Pitchlynn, a politically ambitious young man, predicated his whole career after 1825 upon this general tendency.

The treaties of 1820 and 1825 established educational funds for Choctaw children. Initially the tribe used most of these annuities to support local mission schools but, upon the insistence of some mixed-blood members, determined to appropriate a part of it to maintain an institution that would afford a better education. Pitchlynn, remembering his own academic experience, believed that the new school should be located among the whites, for only there could the Indian learn the white man's ways. Despite the objection of his brother-in-law David Folsom that the money would be better spent within the tribal

[1] Two good examples of this practice are John Ross of the Cherokees and, somewhat earlier, Alexander McGillivray of the Creeks.

area, Pitchlynn's home district adopted his position and elected to enroll its children at a school recently opened in Blue Springs, Kentucky, by United States Senator Richard M. Johnson. Colonel Johnson, a relative of the Choctaw agent and always interested in any venture that might prove profitable, engaged Thomas Henderson, a teacher of "uncommon merit," altered his home to accommodate additional students, and prepared to receive the Choctaws in the middle of October, 1825.[2]

Pitchlynn assumed responsibility for taking the twenty-one selected students, most of whom were mixed-bloods, to Kentucky. After an arduous trip across Tennessee, they reached the five stone buildings of the Choctaw Academy on November 1. What he found at the school pleased him immensely. The commodious facilities "in the bosom of our white brothers," Pitchlynn wrote, promised the advanced education desired for the more capable students of the tribe. Obviously their special abilities entitled them to something more than "the honorable and benevolent exertions of the missionaries" who labored with the less endowed at home.[3] At first glance Pitchlynn seemed to be advocating preferential treatment for the mixed-blood students, which would contradict his always identifying with the general aspirations of the tribe. It did not, however. He wanted the full bloods educated, too; he only wanted to reserve the special opportunities to the Choctaw elite, among whom, most assuredly, he counted himself. Pitchlynn's praise and that of others who visited the school encouraged the Choctaws to continue their support of the academy until 1840, enabling many of those who later became tribal leaders to secure some advanced educational training.

[2] Richard M. Johnson to Secretary of War, September 27, 1825, N.A., O.I.A., Schools, Letters Received, Microcopy 234, Roll 772; David Folsom, Choctaw Nation, to Thomas L. McKenney, May 27, 1826, N.A., O.I.A., Choctaw Agency, Letters Received, Microcopy 234, Roll 169.

[3] Pitchlynn, Blue Springs, to Secretary of War Barbour, November 5, 1825, N.A., O.I.A., Schools, Microcopy 234, Roll 772.

Ironically, the same treaties that gave the Choctaws academic benefits also led to serious political controversy. The land cession provisions of 1820 and 1825 seemed to suggest that the traditional fullblood leadership of the tribe was weakening in its historic opposition to removal. To prevent further capitulation, David Folsom called together the warriors of the Northeastern District in April, 1826, and in their presence accused old Moshulatubbee, a warm friend of the Pitchlynns', of intemperance, misappropriation of tribal school funds, and an inclination to accommodate the United States government. The warriors finally agreed to depose the fullblood chief and to install Folsom in his place. In completing his coup, however, the new chief evoked the animosity of the Pitchlynns, who rallied to the defense of Moshulatubbee and who took pleasure in referring to Folsom as "King David."

Similar transitions of power occurred in the other two districts. Simultaneously with Folsom's rise, Greenwood LeFlore secured his own election as chief in the Northwestern District despite the claim of Robert Cole, a nephew of the recently deceased fullblood leader, Apukshunnubbee. The Southern District experienced its political upheaval in 1828 when John Garland replaced Chief Tapenahomma, the nephew of Pushmataha. In the meantime, in August, 1826, Folsom and LeFlore spearheaded a movement to convene a national council that would frame a tribal constitution. Such a document implied a degree of civilization and might provide a consolidated political authority that would offer effective resistance to further land cessions.[4]

The chiefs and representatives of the three districts met on August 5, 1826, on the banks of the Noxubee River in present Oktibbeha County, Mississippi. Peter Pitchlynn helped represent the Northeastern District and served as secretary of the

[4] Young, *Redskins, Ruffleshirts, and Rednecks*, 9, 26; John to Peter Pitchlynn, April 16, 1827, Pitchlynn MSS, G.M.

council. As written, the constitution called for a decentralized and weak executive, composed of three district chiefs elected for four-year terms, and a national council, consisting of representatives of the three political divisions, that would meet annually and adopt written legislation. At the first session, the council authorized construction of a council house, provided for inheritance through the male line, defined the lawful enclosure of fields, prohibited trespassers, and discouraged polygamy. More important, it enacted a law providing severe punishment for anyone who might sell his country for a bribe.[5]

Although Peter Pitchlynn served as secretary, the record failed to reflect the importance of his role in framing the 1826 constitution. He was only twenty years old, inadequately educated, and a poor penman. Furthermore, men with more ability were present, David Folsom was antagonistic toward him, and in view of his support of Moshulatubbee he was probably not even sympathetic to the basic purpose of the constitution. All these factors point to a less than spectacular role; yet Pitchlynn was there, observing a procedure which he would help re-enact during the critical years after removal.

Contrary to the Choctaws' hopes, the new constitution did not prevent further efforts on the part of the United States government to promote Indian removal. Thomas L. McKenney, chief of the Bureau of Indian Affairs, believed that despite the political changes the tribe might well be responsive to still another treaty of cession. The Choctaw agent, William Ward, had hinted about significant fullblood support for such a treaty, and John Pitchlynn, Jr., had offered to exert his personal influence, "provided my interests can be promoted thereby."[6]

Accordingly, McKenney commissioned John Coffee of Ala-

<hr>

[5] Lester Hargrett, *A Bibliography of the Constitutions and Laws of the American Indians*, 55 (hereinafter *Indian Constitutions and Laws*); Young, *Redskins, Ruffleshirts, and Rednecks*, 26.

[6] DeRosier, *Choctaw Removal*, 89.

bama, Thomas Hinds of Mississippi, and General William Clark of Missouri, as well as interpreter John Pitchlynn, to meet the Indians near the town of Wilson's in the Choctaw Nation in mid-November. The tribal commissioners, thirteen in all, included full bloods General Hummingbird, Red Dog, and Nettuckachee, along with mixed-bloods Peter Pitchlynn, J. L. McDonald, and Israel Folsom, David's brother. As expected, the United States commissioners urged the Choctaws to move to those lands across the Mississippi River ceded to the tribe in 1820, in partial consideration of which the government would pay one million dollars. The Choctaw delegation surprised the commissioners by giving the proposition little consideration and insisting that it was well past time to end all talk about land cessions and westward emigration. The tribe did not want to remove from Mississippi, and as it did not, there was no reason even to continue the discussions. Shortly thereafter the Indian representatives returned to their homes.

Peter Pitchlynn's role in the tribal refusal to treat with the United States is difficult to analyze. Considering his father's earnest support of the Americans and his own advocacy of Moshulatubbee, who was still inclined toward removal, he surely had some reservations about total rejection of the commissioner's proposals. Perhaps it was this hint of reluctance in Peter and fullblood visitors to the treaty grounds that caused the United States delegation to declare: "The government seems to be in the hands of half-breeds and white men who dictate without regard to the interests of the poor Indian."[7]

The events of 1825 and 1826—the visit to the Choctaw Academy, the constitutional convention, and the treaty negotiations—further convinced Peter of his own educational deficiency. As early as January, 1826, he had expressed the desire to attend Transylvania University in Kentucky for two years and then to study law with Colonel Johnson at Blue

[7] *American State Papers: Indian Affairs*, II, 702–17.

Springs. The chief of the Bureau of Indian Affairs had agreed to pay his expenses out of tribal funds as long as the Choctaw chiefs approved.[8] But, caught up in public affairs, Peter did not take advantage of this approval for nearly a year.

Finally, in late January, 1827, Pitchlynn left his wife and child to enroll at Transylvania. He traveled north by way of Florence, Alabama, to Louisville, where friends provided him with letters of introduction to individuals in Lexington. At some point, however, Pitchlynn changed his mind about attending Transylvania and instead entered the Choctaw Academy at the end of February. Superintendent Henderson was delighted to have Peter, describing him as understanding English well and of "a fine mind, dignified and gentlemanly conduct, perfectly sober habits, remarkedly studious, and much intended to piety." Furthermore, he said, Pitchlynn provided a good example for the other young men.[9]

Three months later Peter left the academy and returned home. On the whole his educational experience had been satisfying and had offered him another opportunity to travel among his father's people. Still, the curriculum of grammar, surveying, bookkeeping, geography, reading, and writing was not as advanced as he had wished. The ninety days at the Choctaw Academy thus left his thirst for education unquenched, and he resolved to try again at the earliest possible moment.

At home Peter involved himself again in tribal affairs. In October, 1827, Bureau of Indian Affairs head McKenney visited the Choctaw Nation in another effort to negotiate a removal treaty. Pitchlynn served as secretary pro tempore of the delegation that met with the commissioner. After vigorous dis-

8 Pitchlynn, Choctaw Nation, to Barbour, January 23, 1826, N.A., O.I.A., Schools, Letters Received, Microcopy 234, Roll 773; McKenney, Office of Indian Affairs, to Pitchlynn, February 17, 1826, N.A., O.I.A., Letters Sent, Microcopy 21, Roll 2.

9 Report of the Choctaw Academy, April 30, 1827, N.A., O.I.A., Schools, Letters Received, Microcopy 234, Roll 773.

Pushmataha, famous Choctaw district chief, who died in Washington in 1824. Painting by C. B. King. (Courtesy Gilcrease Institute, Tulsa, Oklahoma)

David Folsom, chief of Northeastern District after deposing Moshulatubbee. (Courtesy Oklahoma Historical Society, Oklahoma City)

Pipe, probably over six hundred years old, smoked at signing of Treaty of Dancing Rabbit Creek. (Courtesy Gilcrease Institute, Tulsa, Oklahoma)

Building once used as temporary council house at Nanih Waiya, near Tuskahoma. (Courtesy Oklahoma Historical Society, Oklahoma City)

Jones Hall, one of four original dormitories of Spencer Academy. (Courtesy Presbyterian Historical Society, Philadelphia, Pennsylvania)

Two studies from George Catlin's original sketchbook: above, Choctaw ball play; below, "Tulloc-chish-ko & Ball Play Dance of the Choctaw Tribe." (Courtesy Gilcrease Institute, Tulsa, Oklahoma)

George Harkins, nephew and successor of Greenwood LeFlore, chief of Apukshunnubbee District. (Courtesy Oklahoma Historical Society, Oklahoma City)

Armstrong Academy at Bokchito, renamed Chahta Tamaha and used as capitol of Choctaw Nation, 1863–83. (Courtesy Oklahoma Historical Society, Oklahoma City)

cussions, the Indians persuaded McKenney that tribal removal at the moment was impossible. With this not wholly unexpected intelligence, he turned his attention to laying the groundwork for a future treaty. He suggested only that the tribe send a delegation to explore the country west of the Mississippi River at the expense of the government. He hoped that such a trip might break down Indian resistance to emigration and demonstrate the desirability of western lands. The Choctaws agreed to the proposed expedition and, at the same time, convinced McKenney that the government could ultimately negotiate a treaty even with the mixed-blood leadership.[10]

Peter Pitchlynn used the occasion of the discussions to visit with McKenney about his continuing interest in higher education and his unfulfilled desire to attend Transylvania. He persuaded the bureau chief for the second time to provide him with financial support to attend the school. In conversations with Peter and his father, McKenney also indicated that young Pitchlynn might qualify to serve on the proposed expedition. Consequently, Peter left the council ground with letters of introduction, a guarantee of financial support, and the prospect of an expedition to the West. For him it had been a fruitful session.[11]

Pitchlynn left almost immediately to pursue his education, leaving his young daughter and his wife, who was again pregnant, to the care of her mother and his father. But for the second time, apparently because of the death of the president of Transylvania, Pitchlynn elected not to attend the school, deciding instead to enter the University of Nashville (now George Peabody College for Teachers). The institution accepted Pitchlynn's application for admission to the session which began on

[10] McKenney, Choctaw Agency, to the Secretary of War, October 17, 1827, in Thomas L. McKenney, *Memoirs, Official and Personal*, 336–37.
[11] Pitchlynn, Nashville, to McKenney, November 2, 1827, N.A., O.I.A., Schools, Letters Received, Microcopy 234, Roll 773.

November 1, 1827, and terminated on April 1, 1828. The dates suited Peter perfectly since he hoped to accompany the exploring expedition the next fall.[12]

Pitchlynn made the best of his opportunity. Using the $500 McKenney had provided for expenses, by the end of November he had bought $116 worth of fabrics for clothes and bedding. For the classroom and his own library he purchased books on the Masonic Order, logic, natural philosophy, synonyms, political economy, chemistry, and moral philosophy. He also secured a volume on the history of Rome and a copy of Milton's *Paradise Lost*. No doubt Peter's course work at the university considerably advanced his education, but one could question his intellectual dedication. Surely a serious student would have planned to stay more than a single term. Pitchlynn pressed his proposal for university level study upon McKenney probably out of a belief that the tribal elite deserved special opportunities. Education outside the Choctaw Nation afforded the preferential treatment he desired and also permitted another excursion into the world of his father's people. Such non-academic motivation was not conducive to disciplined endeavor, and after six months he was ready to leave, taking with him $215 to pay expenses home. Despite the brief enrollment, in 1870 Pitchlynn claimed that he had graduated from the University of Nashville, a statement taken at face value by some Oklahoma historians. Demonstrably, his memory served him false.[13]

[12] Records of the University of Nashville, Vol. I, University of Nashville MSS, Tennessee State Library and Archives; Philip Lindsley, Nashville, to McKenney, November 1, 1827, and Pitchlynn, Nashville, to McKenney, November 2, 1827, N.A., O.I.A., Schools, Letters Received, Microcopy 234, Roll 773.

[13] Accounts, Folder 28–14, Folder 28–7, and Folder 27–11, Pitchlynn MSS, G.M.; Account Book of Philip Lindsley, Vol. X, 71, 78, and Journal of Historical Notes, Vol. IV, University of Nashville MSS, Tennessee State Library and Archives. Also, compare Lanman, "Peter Pitchlynn," *Atlantic Monthly* (April, 1870), 486, with Hargrett, *Indian Constitutions and Laws*

Instead of returning to the Nation, however, Peter went north to the Choctaw Academy at Blue Springs, Kentucky. What motivated him to make this three-month trip is not known, but it is clear that in its wake he left a controversy that resulted in the closing of the academy. After his visit Peter reported to David Folsom, never a real supporter of the school and recently critical of Pitchlynn's educational expenditures, that the food was poorly prepared, consisting chiefly of fat bacon, coarse corn bread, and rye coffee, and was served by three or four insolent, inattentive, and filthy Negroes. He complained also about dirty tablecloths, insufficient lodging, and inadequate bedclothes.[14] In fact, Pitchlynn was so censorious of the academy that Folsom forgot his displeasure with him.

Advised of the charges by Agent Ward, Colonel Johnson responded vehemently. The diet, he declared, consisted of quality food and elegantly prepared rye coffee. The Negroes also waited upon his family, and the lodging and clothing arrangements were as sufficient as the $300 annual per capita allowance would permit. Furthermore, if anybody's actions were questioned, the Choctaws ought to look to Peter. Had he not robbed the tribe of $500 under the false pretense of going to school? Despite Johnson's defense and countercharges, confidence in the school began to diminish, and Pitchlynn became the academy's bitterest enemy.[15]

Having stirred up the controversy, Peter did not remain to answer the charges. He departed for the West in September. The expedition proposed by McKenney had received the sanction of Congress in early 1828, and President Adams had appointed David W. Haley, a trader, to lead the party beyond

55; Joseph B. Thoburn and Muriel H. Wright, *Oklahoma: A History of the State and Its People*, II, 848.

[14] Johnson, Blue Springs, to David Folsom, September 12, 1828, N.A., O.I.A., Choctaw Agency, Letters Received, Microcopy 234, Roll 169.

[15] Johnson, Blue Springs, to McKenney, September 12, 1828, and September 13, 1828, *ibid.*

the Mississippi River. Although Pitchlynn remembered after the Civil War that he had led the group, he was in fact only one of the two men selected from each Choctaw district. In mid-September, after a delay caused by the late arrival of the Chickasaws who accompanied the party, the expedition left for Memphis, where it took passage on a steamboat to St. Louis.[16]

The Choctaws reached the "Crossroads of the West" on October 12. The city teemed with tribes from other areas, one of which, the Sioux, impressed Pitchlynn as "a wild and un-cultivated race, and from every appearance a miserable set."[17] Yet things more important than sight-seeing were at hand. At social events, including dinner with General William Clark, and at a full schedule of meetings, government officials briefed the Indians on the importance of their mission. They also pro-vided traveling outfits and special guides, one of whom was the incomparable Baptist missionary Isaac McCoy. So equipped and so led, the government expected the western tour to per-suade the Indians to remove from their ancestral homes east of the Mississippi.

The forty-one-member expedition left St. Louis on October 18 and, proceeding on a westerly course, crossed the Missouri River first at St. Charles and again at Franklin. But before reaching the Missouri state line, the Choctaw delegation ex-pressed a desire not to continue the tour into the plains of what is now central Kansas but to proceed instead to the resi-dence of their people on Red River. After receiving assurances that the expedition would not go as far west as first contem-plated, the Choctaws agreed to continue.[18]

[16] Thomas H. Hill, Washington, to John Pitchlynn, May 28, 1828, Case 2, Box 5, Gratz Collection, Pennsylvania Historical Society; Lanman, "Peter Pitchlynn," *Atlantic Monthly* (April, 1870), 487; David Folsom, Choctaw Nation, to McKenney, October 14, 1828, N.A., O.I.A., Choctaw Agency, Letters Received, Microcopy 234, Roll 169.

[17] Report, 1829, Folder Un–298, Pitchlynn MSS, G.M.

[18] Isaac McCoy, *History of Baptist Indian Missions*, 349.

On November 3, the party camped just west of the line among the Shawnees. Although McCoy did not record the event in his journal of the trip, Pitchlynn reported after the expedition that there the Choctaws met Tenskwatawa, the Prophet, Tecumseh's famous twin brother. From the Shawnee encampment, the party moved southwesterly and on November 11 reached the Osage River in present eastern Kansas. Two days later, following directions given by the Kauzau Indians, it turned almost due south and reached the Osage Agency on November 17. Recalling this occasion much later, Pitchlynn commented that the Osages showed signs of their ancient enmity toward the Choctaws and that only a slashing oration by him brought about the desired council of peace. McCoy recorded no such incident, remarking instead that in speechmaking the "Osage exhibited more native eloquence and acquitted themselves with much more credit than our civilized and half-civilized Indians." As a matter of fact, McCoy mentioned Pitchlynn only as "an intelligent, sensible man" who frequently borrowed his Bible and asked why Christians differed so much in opinion.[19]

On November 22 the expedition, accompanied by a local escort, left the Osage villages. On the twenty-sixth it reached the junction of the Arkansas and Verdigris rivers near present Muskogee, Oklahoma. Having spent two months on the trail, the Indians now exhibited a strong desire to end the expedition without exploring the area ceded to the Choctaws in the treaty of 1820 and envisioned as a future home.[20] After a buffalo hunt

[19] Report, 1829, Folder Un–298, Pitchlynn MSS, G.M.; McCoy, *History of Baptist Indian Missions*, 354–58; Lanman, "Peter Pitchlynn," *Atlantic Monthly* (April, 1870), 488.

[20] Surprisingly, Professor Arthur DeRosier, Jr., writes of the expedition: "[It] arrived in the Kiamichi area late in September," and "throughout October and November the exploring party toured the new land from one end to the other." *Choctaw Removal*, 97, 98. As he cites documents which either relate to the early phases of the expedition or cannot be located as identified, he must be confusing the exploring group of 1828 with one unknown to this writer.

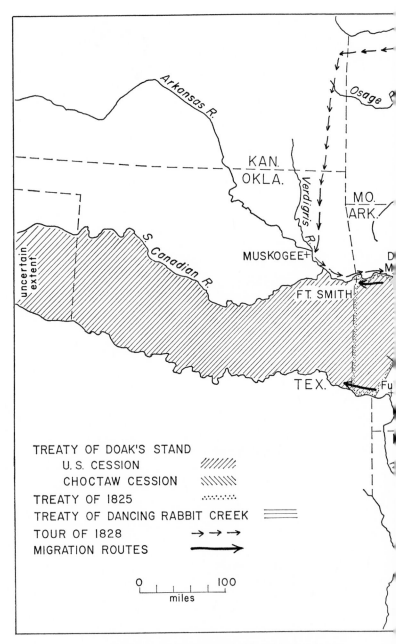

LAND CESSIONS AND MIGRATION ROUTES

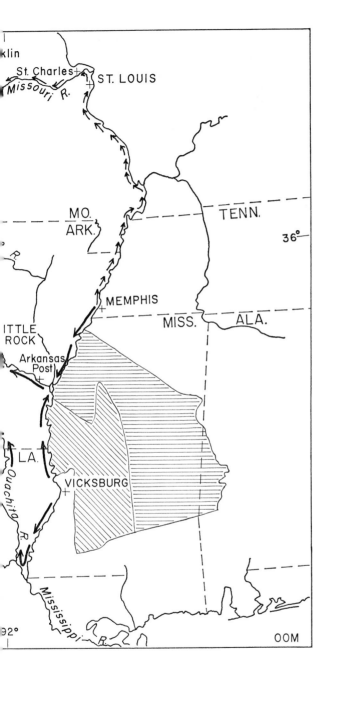

klin
St. Charles
Missouri R.
ST. LOUIS

MO.
ARK.

TENN.

36°

MEMPHIS

MISS.

ALA.

ITTLE
ROCK

Arkansas
Post

LA.

Ouachita R.

VICKSBURG

Mississippi R.

92°

OOM

in early December, the party turned east along the Arkansas River and arrived at the Choctaw Agency West near present Fort Smith on December 9. Pitchlynn later hinted of severe skirmishes with Comanches in the course of the trip, and H. B. Cushman, a contemporary historian, recorded an incident in which the young "colonel" saved the entire party from decimation. Both accounts were fabrications. The Comanches seldom ranged that far east, and Cushman always followed Pitchlynn's reminiscences except for this incident.[21]

The expedition terminated at the Choctaw Agency and all but Peter and a friend arrived home in early January, 1829. Peter may have remained to explore the area south of the Arkansas River; in any event, on January 7 he was at old Dwight Mission, near present Russellville, Arkansas. There he borrowed money for passage back to Mississippi.[22]

Though the trip was not as romantic as Pitchlynn later remembered, it was significant. First, it represented one of the earliest exploring parties of Indians sponsored by the federal government. Second, the Choctaws established peaceful relations with the Osages. Finally, a select few of the tribe did have an opportunity to see the West. Still, the trip failed to serve the purpose that McKenney had hoped it would: the Choctaws did not explore the 1820 cession, and tribal appetite for western lands remained unwhetted.

Despite the failure of the government in this instance, the policy of removal continued. Andrew Jackson's election in 1828 increased the urgency for general Indian emigration. The Choctaws reacted to the increased pressure by dividing into political factions. Moshulatubbee, struggling to retain his position of leadership and allied with the Pitchlynns, led the

---

[21] Lanman, "Peter Pitchlynn," *Atlantic Monthly* (April, 1870), 489; Cushman, *History of the Indians*, 337.

[22] Pitchlynn, Dwight [Mission], to Edmund Folsom, January 7, 1829, Pitchlynn MSS, G.M.

Republicans, and David Folsom and Greenwood LeFlore headed the Christian party. In September, 1829, at the direction of the government, Agent Ward confronted tribal leaders with another plan of removal. The Christian party, largely mixed-bloods, immediately rejected the proposal, but in early December, Moshulatubbee, worn out from the struggles, consulted his fullblood supporters and agreed to emigrate. In this decision John Pitchlynn supported the Republicans, but Folsom vigorously objected and to counter the move had himself proclaimed chief for life.[23] The confused situation for the moment postponed the day of removal.

The platform and the alignment of the Choctaw parties radically altered in January, 1830, when the state of Mississippi further extended her laws over the tribe. "Rights, privileges, immunities and franchises of the Indians" were repealed by the state, and if the Choctaws did not comply with the law they would be fined $1,000 and sentenced to twelve months in prison. Folsom now did an about-face and announced his willingness to consider emigration, while Moshulatubbee prepared to remain in Mississippi as a citizen of the state, even pathetically offering himself as a candidate for Congress. Fearful of the effect of state law upon tribal society and its own honored political position, on March 15 the Christian party hurriedly elected Greenwood LeFlore as chief of the entire Nation, drew up a treaty of emigration, sent it to President Jackson for ratification, and prepared to remove.[24]

Moshulatubbee reacted to the election by becoming for the moment antimissionary—Alexander Talley, a Methodist minister, had written the proposed treaty—and even more committed to nonremoval. His young ally, Peter Pitchlynn, adopted

---

[23] Ward, Choctaw Agency, to John H. Eaton, December 29, 1829, N.A., O.I.A., Choctaw Agency, Letters Received, Microcopy 234, Roll 169.
[24] Young, *Redskins, Ruffleshirts, and Rednecks*, 29; *Niles' Register*, Vol. XLVIII (1830), 362–63; Debo, *Rise and Fall*, 52.

the same positions. In a demagogic exercise, Peter castigated David Folsom for his support of the missionaries. The preachers, he declared, came with soft words and pleasant manners only to swindle the Choctaws of their wealth. They were responsible for the deplorable conditions of the tribe. "Why then," he cried, "do we nourish in the bosom of our country a set of beings that do nothing except excite separation amongst us?" He also accused Folsom and LeFlore of quietly bargaining the country away and then having the audacity to say it was done in a national council. "Will you my brave countrymen," he asked, "submit to all this?" Then in a classic understatement: "Do not think from what I have said that I am here to stir your hearts with separation." He desired only to admonish them to stand united in opposition to the Christian party, to land cession, and to Folsom. "We are free men and we intend to remain so," he concluded.[25]

After all the excitement the federal government did not accept the treaty proposed by the Christian party, presumably because of its fifty-million-dollar price tag. A Republican council, in a message written by Peter Pitchlynn, congratulated Secretary of War John Eaton on the action and suggested that if the United States really desired a treaty, commissioners should be sent to the Choctaw Nation to meet with the whole tribe. President Jackson, on vacation in Tennessee, initially rejected this advice and decided to meet personally with the tribe, inviting the chiefs to Franklin in August, 1830. Such a meeting at first seemed feasible, but some tribal factions refused to cooperate, and no delegation was sent. Instead, the Republicans asked John and Peter Pitchlynn and three others to call on the President personally and explain why the chiefs failed to appear. Probably the Republican delegation never spoke to Jackson, for the President returned to Washington almost immediately after issuing his invitation. But removal, especially after

[25] Pitchlynn's Speech [1830], Folder Un–277, Pitchlynn MSS, G.M.

congressional approval on June 30, 1830, was very important to his administration, and he left instructions for General John Coffee and Secretary of War Eaton to meet the Choctaws in general council.[26]

Six thousand Choctaws gathered at Dancing Rabbit Creek in Noxubee County, Mississippi, on September 15, 1830, to greet the two commissioners. After denying the missionaries permission to attend the council, Coffee and Eaton declared to the Indians in a message interpreted by John Pitchlynn that they had come seeking not their lands but their happiness. They asked whether the Choctaws were willing to be subject to the white man's law and, if not, urged them to remove beyond the Mississippi River. Considering the interest in removal manifested by different tribal leaders in the previous year, the United States commissioners were somewhat surprised by the response of many of the chiefs and most of the full bloods, including Moshulatubbee and Peter Pitchlynn, now secretary of the tribal delegation responsible for conducting the negotiations: the terms of the United States were "insufficient."[27]

The reply so infuriated Eaton that he addressed the Choctaws in angry language reminiscent of Jackson's at Doak's Stand. Some of the tribe left the council grounds in indignation, but others, under pressure from Greenwood LeFlore and aware that they had no realistic alternative, agreed to negotiate. Those who remained, including Peter, submitted a list of terms upon which they would be willing to treat. Eaton and Coffee rejected even these proposals, presenting their own compromise

[26] Choctaw Chiefs, Choctaw Nation, to John H. Eaton, June 2, 1830, and Choctaw Chiefs, Council Grounds, to Jackson, August 16, 1830, N.A., O.I.A., Choctaw Agency, Letters Received, Microcopy 234, Roll 169; Jackson, Hermitage, to Pitchlynn, August 5, 1830, in Bassett, *Correspondence of Andrew Jackson*, IV, 169.
[27] 23 Cong., 1 sess., *Sen. Doc. 512*, II, 255–58; Letter to the Commissioners [1830], Folder 30–18, Pitchlynn MSS, G.M.

draft that called for the removal of the tribe from Mississippi, protection by the United States in their new home, additional annuities, and land gifts to the chiefs and those tribal members who wished to remain in the ancestral home. When the Indians still withheld consent, the United States commissioners promised to provide additional land reservations for the "deserving" in a separate document. Accordingly, on September 27, 1830, the Choctaws reluctantly signed the Treaty of Dancing Rabbit Creek, to which on the following day were added the supplementary articles that gave lucrative land assignments to prominent tribal families. The two documents together signaled the tribe's recognition of the inevitable: they must leave their old homes for new ones beyond the Mississippi.[28]

The supplementary articles and certain provisions of the original treaty suggested that the United States secured acceptance of an unpopular treaty by the Choctaws by bribing the leadership. The Pitchlynns, for example, received at least 5,120 acres of land. As Peter had just recently opposed removal, did these special provisions mean that he had sold out? Absolutely not. Out of political considerations all prominent men of the tribe had been on both sides of the removal question at one time or another and never entirely committed to either. When it became obvious in September, 1830, that no reasonable alternative to removal existed, the leadership of the different factions closed ranks and determined to profit individually. To do so proved to be extremely easy as the United States commissioners not only acquiesced in their desires but encouraged them.

To accept preferential treatment, however, implied more of a realization of the inevitable than support of the signed document. The rank and file of the Choctaws were forestalled from

---

[28] Letter of the Choctaw Commissioners, September 25, 1830, and Terms [1830], Folder 30–10, Pitchlynn MSS, G.M.; W. S. Halbert, "Story of the Treaty of Dancing Rabbit," *Publications of the Mississippi Historical Society*, Vol. VI, 391. *Statutes At Large*, VII, 333–41.

revolting at the council ground only when George S. Gaines, at the suggestion of John Pitchlynn, was appointed to lead an exploring party to survey the location of their new homes. This action seemed to assuage the immediate anxieties of the Indians, but once copies of the concordat filtered back into the Nation, opposition, centering around Peter Pitchlynn, sprang up anew.

In its wake, Peter became a vigorous foe of the treaty. Forgetting his own acceptance of two sections of land and his quarrel with the missionaries, he piously accused David Folsom of being unable to withstand the temptation of land reservations and aligned himself with the Presbyterian missionary Loring S. Williams in the general opposition to tribal removal. Pitchlynn even planned a trip to Washington, but two incidents canceled these plans and served to nullify his opposition. Agent William Ward, learning of the collaboration, went immediately to Williams and threatened to expel the whole Presbyterian mission from the Choctaw Nation if he continued to support Peter. In addition, the secretary of war sent a company of troops into the Choctaw country to discourage any prospect of an armed uprising. The action of Ward and the army wholly intimidated Pitchlynn, who had nothing more in mind than a polite protest to the President which would endear him to the full bloods of his district. He forgot about his trip to Washington, but he hoped that the tribe would not.[29]

With the treaty signed and opposition quelled, the process of removal began as early as October, 1830, in LeFlore's Northwestern District. A conflict over leadership prevented such dispatch in Moshulatubbee's Northeastern District. There, in

[29] Pitchlynn, Choctaw Nation, to Folsom [1830], Folder Un–278, and J. L. McDonald, Jackson, to Pitchlynn, November 2, 1830, Pitchlynn MSS, G.M.; *Missionary Herald*, Vol. XXVII (January, 1831), 18; Ward, Choctaw Agency, to Eaton, December 2, 1830, N.A., O.I.A., Choctaw Agency, Letters Received, Microcopy 234, Roll 169; Arthur H. DeRosier, Jr., "Andrew Jackson and Negotiations for the Removal of the Choctaw Indians," *The Historian*, Vol. XXIX (May, 1967), 361.

January, 1831, at the suggestion of the old Republican chief, his supporters replaced him with Peter Pitchlynn.[30] Apparently Peter's role following the treaty had been well received. The Christian party of earlier days, however, denied the election and continued to look to David Folsom as captain and chief.

Despite the contest over his credentials, Pitchlynn, now twenty-four, assumed a degree of leadership. With others he urged the approval of the sale of unsurveyed individual reservations as provided in the treaty and the construction of a road which emigrants could use to drive cattle and other stock across the swamps of Mississippi and Arkansas. Looking to the time after removal, Pitchlynn also planned for some kind of educational facilities. He even wrote to his friend, teacher Henry Vose, about assuming the superintendency of such a school. Peter also dreamed of a new constitution, the construction of which he would supervise once the removal was completed. Further, to support his own family in the new country, he tentatively arranged with Natchez merchants to finance a mercantile business.[31]

To supervise the Choctaw emigration east of the Mississippi the United States selected George S. Gaines. This selection sorely disappointed Pitchlynn since some of his people had urged his appointment as their leader in the West. Yet he did gain permission to organize a party of emigrants, with the purse entrusted to Thomas McGee, a white man from Alabama. Those who planned to emigrate gathered at Peter's home at the end of October, 1831, after the fall harvest. He assisted in hurrying up the latecomers and also provided the party with corn, fodder, and beef, for which he received nearly $200.

[30] Choctaw Council, Dancing Rabbit Creek, to John H. Eaton, January 16, 1831, N.A., O.I.A., Choctaw Agency, Letters Received, Microcopy 234, Roll 169.

[31] Choctaw Chiefs to Ward, May 18, 1831, *ibid.*; Henry Vose, Natchez, to Pitchlynn, September 19, 1831, Pitchlynn MSS, G.M.

Notwithstanding all the preparation, Peter did not expect to move his own family. He was slow to liquidate his own assets, and, furthermore, he saw wisdom in first surveying the land as a leader of emigrants before taking out his wife and family. As the figurative head of a party of more than four hundred, Pitchlynn left the Tombigbee River settlements for Memphis in late October. Thirty days later his party reached the Tennessee city, loaded their ponies on flatboats, and boarded the steamboat *Brandywine* for a trip to the mouth of White River.[32]

The progress of the emigrants from Memphis across Arkansas Territory slowed considerably. On December 28 they were stranded because of low water at the Post of Arkansas, a point very near the mouth of the Arkansas River. In addition to Pitchlynn's group there were more than two thousand other Choctaws at the post, most of whom were forced to brave the winter weather without proper clothes or facilities. In late January the *Reindeer* took Pitchlynn's party aboard and headed up the river for Fort Smith. Ninety miles below the post, low water again halted the boat, and the Choctaws disembarked to begin an encampment that lasted through one of the coldest periods ever known in Arkansas. Finally, on February 20, 1832, the *Reindeer* deposited Pitchlynn and his party at their destination. They settled just south and west of Fort Smith along the Arkansas River, an area already selected for emigrants from the old Northeastern District. It was named Moshulatubbee, and it was also the location of the newly constructed agency, Skullyville. Most of the other parties emigrated to north of the Red River where the region east of the Kiamichi River had been reserved for residents of the old Northwestern District and the area west for those from the extinct Southern District.

---

[32] Accounts of Thomas McGee, Last Quarter of 1831, in 23 Cong., 1 sess., *Sen. Doc. 512*, I, 982; Thomas McGee, Demopolis, Alabama, to George S. Gaines, January 2, 1831, Letters Received, Records of the Commissary General, Bureau of Indian Affairs, N.A.

The new political units were named Oklafalaya and Pushmataha, respectively.[33]

Pitchlynn stayed in the West serving as district chief throughout the winter and early spring of 1832. He devoted most of his energies to selecting home sites for members of his party, seeing that they registered at the agency and drew their provisions and that some system of government was created which would sustain the group in his absence. He also probably chose the future location of his own home, near present Spiro, Oklahoma, which he designated New Hope. In mid-April he left the West and returned to Mississippi.

As he prepared to make arrangements for the fall emigration of 1832, two problems confronted him: a disputed political position among his people and the liquidation of his assets. To solve the former, he addressed a letter to the secretary of war about problems associated with removal. He asked official recognition of his position as chief of the Moshulatubbee District in the West and favorable consideration of his recommendations:

> For a whole nation to give up their whole country, and to remove to a distant, wild, and uncultivated land, more for the benefit of the Government than the Choctaws, is a consideration which, I hope, that the Government will always cherish with the liveliest sensibilities. The privations of a whole nation before setting out, their turmoil, and losses on the road, and settling their new homes in a wild world, are all calculated to embitter the human heart. These can be softened by a generous fulfillment of the treaty, a few thousand dollars more in a liberal fulfillment of that instrument, will be more than counterbalanced by keeping alive forever generous feeling which has always existed in the bosom of the Choctaws toward their white brethren.[34]

[33] Little Rock *Arkansas Gazette*, December 28, 1831, p. 3; Grant Foreman, *Indian Removal*, 51–52.

[34] Pitchlynn, Choctaw Nation, to Hon. Lewis Cass, July 10, 1832, N.A., O.I.A., Choctaw Emigration, Letters Received, Microcopy 234, Roll 185.

The historian of the Choctaws, Angie Debo, points to this letter as indicative of Pitchlynn's bitterness and education. It was indeed a good letter and reflected the sentiments of most tribesmen; unfortunately, Peter did not write it. The rough and even the final drafts were in the handwriting of his friend Henry Vose. The incident amply illustrates Pitchlynn's life-long practice of using the pens and talents of others.[35] The letter wore well as a state paper, but it failed to achieve its immediate purpose. Because Pitchlynn was elected in the East, the War Department refused to recognize him as chief beyond the Mississippi and accordingly denied him the $250 annual stipend provided in the treaty of 1830 (the Treaty of Dancing Rabbit Creek).[36]

In addition to his political activities, in the spring and summer of 1832, Peter converted his sizable estate into cash and transportable goods. The tax rolls of Lowndes County, Mississippi, in 1831 credited him with 4 slaves and eighty acres of cultivated land. But the government census of the Choctaws taken by F. W. Armstrong in 1831 assigned 10 slaves to him and 50 to his father. The number of slaves was significant, since Greenwood LeFlore, considered one of the richest men among the Choctaws, had only 32, while in all of the three districts there were only 521. In terms of slaves John Pitchlynn was the wealthiest man in the tribe.[37]

Peter had even more valuable assets. He had received two sections of land under the terms of the supplementary articles to the treaty of 1830. These he sold to Booth Malone in April, 1832, along with his improvements, fifty head of cattle, other livestock, and full cribs of corn for $6,000 cash plus cancella-

[35] *Ibid.*; Draft of a letter to Lewis Cass, May 2, 1832, Pitchlynn MSS, G.M.
[36] John Robb, Acting Secretary of War, to Pitchlynn, July 28, 1832, N.A., O.I.A., Letters Sent, Microcopy 21, Roll 9.
[37] Lowndes County Tax Roles, 1831, Miss. Archives; Armstrong Role, 1831, Records of the Commissary General, Bureau of Indian Affairs, N.A.; 23 Cong., 1 sess., *Sen. Doc. 512*, III.

tion of a $12,000 note. In August he converted some of the cash into slaves, purchasing five Negro girls ranging in age from eleven to thirteen years old and in price from $275 to $450. On other occasions he made similar transactions in partnership with his father, and by October he owned or had an interest in forty-five Negroes, all of whom prepared to make the trip west.[38]

Having turned his assets into either cash or slaves, young Colonel Pitchlynn readied his family to emigrate in the fall of 1832. Nearly twenty-five hundred Choctaws of the Northeastern District rendezvoused on October 3 at the old council house, where they were divided into two groups, one led by Moshulatubbee and the other by David Folsom. Their first destination was Memphis. From there Moshulatubbee's party would make its way to the Choctaw Agency at Skullyville, either overland or up the Arkansas River, and Folsom's would go to the Red River country.[39] Pitchlynn declined to accompany either party. He preferred to make his own arrangements, the expenses for which the government would reimburse him.

There are several reasons why he chose to travel with only his family. First, the extension of Mississippi state law over the Choctaws had made him liable to lawsuits involving the ownership of a slave and a roan horse. To avoid the legal entanglements speed was important, and a small group traveled faster. Second, Pitchlynn hoped to avoid the frustrations of delay he had experienced on his 1831 trip. Third, he feared the diseases that seemed to afflict large emigrating parties; in this respect he was wise, for cholera decimated the group with which he would have traveled. Fourth, if judiciously managed, the government stipend of ten dollars per capita, including slaves,

---

[38] Deed Record, Book 1–2, Records of the Chancery Court, Lowndes County; Bill of Sale, Columbus, Mississippi, August 18, 1832, Pitchlynn MSS, G.M.

[39] John T. Fulton, Little Rock, to General George Gibson, September 25, 1832, in 23 Cong., 1 sess., *Sen. Doc. 512*, I, 688.

might make the trip profitable. And, finally, traveling alone freed him from the orders of government officials.

Although Pitchlynn managed to avoid the principal evils of emigration, the Choctaws generally, like any group forced to leave their homes, were sorely tested. Alexis de Tocqueville caught the pathos of that test when he observed the Choctaws at Memphis crossing the Mississippi during the same period that Peter crossed:

> . . . in the whole scene there was an air of ruin and destruction, something which betrayed a final and irrevocable adieu; one couldn't watch, without feeling one's heart wrung. The Indians were tranquil, but sombre and taciturn. There was one who could speak English and of whom I asked why the Choctaws were leaving their country. "To be free," he answered.[40]

If some of the tribe were tranquil and taciturn, others were bitter. In less refined language than that of the Frenchman, members of Pitchlynn's party expressed their resentfulness in a song composed as they marched west:

> *Jackson sent the Secretary of War*
> *To tell Indians of the law,*
> *Walk oh jaw bone walk I say*
> *Walk oh jaw bone walk away.*
>
> *On my way to the Arkansas*
> *G——d d——m the white man's law,*
> *Oh come and go along with me*
> *Oh come and go along with me.*
>
> *It snowed, it hailed, I do you tell*
> *And I thought it would pelt us all to hell,*
> *Oh the hard times we did see*
> *Oh the hard times we did see.*
>
> *The salted pork and damned poor beef*
> *Enough to make the devil a thief,*

[40] Quoted in George Wilson Pierson, *Tocqueville in America*, 380.

This is hard times I do say
This is hard times I do say.

We have gone to the West
You will say tis for the best,
We shall never think it so
We shall never think it so.[41]

The song more nearly stated the circumstances of Pitchlynn's 1831 trip, for the Colonel reached Skullyville on November 1, 1832, well before the bitter weather of winter.[42] He moved his hands and family to New Hope and began the task of erecting new cabins and preparing new soil. By the time Moshulatubbee's party arrived in mid-December enfeebled by cholera and struggles against the elements, he had so arranged his personal affairs that he could assume a measure of leadership. He joined with others in asking for the removal of a whisky-selling white interloper[43] and in appealing for additional government assistance to alleviate starvation. The government directed the agent to issue surplus condemned pork. "They will, no doubt, willingly accept, under present circumstances, what they formerly rejected," wrote the commissary general.[44] Such conditions of course stifled concern about public affairs, Pitchlynn's principal interest. But he could wait until men's stomachs were full and their crops abundant. Then he would capitalize upon the support of those full bloods who remembered his leadership and take a formative role in rebuilding his nation.

[41] Draft of a Song, Folder Un–348, Pitchlynn MSS, G.M.

[42] Choctaw Muster Roll 5, Records of the Commissary General, Bureau of Indian Affairs, N.A.

[43] Pitchlynn et al., to Lieut. G. L. Raines, n.d., N.A., O.I.A., Agency West, Letters Received, Microcopy 234, Roll 184.

[44] General George Gibson, Washington, to G. L. Raines, May 6, 1833, Letter Book of the Commissary General, Bureau of Indian Affairs, N.A.

CHAPTER III

Rebuilding the Republic

In November, 1832, the Pitchlynn family resided at New Hope, near the Choctaw Agency at Skullyville, but the site did not fulfill the promise of its name. Arriving too late in the year to plant, Peter engaged his slaves in clearing fields for spring cultivation. Corn was sown in the new ground by mid-May, 1833, and was sprouting by the first of June. But just when Pitchlynn was counting on an abundant harvest, the Arkansas River rose to inundate and kill all of his crops. There was also almost total destruction of his cows and calves, beef cattle, and hogs in what proved to be one of the worst floods in the history of that stream. For many of the less fortunate, the high water meant total destitution, starvation, disease, and death. In a five-week period ending in September, 1833, six hundred in the vicinity died from fever alone.[1] Confronted by this disaster and the continuing expense of his slaves, Pitchlynn had doubts about the wisdom of leaving Mississippi. But before he made

[1] Foreman, *Indian Removal*, 96–99; F. W. Armstrong, Choctaw Agency, to Elbert Herring, September 20, 1833, N.A., O.I.A., Choctaw Agency, Letters Received, Microcopy 234, Roll 170.

a decision to return, he resolved to search out the rest of the new country.

In the fall of 1833 he traveled south over the Kiamichi Mountains to the Red River. There he found a region prospering agriculturally and unaffected by the floods and diseases that ravaged farther north. Many of the residents were old friends, acquaintances, and relatives, most of whom had emigrated in David Folsom's party the year before. Furthermore, the Presbyterian missionaries who had removed with the Choctaws had established stations in the area. Considering the primitive conditions on the Arkansas River, the southern reaches of the new Choctaw Nation seemed to Pitchlynn most ideal. He returned to New Hope convinced that he should move his family to a location he had selected on Mountain Fork River near present Eagletown, Oklahoma.

Peter's decision to move to the Red River area was not an easy one to make. It involved altering his residence from the Moshulatubbee District, with which his family had long been identified, to the Oklafalaya District, where he was not so well known. But because of the capricious removal process that had paid little attention to old tribal ties, such a relocation was entirely feasible in the new country. Consequently, Pitchlynn moved his family to Mountain Fork in the summer of 1834. After his slaves began the process of building new cabins and clearing new ground, he left for a three-month buffalo hunt on the western prairies. When he returned, he had a reasonably commodious home, the first of two he selected in the region. In 1837 or 1838, he moved south to a site near Wheelock Mission, in the vicinity of present Tom, Oklahoma. Throughout the 1830's and 1840's the family alternated between the two locations, though more time was spent at the Wheelock home.[2]

[2] Notebook, n.d., Folder 79–39, Pitchlynn MSS, G.M.; L. S. Williams, Eagletown, to D. Greene, August 8, 1834, Box 35, p. 514, Foreman Collection, G.M.

Back in Mississippi, John Pitchlynn's life had been just as unsettled as that of his son in the Choctaw Nation. Deciding first against and then in favor of selling his assets and emigrating west, John ultimately moved to the Chickasaw country about ten miles from Columbus, Mississippi. From there he appealed to his son to return and live near him. But Peter hesitated, and in late May, 1835, he learned that his father had died. John Pitchlynn's estate, composed largely of slaves, was valued at over $35,000, and Peter's family encouraged him to direct the liquidation of it. For some unknown reason, however, he refused and in the division of the estate, Peter realized only $1,000,[3] having already received a substantial inheritance in slaves.

The death of John Pitchlynn removed the doubts of other members of his family about moving west. Peter's sister's husband, mixed-blood Samuel Garland, who had earlier emigrated and then gone back to Mississippi, made plans to return to the new country. In June, 1836, another brother-in-law, William R. Harris, asked Pitchlynn to select a farm for him as near Mountain Fork River as possible, and in the summer of 1837, his mother emigrated with his youngest sister. Finally, Calvin Howell, another brother-in-law and founder of Plymouth, Mississippi, who longed for the society of "unsophisticated sons of the forest," removed in 1837. For all, Pitchlynn served as advance agent, selecting sites for his relatives near his own home at Eagletown.

Peter failed to record how he supported his family in the West. He went prepared to pursue agricultural activities, but because of the failure on Arkansas River and the move to Mountain Fork in 1834, he certainly realized little profit from that endeavor. At one time he had considered opening a store, a

---

[3] Case of John Pitchlynn, Estate Docket 92, Chancery Court Records, Lowndes County; Samuel Garland, Chickasaw Nation, to Pitchlynn, May 20, 1835, and March 6, 1836, Pitchlynn MSS, G.M.

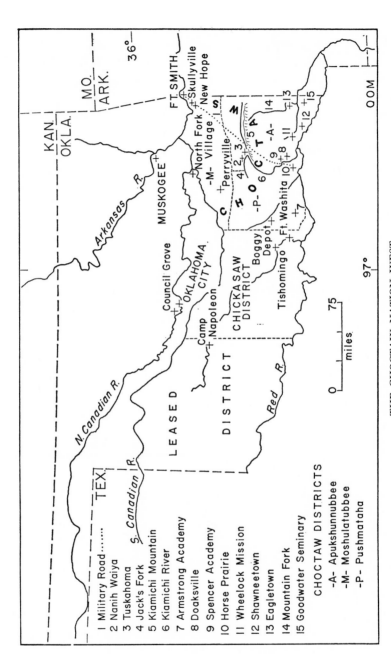

THE CHOCTAW NATION WEST

CHOCTAW DISTRICTS

-A- Apukshunnubbee
-M- Moshulatubbee
-P- Pushmataha

1 Military Road ....
2 Nanih Waiya
3 Tuskahoma
4 Jack's Fork
5 Kiamichi Mountain
6 Kiamichi River
7 Armstrong Academy
8 Doaksville
9 Spencer Academy
10 Horse Prairie
11 Wheelock Mission
12 Shawneetown
13 Eagletown
14 Mountain Fork
15 Goodwater Seminary

possibility that continued to intrigue him even as late as 1839. Yet the mercantile business required constant attention, and Peter did not have that kind of dedication. The government provided an occasional annuity and also subsistence for one year after removal, but neither measure wholly supported the family. For example, in 1838, Pitchlynn purchased additional goods amounting to nearly $1,100.[4] Once he had moved south of the Kiamichis, he relied upon cotton as a source of income, but if his farm supported his family it was not because of his careful attention. Pitchlynn was more interested in public affairs.

The removal of the Choctaws officially ended in the spring of 1834. Until then the tribe could accomplish little toward forming a government and was discouraged from even trying by the United States. Finally, on June 3, 1834, representatives gathered to establish some kind of permanent government at a point "near Turnbull's Stand on Jack's Fork of Kiamichi where the Military road leading from Fort Smith to Horse Prairie crosses that stream." Presently the Choctaws named the location Nanih Waiya after their sacred ceremonial mound in Mississippi, and there they proceeded to write Oklahoma's first constitution.[5]

Pitchlynn had long planned for the convention day. Using as models the constitutions of several American states, especially that of Mississippi, he and his fellow delegates drafted a document providing for a unicameral council composed of ten representatives from each of the three districts, which would meet annually on the first Monday in October. Each district elected a chief to a four-year term, and the three sitting together served as an executive body vested with veto power. The document set forth a bill of rights, extended suffrage to every male

---

[4] Statement of George F. Lawton, February, 1836, to January, 1837, Pitchlynn MSS, G.M.

[5] Constitution, June 3, 1834, *ibid.*

over sixteen years of age, and established a judiciary whereby each district chief appointed judges who held court at stated intervals.[6] To say that Pitchlynn played the decisive role in the convention ignores the contributions of others, yet few Choctaws possessed as much ability or had planned so long for the occasion. He should receive credit for this milestone in the constitutional development of the American Indian.

Pitchlynn took an even more active part in public affairs after the formation of the constitution. For example, he acted as principal Choctaw commissioner during the negotiations with the Chickasaws in January, 1837, at Doaksville. The Chickasaws ceded their Mississippi lands to the United States in 1832, after which time the federal government sought to provide a home for them among their relatives, the Choctaws. During the parley the Chickasaws offered to purchase a part of the Choctaw lands, a proposal refused under Pitchlynn's leadership. The smaller tribe then requested the privilege of forming a district within the limits of the other's country to be called the Chickasaw District. After additional discussion, during which the Choctaws proved themselves consummate negotiators, the Chickasaws received a district west of the Choctaw settlements for which they agreed to pay $530,000.[7]

With the Chickasaws now a part of their nation, the Choctaws met at Nanih Waiya in their newly constructed council house in October, 1838, to write another constitution, a practice that soon became a habit. Of the council that gathered, Peter Pitchlynn served as speaker. He also wrote the rough draft of the constitution ultimately adopted. It differed little from the constitution of 1834 but did provide a chief and coun-

[6] *Ibid.*; *Report of the Commissioner of Indian Affairs, 1838*, 509; Hargrett, *Indian Constitutions and Laws*, 56.

[7] Correspondence between the Choctaw and Chickasaw Delegations, Doaksville, Choctaw Nation, January 11 through 18, 1837, N.A., O.I.A., Choctaw Agency, Letters Received, Microcopy 234, Roll 172; Kappler, *Indian Affairs: Laws and Treaties*, II, 486–88.

cil representation for the Chickasaw District. Oklafalaya District was redesignated Apukshunnubbee and as the largest of the four political units was given thirteen representatives in the council instead of the nine assigned to the others.[8] This constitution, however, was remembered more for the praise it elicited than for its legal qualities. The English trader Thomas J. Farnham, visiting the Choctaws, obtained a copy of the instrument and was so moved by Pitchlynn's handiwork that he wrote:

> At the time when the lights of religion and science had scarcely begun to dawn upon them, even while the dust of antiquated barbarism was still hanging on their garments, they read on all the holy battlements, written with beams of living light, "all men are, and of right ought to be, free and equal." This teaching leads them . . . to rear in the Great Prairie wilderness a sanctuary of republican liberty.[9]

On the basis of his constitutional contributions Pitchlynn entered the race for the office of chief for the Apukshunnubbee District in 1840. This was a bold venture for several reasons. First, his family was traditionally linked with another district, and, second, he was a mixed-blood among a people who knew nothing of his earlier alliance with the full blood, Moshulatubbee. Furthermore, many of those living in the district had belonged to David Folsom's faction in pre-removal days and remembered Peter's vitriolic opposition to "King David." These obstacles proved insurmountable; although the election was close, Pitchlynn was defeated. This setback embittered him for a time, but he continued his public service and in 1841 was appointed one of the captains of his district.[10]

[8] Manuscript of the Constitution, October 3, 1838, Folder 42–55, Pitchlynn MSS, G.M.; *The Report of the Commissioner of Indian Affairs, 1838*, 510; Hargrett, *Indian Constitutions and Laws*, 55.

[9] Thomas J. Farnham, *Travel in the Great Western Prairies*, in Reuben Gold Thwaites, *Early Western Travel*, 124.

[10] Loring S. W. Folsom, Mount Pleasant, to Pitchlynn, July 12, 1840, Pitch-

Removal forced not only personal and governmental re-orientation upon the Choctaws, but readjustment to different neighbors as well. The so-called wild tribes, including Kiowas and Comanches, ranged over lands now assigned to the Choctaws. The buffalo hunt in which Pitchlynn participated in late 1834 was designed to ease relations with these wandering tribes. The hunt lasted some three months and made contact with the western bands, but relations failed to improve until the conclusion of the Treaty of Camp Holmes in August, 1835.[11]

Removal also altered affiliations with the other civilized tribes who followed the Choctaws to Indian Territory. In closer proximity in the West the tribes consulted more often and friction between them occurred less frequently. Intertribal ball plays indicated the closer relations, and at one such event in 1834, Pitchlynn met George Catlin, who was on a tour through the Indian country. The artist, impressed with the game and with Pitchlynn, painted both. Peter always expressed great pride in this encounter, even mentioning it to Charles Dickens some years later.[12]

But the cordiality noticed by Catlin on the occasion of the ball play did not always characterize intertribal relations. In 1837 the Choctaw agent, William Armstrong, recruited warriors to fight the Seminoles, who were resisting removal from Florida. Pitchlynn opposed Choctaw involvement, but the offer of $270 for each enlistment brought five hundred volunteers. When the War Department reduced the pay to only $72.72, interest waned, and Armstrong mustered the Choctaws out of

---

lynn Memorandum Book, Mountain Fork, 1841, Folder 41–61, and Tishomingo Company under Peter Pitchlynn, 1842, Folder 42–50, Pitchlynn MSS, G.M.

[11] F. W. Armstrong, Washington, to Secretary of War Lewis Cass, May 17, 1834, N.A., O.I.A., Choctaw Agency, Letters Received, Microcopy 234, Roll 170.

[12] Catlin, *Letters and Notes*, II, 140–46; *Annual Report of the Smithsonian Institution, 1885*, 212.

the service.[13] The Seminole incident was an exception to the general rule of harmony among the civilized tribes.

Although the treaty of 1830 called for Indian isolation from the white man, disputes with Texans occurred frequently. Efforts of Mexican agents in 1836 to recruit Choctaw troops to oppose the Texas revolutionaries greatly amplified the ill will generated earlier when Choctaw hunters south of Red River were fired upon by white settlers. Strained relations continued throughout the life of the Texas Republic as Texans habitually disregarded the Indian border and among other things engaged in commerce without the proper license. But the controversy was really more smoke than fire, and when the Mexican War began in 1846, Pitchlynn, in Mississippi at the time, boasted of his intention to raise five thousand warriors and offer their services to the government to march across Texas against Mexico. Texas statehood had eased whatever real tensions existed.[14]

Pitchlynn's pronouncements in regard to Texas reflected phases of a new career that began in 1840 and found him frequently on missions outside the Choctaw Nation. His first task on behalf of the tribe grew out of his historic interest in education and the Choctaw Academy. The educational system of the tribe, despite the efforts of missionaries and government teachers, failed to regain its former stature after removal. Dissatisfaction with the general school program, and especially with the academy, existed in all quarters. Thomas LeFlore, a prominent tribal leader, complained that his son received terrible

[13] Armstrong, Choctaw Agency, to J. W. Poinsett, Secretary of War, August 25, 1837, and Armstrong to C. A. Harris, Commissioner of Indian Affairs, November 10, 1837, N.A., O.I.A., Choctaw Agency, Letters Received, Microcopy 234, Roll 170; Notebook, n.d., Folder 79–39, Pitchlynn MSS, G.M.

[14] Armstrong, Fort Towson, to T. Hartley Crawford, Commissioner of Indian Affairs, February 4, 1839, N.A., O.I.A., Choctaw Agency, Letters Received, Microcopy 234, Roll 171; Ebenezer Hotchkins, Goodwater, to David Greene, July 23, 1838, Box 35, p. 556, Foreman Collection, G.M.; Clarksville (Texas) *Northern Standard*, November 5, 1842; Van Buren *Arkansas Intelligencer*, May 30, 1846, p. 3.

treatment at the Kentucky school and learned the vices of gambling and drinking.[15] Josiah Gregg, who visited among the Choctaws in the early 1840's, recorded that students forgot their customs, their relatives, and their national attachments, and frequently acquired indolent, effeminate, and vicious habits.[16] Several returning students, estranged from the rest of the tribe, even committed suicide.[17]

Colonel Richard M. Johnson, who had been elected vice-president of the United States in 1836, perceived the growing opposition to his school. In January, 1840, he urged the United States government to continue its support of the academy for at least two more years and encouraged its superintendent, Thomas Henderson, to invite Peter Pitchlynn to assist in the operation of the institution. Johnson believed that if he could induce Pitchlynn to support the school, its chances for survival would improve accordingly. Coincidentally, in October, 1840, the Choctaws appointed Peter to visit the academy, investigate the situation, and report back to the council. He undertook the assignment that December.[18]

From the beginning, Pitchlynn showed little objectivity. Two reasons prompted his attitude: he wanted to build a similar school at home, and he wanted to be the superintendent. But Johnson, unaware of Peter's ambitions and hoping to gain the tribe's support, offered Pitchlynn the superintendency of the Kentucky school and encouraged him to go to Washington to discuss the future of the academy. Pitchlynn accepted the invitation and after a brief visit to the school arrived in the

[15] Thomas LeFlore to William Armstrong, January 14, 1840, N.A., O.I.A., Schools, Letters Received, Microcopy 234, Roll 779.

[16] Josiah Gregg, *Commerce of the Prairies* (ed. by Max L. Moorhead), 402.

[17] *Report of the Commissioner of Indian Affairs, 1842,* 507.

[18] R. M. Johnson, Washington, to Joel Poinsett, Secretary of War, January 12, 1840, N.A., O.I.A., Schools, Letters Received, Microcopy 234, Roll 779; Johnson to Henderson, June 1, 1840, Box 35, p. 579, Foreman Collection, G.M.

national capital in late February, 1841. With regard to the academy he discreetly reported to the commissioner of Indian affairs that he found conditions much better than he had anticipated. Yet, in the same report, he did not deny that the Choctaw Nation wanted its own school within its own borders.[19]

Johnson misunderstood Pitchlynn's friendly attitude. He tendered him the appointment as superintendent of the Choctaw Academy plus a personal guarantee of a $1,500 annual salary. On March 15, 1841, Peter accepted, but he also remained true to his convictions, taking the position with the understanding that his action would not prolong the existence of the school beyond the two years agreed upon.[20]

Peter returned to the Choctaw Academy in March, 1841, reorganized it, and then hastened to Indian Territory, supposedly to pick up his family. However, his sojourn with the tribe lasted until late July. In the interim he consulted with tribal leaders and made further arrangements concerning the new school planned for the Nation. Pitchlynn also learned to his dismay that Agent Armstrong questioned his credentials to head such an institution. Feeling that a popular endorsement was essential to offset Armstrong's opposition, he initiated a petition campaign in his own behalf urging his appointment as superintendent.[21] But Pitchlynn had to return to Kentucky in late summer without any assurances that he would direct the proposed school. Nonetheless, he was just as committed to severing relationships with the academy as before.

[19] Peter, Choctaw Agency, to Rhoda Pitchlynn, December 11, 1840, and Letter Fragment, n.d., Folder Un–155, Pitchlynn MSS, G.M.; Johnson, Washington, to Thomas Henderson, February 21, 1841, Box 35, p. 482, Foreman Collection, G.M.; Pitchlynn to Crawford, March 2, 1841, N.A., O.I.A., Schools, Letters Received, Microcopy 234, Roll 780.

[20] Agreement between Johnson and Pitchlynn, March 10, 1841, and Pitchlynn to Crawford, March 15, 1841, N.A., O.I.A., Schools, Letters Received, Microcopy 234, Roll 780; Crawford to Pitchlynn, March 13, 1841, N.A., O.I.A., Letters Sent, Microcopy 21, Roll 30.

[21] Letter Draft, n.d., Folder Un–155, Pitchlynn MSS, G.M.

In Kentucky, an incident in mid-September provided the pretext Peter desired to end the tribal attachment to the school. After one of Johnson's Negro servants and a Choctaw student came to blows over a cockfight, Pitchlynn flew into a violent rage, profanely advised the boys to avoid Negro associations, and threatened to break up the school if it happened again. Johnson, who had returned to Kentucky, now realized that his Indian superintendent intended to destroy the academy. To prevent total decimation of enrollment and the withdrawal of students from other tribes, he ultimately agreed, under pressure from Pitchlynn, that some of the Choctaws and Chickasaws could leave the last of October. Concurrently, the Choctaw chiefs advised the secretary of war that they wished to terminate their association with the academy on April 1, 1842, and that they wanted Pitchlynn to effect that objective in Washington. Sustained now by the tribe, Peter moved quickly to ensure the removal of the Choctaw students. He resurrected his old charges of insufficient food and clothing, filthy beds, an unqualified physician, and the dilapidated condition of the school. Johnson, who had second thoughts about student withdrawals, responded as of old that Peter was unqualified, callous, and self-willed. Finally, however, he agreed to the departures and to provide $750 for the boys' expenses home but only if no more than thirty students withdrew. Though Pitchlynn apparently gave his word to this, on November 25 he arrived in Louisville with forty-one students. Johnson sent an agent after the extra eleven, but his efforts availed nothing, as Peter, like Moses, was determined to deliver the boys from bondage. He placed the youngsters on a steamboat going down the Ohio while he boarded another that traveled up the river. His destination was Washington.[22]

[22] David Vanderslice, Choctaw Academy, to Sir, October 31, 1841, Agreement between Johnson and Pitchlynn, September 25, 1841, Choctaw Chiefs, Choctaw Nation, to John Bell, October 8, 1841, Chiefs of the Choctaw Nation

As it had twelve years before, controversy followed in Pitchlynn's wake. Johnson secured affidavits that Peter had provided whisky for the boys and was frequently drunk himself. On the other hand, Pitchlynn condemned the academy as "the nursery of violence and degradation." But that was not all. In the spring of 1842 he stopped by Kentucky on his way home and withdrew the remaining Choctaw students, leaving only 39 scholars from other tribes of the original 122 at the academy.[23]

Peter Pitchlynn ruined the Choctaw Academy despite its record as the chief educational institution of the Choctaws for fifteen years. He opposed it after 1828, and when he accepted the superintendency in 1841, it was to end the school rather than to advance it. Certainly his personal hostility was not unique; yet he capitalized on the growing opposition of full bloods to Johnson's school to secure the establishment of a new academy that he expected to superintend. His actions provide another example of Pitchlynn's using the prejudices of the full bloods to advance his own personal interests.

At the height of the school controversy the chiefs had directed Pitchlynn to go to Washington on tribal business. Arriving in December, 1841, he re-emphasized to the government the desire of the tribe for its own national academy and requested that the funds recently channeled to Kentucky now be applied to support the school envisioned for the Nation. He asked also for an appropriation from the government's Indian Civilization Fund for the education of Choctaw girls at Wheelock, a school administered by Presbyterian missionaries. "The surest way to civilize and improve the condition of our

to Pitchlynn, October 8, 1841, Pitchlynn to William S. Crawford, October 21, 1841, Johnson to Secretary of War John Spencer, November 25, 1841, and O. P. Road to R. M. Johnson, November 28, 1841, N.A., O.I.A., Schools, Letters Received, Microcopy 234, Roll 780.

23 John W. Forbis, White Sulphur Springs, to R. M. Johnson, December 21, 1841, and Pitchlynn, Washington, to Crawford, January 13, 1842, *ibid.*

people is to educate our females," he wrote. To both requests the government responded tentatively but encouragingly.[24]

Other matters of interest related to claims against the government, both individual and national, for nonfulfillment of treaty obligations. Pitchlynn inquired when the Choctaws who lost cattle during the tribal removal would be compensated. He demanded that some accommodation be made for the Indians who desired to stay in Mississippi as permitted by the treaty of 1830 but were prevented from doing so by the fraudulent actions of the agents. Peter also asked that orphans provided for in the removal treaty receive the benefits stipulated, and he urged that the Choctaws be allotted the looms and the spinning wheels promised in the same agreement.[25]

Other items of a more general nature also interested Pitchlynn. He wanted the government to issue a patent to the Choctaws for their land which would give them undisputed legal title to their new home. He urged Congress to seat a delegate from Indian Territory, contested the congressional award to Joseph Bogy, a trader whose property in the Osage country was raided by Pushmataha's band in 1807, and asked the government to distribute the annuity in summer rather than fall. Finally, he vigorously protested the action of the Texans who, he charged, indiscriminately murdered Choctaw Indians.[26]

All things considered, Pitchlynn's mission to Washington in 1842 succeeded moderately. He laid the groundwork for

[24] Pitchlynn to John C. Spencer, January 6, 1842, *ibid.*

[25] Memorandum Book, Mountain Fork, 1841, Folder 41–61, and Pitchlynn, Washington, to Senator James T. Moorehead, January 3, 1842, Pitchlynn MSS, G.M.; Crawford to Pitchlynn, three letters dated March 14, 1842, N.A., O.I.A., Letters Sent, Microcopy 21, Roll 32; Pitchlynn to Spencer, February 14, 1842, N.A., O.I.A., Choctaw Agency, Letters Received, Microcopy 234, Roll 171.

[26] Crawford, Washington, to William Armstrong, March 28, 1842, Pitchlynn, Washington, to Congress [1842], Folder Un–282, Memorandum of Pitchlynn to Congress, n.d., Folder Un–177, and Pitchlynn, Washington, to the Hon. John C. Spencer, March 25, 1842, Pitchlynn MSS, G.M.

the future educational system of the Choctaws, secured a patent for the western lands, and received governmental promises to pay the annuity earlier and to supply the looms still due. And significantly, questions of claims based upon nonfulfillment of treaty provisions were set aside for future consideration by the government.

On the trip home Pitchlynn had the pleasant experience of meeting the English novelist Charles Dickens on the steamboat between Cincinnati and Louisville. Learning of Dickens' presence, the Choctaw sent him one of his cards, something that the Englishman found unique, as he did Peter's facility with the English language and his common, everyday clothes. Further, Pitchlynn impressed Dickens as a person. "He was a remarkably handsome man," the novelist wrote, "with long black hair, an aquiline nose, broad cheek bones, a sunburnt complexion, and a very bright, keen, dark, and piercing eye." To him Peter was "as stately and complete a gentleman of Nature's making as ever I beheld, moving among the people in the boat as another kind of being." Dickens saw the American Indian as a romantic being, and he so described Pitchlynn.[27] This kind of identification by non-Indians complicated Peter's role in life. More white than red, he was nonetheless confined to a society that did not entirely trust him nor wholly desire his services. No wonder he came to see his personal interests as more important than all others.

Back in the Nation by the summer of 1842, Pitchlynn offered himself as a candidate for the council from his district. Defeated for chief two years earlier, he conducted a vigorous campaign that included at least two speeches on temperance and one on patriotism. Successful in the bid, he took his seat in the council that convened at Nanih Waiya in October, 1842, and was again elected speaker of the unicameral legislature that met according to the constitution of 1838. He soon dissolved

[27] Charles Dickens, *American Notes*, 191–93.

this gathering into a convention which, under his watchful eye, wrote and adopted another constitution on November 10, 1842. Pitchlynn had been impressed by the organization of Congress at Washington, and he saw it as an answer to the complaints of the smaller Choctaw districts that their influence in the council suffered because of the larger representation of the more populous district. Accordingly the new document provided for a bicameral council. It called for a senate composed of three members from each district elected for two-year terms and a house of representatives elected annually and apportioned among the districts according to population. The executive and judicial branches of the government remained unaltered. As this constitution was the third one written in eight years, the experimenting Choctaws agreed to call a halt and provided that no alteration could be made in the new document for eight years.[28]

The council of 1842 also passed an educational act which provided for two male academies and four female seminaries. The institution most favored in appropriations was Spencer Academy, the national school of which Pitchlynn had so long dreamed. For the maintenance of all the schools the council appropriated nearly $20,000 out of annuities normally distributed per capita, the first such educational appropriation in American Indian history. It placed one school under the direction of the Methodist Missionary Society and assigned the four female seminaries to the American Board of Commissioners for Foreign Missions. It elected, however, to retain direct control of Spencer Academy.[29] Together with the adoption of other educational measures, the School Act suggested an enlightened and concerned tribal leadership that deserved much praise. But most of the credit belonged to Peter Pitchlynn and, though it was somewhat self-serving, the legislation of 1842 comprised his single most significant contribution to the Choctaw Nation.

[28] Hargrett, *Indian Constitutions and Laws*, 57; Debo, *Rise and Fall*, 74–75.

To administer the educational system the council established a board of trustees and appointed Peter its president. Although he was responsible for all the schools, he made Spencer Academy his special project. He had always envisioned himself as superintendent, but, denied that post because of the overpowering influence of the tribal agent, Pitchlynn determined to make as much of his official power as he could. With the advice of the trustees and the agent, he appointed Edmund McKinney, a Presbyterian missionary, as superintendent and then worked to have the academy opened by January, 1844. Successful in meeting the target date, Peter's enthusiasm knew no bounds when he enrolled his oldest son and several of his nephews in the first class.

Yet for all of its promise, tribal control of Spencer proved very disappointing. The superintendent and the trustees frequently antagonized one another. Pitchlynn appointed a nephew, Jacob Folsom, farmer for the academy at a salary which McKinney considered extravagant. On the other hand, Folsom thought the superintendent rather "green" and objected to the purchase of a large mirror for the school. "Our sons will turn out to be real fops," he wrote. "It puts me in mind of the Roman Catholic chapels."[30] Pitchlynn on one occasion interfered in the letting of a contract for the construction of a dormitory, and on another considered withdrawing his son in protest to the administration.[31] His authority so challenged, McKinney resigned in October, 1845, whereupon the council placed Spencer under the direction of the Presbyterian Board of For-

[29] Joseph P. Folsom, *The Laws of the Choctaw Nation, 1869* (New York, 1869), 78–81.

[30] McKinney, Spencer, to Walter Lowrey, July 18, 1845, Box 9, Vol. II, American Indian Correspondence MSS, Presbyterian Historical Society; Folsom, Spencer, to Pitchlynn, December 17, 1843, Folder 45–47, Pitchlynn MSS, G.M.

[31] *Ibid.*; McKinney, Spencer, to Pitchlynn, [1844], Folder 44–55, Pitchlynn MSS, G.M.

eign Missions, Philadelphia, Pennsylvania. In concurring in this decision, Pitchlynn admitted that he and the Nation were unprepared to direct a school with an enrollment of one hundred students.

Peter's interest in Spencer continued throughout the 1840's. He looked upon the school as the only suitable educational institution for his children and as the best hope of the tribe, despite the fact that in 1847, for the second time, he sought to reprimand the school's administration for disciplining his son. In 1849 he alone among men of stature opposed the division of the student body into smaller groups. But by 1854, Pitchlynn had largely lost interest in the academy, as his sons and the sons of his mixed-blood friends refused to accept the discipline of the missionaries and left the school. Fullblood Choctaws soon filled the vacant places, and Peter's visits ceased. To the missionaries it appeared that he retained his interest only as long as the school benefited his own family.[32]

Yet, by 1850, other educational matters vied for Pitchlynn's attention. The treaty of 1830 had provided a twenty-year annuity for the education of forty Choctaw young men. When the tribe deserted that institution, the funds once channeled to the Choctaw Academy were available for expenditure elsewhere in the United States. In 1842 the council suggested that the forty youngsters be sent to four different schools, including Ohio and Asbury universities. The tribe took no immediate action, and in May, 1844, Pitchlynn and his colleagues wisely decided to wait until their scholars received additional training in the tribal schools. Four years later they thought their students were adequately prepared, and the trustees selected seven Spencer-trained boys, including Pitchlynn's son and two nephews, to attend eastern schools. Peter preferred

[32] James R. Ramsey, Spencer, to Lowrey, October 13, 1847, Alexander Reid, Spencer, to Lowrey, August 7, 1849, and Reid, Spencer, to Lowrey, January 6, 1854, Box 9, Vol. II, American Indian Correspondence MSS, Presbyterian Historical Society.

unpretentious schools since, he claimed, Princeton, Yale, and Harvard were all "dissipated and full of wild fellows." Ultimately in March, 1848, the Choctaw students were enrolled in Delaware College in Newark, New Jersey, a school with a student body of less than seventy-five.[33]

The Choctaws continued to send students to schools in the United States throughout the 1850's. Pitchlynn provided them with fatherly counsel and administered the funds appropriated for their maintenance. His concern for their welfare was genuine, but when they besieged him with requests for additional money, more often than not their letters were unanswered. Yet Pitchlynn always managed to retain the respect and gratitude of the scholars and their families. The selection of a student for study in the "states" as well as in the Choctaw Nation relieved the parents, both mixed-blood and fullblood, of a great financial burden and placed them in Pitchlynn's debt, an obligation they repaid by support of his political ambitions. Still, the educational program interested Peter for its intrinsic value, and the tribe recognized him as the system's architect.

Between 1845 and 1847, Pitchlynn devoted himself to affairs designed to increase his personal fortune, but in late 1847 he traveled to Washington on his third official mission. In addition to the placement of Choctaw students in eastern schools and personal speculation, two things occupied his time: a $5,000 claim against the Chickasaws and proposed legislation in Congress for an Indian Territory. The claim against the brother tribe stemmed from the Treaty of 1837, terms of which obligated the Chickasaws to pay the Choctaws $530,000. The

---

[33] Pitchlynn, Doaksville, to Armstrong, December 12, 1842, and James P. Wilson, Delaware College, to William Medill, Received November 10, 1848, N.A., O.I.A., Schools, Letters Received, Microcopy 234, Roll 784; Trustees to Armstrong, May 15, 1844, and Minutes of the Meeting of the Trustees, January 13, 1848, Pitchlynn MSS, G.M.; Pitchlynn, Washington, to Thompson McKenney, December 13, 1848, H-44, J. L. Hargett MSS, Western History Collection, University of Oklahoma Library (hereinafter U.O.L.).

smaller tribe paid $30,000 in cash immediately and transferred to the Choctaws $500,000 in bonds held in trust by the government. But the Choctaws maintained that the treaty envisioned a completely cash payment, with which they might have purchased $750,000 in bonds. They reasoned they had been cheated out of $250,000 in invested funds. Even more significant, the Chickasaws had paid only $495,000 for the bonds used to settle the $500,000 debt. The complaint about receiving bonds instead of cash gained little consideration in Washington, but Pitchlynn and his colleagues did bring the $5,000 discrepancy to the attention of the United States Senate. After some vigorous lobbying by Pitchlynn, the Senate resolved on January 26, 1849, that the Choctaws ought to receive from the Chickasaws $5,000 in additional funds and referred the matter for a final decision to President James K. Polk. On February 20, 1849, Polk ruled that the Choctaws should receive the $5,000, but no interest. For Pitchlynn the decision represented a rather small return on a great deal of work.[34]

Congressional proposals for Indian Territory also demanded Peter's attention. With the very first Indian removals beyond the Mississippi River the federal government had hoped to establish some type of Indian state that would include all of the tribes. Pledges in the removal treaties momentarily restrained specific legislation, but interest in that type of arrangement increased in the late 1840's. To forestall any legislative action Pitchlynn filed a protest with Congress on February 3, 1849. The document pointed to the impossibility of an Indian state because of different tribal laws and customs, and it maintained that the tribes were doing well on their "fruitful farms and flourishing villages." To be sure, the territorial scheme was beautiful in theory, but it was the beauty of a summer cloud

---

[34] Pitchlynn, Washington, to William Medill, January 31, 1849, Resolution of the United States Senate, January 26, 1849, and Office of Indian Affairs, Washington, to Pitchlynn, February 23, 1849, Pitchlynn MSS, G.M.

with borders tipped in sunlight. In the cloud, forked lightning and thunderbolts scattered death around.[35]

The House of Representatives did not consider favorably the legislation to which Pitchlynn addressed himself. But Peter's personal contribution to the defeat of the measure can be over-emphasized.[36] His memorial registered well the objections of the Choctaws, but in view of his practice of having important state papers prepared for him, it is doubtful that he wrote the document. The inspiration may have been his and even some of the imagery, but surely the drafting was done by others.

In August, 1849, Peter completed his personal and private business in Washington and returned to the Choctaw Nation to look after his farms. He took time to serve in the council that met in 1849 and in the constitutional convention of 1850. The latter convention met at Nanih Waiya in October, and once more under his leadership adopted a constitution that differed only moderately from earlier documents. The Choctaws retained the executive made up of four district chiefs, increased the term of service of senators to four years, and provided for a judicial system that established a supreme court, four district circuit courts, and county courts, the judges of which were selected by the general council. Ratifying its own creation, the convention then constituted itself as the first government operative under the constitution and passed legislation that among other things divided the nation into different counties and moved the capital to Doaksville. Such questionable methods of ratification nearly caused civil war in the late 1850's, but for the moment no one opposed Pitchlynn's fourth constitution.[37]

[35] 30 Cong., 1 sess., *House Misc. Doc. 35*, 1–4.

[36] Debo, in *Rise and Fall*, 67, refers to Pitchlynn's "desperate eloquence" and Grant Foreman, in *Advancing the Frontier*, 191–94, notes his "devastating presentation" in attacking the measure. These assessments overstate his personal contribution.

[37] *Choctaw Intelligencer*, October 30, 1840, a. col. 2; *Constitutions and Laws of the Choctaw Nation* [Doaksville, 1852], in Folder 52–15, Pitchlynn MSS, G.M.

CHAPTER IV

The Jackson Man and Family Man

Richard Hofstadter has described the "Jackson man" as "an expectant capitalist, a hardworking, ambitious person for whom enterprise was a kind of religion." He "everywhere found conditions that encouraged him to extend himself."[1] Further, Thomas P. Abernethy has suggested that if the Jackson Age leader could contrive to make his public position contribute to his private fortune, he was not condemned for his action.[2] In terms of these criteria, Peter Pitchlynn was a Jackson man. Circumstances of the era excited in him prospects of profit, and, like his white contemporaries, in pursuit of his official duties he was never unmindful of his own interests.

Peter Pitchlynn's most speculative endeavors grew out of the removal treaty signed at Dancing Rabbit Creek in 1830. That concordat provided for three varieties of Indian land allotments. First, under the nineteenth article, 1,250 heads of

[1] Richardson Hofstadter, *American Political Tradition*, 57. For a related discussion of the mountain man see William R. Goetzmann, "The Mountain Man as Jacksonian Man," *The American Quarterly*, Vol. XV (Fall, 1963), 402–15.

[2] Thomas P. Abernethy, *From Frontier to Plantation in Tennessee*, 227.

families received grants of land equal to the amount they generally cultivated. The government expected that the individual holding such a reservation would sell immediately to finance removal. Second, influential Indians, white men, and mixed-bloods were granted "special reservations" which they might either sell or keep. In accordance with this provision, as already noted, Pitchlynn received two such sections. Finally, the fourteenth article awarded 640 acres to any head of family who wanted to remain in Mississippi and granted title of the land to him after five years' residence.[3] Both the beneficiaries of the treaty and white purchasers experienced difficulty in securing unclouded titles. For example, Pitchlynn sold his two sections to Booth Malone in 1832 for $6,000 and the cancellation of a $12,000 note. By February, 1839, Malone had not yet received the patent, even though he had sold the property. Finally, the government issued the patent to Peter, who in turn delivered it to Malone, but not until the latter paid an additional $3,005.[4] By threatening to retain the patent, Pitchlynn forced an upward adjustment of the original price, a process repeated many times in Mississippi.

There were other possibilities for profit. The Choctaw agent had prevented vast numbers of the tribe who wanted to remain in Mississippi from selecting the 640-acre reservation provided by the fourteenth article. Denied the land, about six thousand Choctaws stayed anyway. Self-appointed white "guardians" of the Indians learned of the situation, located independently the lands not yet entered in Mississippi for the dispossessed, and then worked to get the government's approval of the assignment.[5] In return they asked for half of everything the Indians

[3] Kappler, *Indian Affairs: Laws and Treaties*, II, 310–18.
[4] Deed Records, Book 1–4, p. 108, Book 12, p. 1, and Book 22, p. 340, Records of the Chancery Court, Lowndes County; T. Hartley Crawford, Washington, to Senator T. H. Williams, February 9, 1939, N.A., O.I.A., Letters Sent, Microcopy 21, Roll 26.
[5] Young, *Redskins, Ruffleshirts, and Rednecks*, 47–72.

secured. This type of activity represented the most common speculative endeavor after Choctaw removal.

On his mission to Washington in 1841 as superintendent of the Choctaw Academy, Pitchlynn met some of the white guardians interested in Indian claims. These gentlemen recognized immediately the contribution Peter as an influential Choctaw could make to their operation and worked to interest him in the possibilities of speculation. The schemes of Reuben Grant impressed Pitchlynn the most. Grant had traded among the Indians prior to 1830, but now was interested in aspects of the Chickasaws' removal. This tribe had suffered a fate similar to that of the Choctaws and, after ceding their lands in 1832, many found themselves swindled out of reservations granted by the government. Grant wanted to bring this injustice to the attention of the federal authorities and to demand some financial adjustment, which if properly handled might pay the Chickasaws $6,000,000 to $10,000,000. In that case, Grant believed that the tribe would not object to paying two "attorneys" $125,000 each. Peter's job was to see that he and his partner received a contract from the Chickasaws to press the claims.[6]

In the spring of 1841, after a quick stop at the Choctaw Academy, Pitchlynn made overtures to the Chickasaws and generated some interest in the scheme. But having been initiated into the speculative fraternity, Peter decided to drop his role subordinate to Grant's and go into business for himself. He and a friend, Thomas Wall, purchased two of the four sections of Mississippi land allotted by the 1830 treaty to the deceased chief, Moshulatubbee. Both knew that the chief had sold the 1,280 acres in 1834 for more than $4,200, but that modest sum only enhanced the speculative possibilities. In September, Peter protested to the Office of Indian Affairs against the issuance of a patent to the original purchasers, demanding instead that

[6] Grant, Macon, to Pitchlynn, April 28, 1841 and April 29, 1841, Pitchlynn MSS, G.M.

the patent be issued to him. Such action by the government would cloud the title and open the possibility of a settlement. Pitchlynn succeeded in delaying the issuance of the patent, but his protest ultimately failed, largely because his father and wife had both witnessed the original transaction.[7]

Peter's visit to Washington in early 1842 proved unsatisfactory for speculative purposes, but his third mission in 1845 was more fruitful. Since his plans with the Chickasaws had failed to materialize, he devoted his attention to the so-called orphan claim. The treaty of 1830 granted to each Choctaw orphan a quarter-section of Mississippi land and directed the President of the United States to locate, sell, and apply the proceeds to the benefit of the orphan. In 1837, 134 quarter-sections were sold for $131,762.81 on a credit of two, four, and six years. When the notes fell due, however, with few exceptions the purchasers failed to meet their obligations. In March, 1842, of the total purchase price only $25,000 had been paid. Furthermore, the government refused to release the money to the orphans until all was collected. In March, 1843, President John Tyler initiated proceedings in the United States District Court to collect from the purchasers the balance due, but, to the surprise of all, the court ruled that the executive had no authority to sell the land in the first place as that right was retained by the individual orphan. The government appealed the decision to the United States Supreme Court, but in the meantime the legal action clouded all titles to the land in question.[8]

Pitchlynn and his friends moved to take advantage of the

[7] Contract between Pitchlynn and Wall, June 29, 1841, D. Kurtz, Office of Indian Affairs, to Pitchlynn, September 30, 1841, and L. N. Hatch, Columbus, Mississippi, to Pitchlynn, December 28, 1841, *ibid.*

[8] T. Hartley Crawford, Washington, to Pitchlynn, March 22, 1842, and Pitchlynn, Washington, to Crawford, February 14, 1842, N.A., O.I.A., Choctaw Reserves, Letters Received, Microcopy 234, Roll 191; John A. Rogers, Fort Smith, to William Armstrong, June 5, 1844, N.A., O.I.A., Choctaw Reserves, Letters Received, Microcopy 234, Roll 194.

controversy. In February, 1845, he concluded a questionable agreement with Reuben Grant and John N. Nail in Mississippi. Previously Nail had located the Choctaw orphans or their representatives, purchasing at a pittance whatever claim the district court now ruled they had to reservations in Mississippi. Nail paid only part of the agreed-upon price and promised to pay the rest when the government approved his purchase. In Nail's contract with Pitchlynn and Grant, the latter two agreed to go to Washington and demand presidential confirmation of Nail's acquisitions.[9] As the opportunity for profit was considerable and the title to thousands of acres in the balance, Peter hastened to Washington in early 1845.

Influential Choctaws criticized the whole orphan scheme. Despite the ruling of the lower court, they believed that the government's sale of the land was final. How, they asked, could Nail and Pitchlynn now purchase land that the government had already sold to others? In Washington, Peter attempted to quiet this criticism by urging the Office of Indian Affairs to distribute among the orphans the money already collected from the presidential sales. But, pending the decision of the Supreme Court, the government rightly refused to release money that might have to be returned to the original purchasers.[10]

With the request, an even more lucrative scheme than Nail's occurred to Pitchlynn. If he secured the payment to the orphans of funds already in the treasury, the tribal council ought to be so thankful that it would reward him with a contingent fee. After sounding out R. M. Jones, a prominent Choctaw planter and trader, Peter hurried home to cash in on his growing number of "educational" I.O.U.'s and to organize a pressure group that would secure authorization for such action. His plan suc-

[9] Agreement between Nail, Pitchlynn, and Grant, Noxubee County, Mississippi, February, 1845, Pitchlynn MSS, G.M.
[10] Israel Folsom, New Hope, to Pitchlynn, March 4, 1845, *ibid.*; Pitchlynn, Washington, to Crawford, April 3, 1845, N.A., O.I.A., Choctaw Reserves, Letters Received, Microcopy 234, Roll 194.

ceeded, and on October 8, 1845, the council ordered Pitchlynn back to Washington and agreed to pay him 10 per cent of all orphan monies paid into the Choctaw treasury.[11]

A visit with President James K. Polk in December finally convinced Pitchlynn that he could not demand payment of the orphan claim and assist Nail at the same time. Nail's scheme prevented the initial purchasers of the land from continuing payment and the government from releasing those funds already in the treasury. Thus, in 1845, Peter abandoned Nail and supported the view that the presidential sales were final. But other matters prevented progress until 1848.[12]

In that year Pitchlynn and George W. Harkins, a prominent district chief of the Choctaws, returned to Washington with special instructions to secure the release of orphan funds held by the United States. They hired attorney Joseph Bryan to protect the tribal interest in the case pending before the Supreme Court, which in its January, 1849, term reversed the lower court's decision and held that the presidential sales were final. So supported, in June the government proceeded to collect the unpaid amounts from buyers or foreclose. Purchasers of nearly half of the 134 quarter-sections paid up, while the government foreclosed and remarketed the remainder.[13]

This action increased the amount in the United States treasury credited to the Choctaw orphans. Pitchlynn now acted to get the funds transferred to the tribe so that he could collect

11 Jones, Choctaw Nation, to Pitchlynn, August 16, 1845, August 29, 1845, and Resolution of the National Council, October 8, 1845, Pitchlynn MSS, G.M.

12 Pitchlynn, Washington, to William Medill, December 16, 1845, N.A., O.I.A., Choctaw Reserves, Letters Received, Microcopy 234, Roll 194; Richard Evans, Columbus, Mississippi, to Pitchlynn, April 22, 1846, Pitchlynn MSS, G.M.

13 Pitchlynn, Washington, to Thomas McKenney, December 13, 1848, H–44, J. L. Hargett Collection, Western History Collection, U.O.L.; G. W. Manypenny, Commissioner of Indian Affairs, to Secretary of Interior R. McClelland, July 21, 1854, N.A., O.I.A., Choctaw Agency, Letters Received, Microcopy 234, Roll 173.

his 10 per cent. After extended petitioning, the government released the money in the spring of 1850, and Pitchlynn and Harkins collected $9,123 for their services. The return was small considering the ten years of hard work and prolonged absences from home, but to Peter it was only the first of an anticipated series of dividends.[14]

Pitchlynn had speculative interests other than the orphan claim. One grew out of the fourteenth article of the treaty of 1830 which gave 640 acres to Choctaws who wanted to remain in Mississippi. Because many Indians claimed they had been prevented from taking advantage of that prerogative, Congress had established two commissions, in 1837 and in 1842, to investigate the circumstances. Indian claimants appeared before the second commission, and if their eligibility for fourteenth article benefits was established and the government had not disposed of land they claimed, it was awarded to them. But where the land had been sold or not enough was available to satisfy individual claims, the commission awarded land scrip to the defrauded Indians at the rate of $1.25 an acre. The government land offices in Mississippi, Alabama, Louisiana, and Arkansas all negotiated the issued paper. The scrip was paid, however, only if the claimant moved to the West, and even then he received just one half of the amount due, the other half to be delivered after emigration.[15] With a number of claims adjudicated in September, 1844, the government contracted with private parties to remove those Choctaws eligible for the scrip.

Able lobbying on the part of the Indian guardians was required even to gain recognition of the claims. The chore completed, they arranged to harvest the profits. But the ladder to financial success had three steps: establish the claim, get the

---

[14] John Drennen, Choctaw Agency, to Orlando Brown, Commissioner of Indian Affairs, May 16, 1850, N.A., O.I.A., Choctaw Agency, Letters Received, Microcopy 234, Roll 171.

[15] Franklin L. Riley, "Choctaw Land Claims," *Publications of the Mississippi Historical Society*, Vol. VIII, 366–67.

Indian to remove west, and then get the first half of the awarded scrip as an attorney fee. Control of at least one of the first two steps increased the chances of achieving the third. Accordingly, two groups of speculators evolved: one attempted to gain the scrip by establishing the claim, while the other hoped to obtain the paper by controlling the removal process. Pitchlynn associated with both groups, but his duties were always the same— influence the Mississippi Choctaws to remove west. As scrip was paid only if the Indian emigrated, he played a crucial role to the success of either group.

Daniel Saffarans, a Tennessee merchant once a friend of Andrew Jackson, dominated one of the two speculative groups with which Pitchlynn worked. As a means of obtaining the scrip Saffarans gained control of the government contract for removal. He sent Pitchlynn to Mississippi during the fall and spring of 1846 and 1847 to locate those Choctaws eligible for scrip, persuade them to move west, and then lead them to a rendezvous where government agents paid the scrip due. Once the agent handed over the land warrants, the Indians turned to face a table piled high with coin and currency. With Pitchlynn standing by, they frequently agreed to exchange their scrip for money at prices of less than thirty-one cents an acre. Having successfully used their official position, the removal contractors hurried the Choctaws over the river and then marketed the scrip at a higher price.[16]

The success of the speculators who controlled the removal contract was frequently spoiled by those interests who had

[16] B. J. Jacoway, Coffediliah, Mississippi, to Pitchlynn, August 18, 1846, A. Harris, Union, Mississippi, to Pitchlynn, November 13, 1846, and W. P. Stone, New Orleans, to Pitchlynn, March 6, 1847, Pitchlynn MSS, G.M.; Thompson McKenney, Washington, to Luke Lea, Commissioner of Indian Affairs, May 6, 1852, N.A., O.I.A., Choctaw Reserves, Letters Received, Microcopy 234, Roll 196; H. L. Martin, Washington, to W. Medill, Commissioner of Indian Affairs, July 24, 1847, 34A–HA, Records of the United States Senate, N.A.

established the individual Indian's claim before the commission. Thus, the Choctaws Pitchlynn and others brought into camp were generally represented by one specific "guardian" who expected payment for his attention. When the government paid the scrip, the amount being half of the total award, the guardian demanded all of it and objected strenuously to efforts by the removal contractor to purchase the paper from the Indians. Furthermore, unless he got his fee, he prevented the Choctaws he influenced from emigrating, thereby destroying the entire purpose of the scrip payments.[17] Pitchlynn, of course, generally opposed this class of speculator, and to the uninitiated his efforts seemed worthy of great praise. One woman missionary who in January, 1847, observed the removal process in Mississippi referred to Peter as "a faithful friend and guide to the Indians" who sought to forestall the "pettifoggers" who wanted to rob the emigrants of their scrip.[18]

To deliver the Indians from the clutches of the guardians, Choctaw Agent William Armstrong recommended in March, 1846, that all land warrants be paid in the West. He believed that the Choctaws ought to realize something for their land, even if but a fraction of the true value.[19] Pitchlynn and his friends, the removal contractors interested only in purchasing the scrip, concurred in such a policy as it placed the Indians beyond the influence of guardians and increased the possibilities of scrip purchase. Furthermore, since the removal contract expired on June 1, 1847, operations in the West might produce faster returns on a smaller investment.

The decision of the government in the summer of 1847 to

[17] A. Harris, Vicksburg, to Pitchlynn, December 25, 1846, Pitchlynn MSS, G.M.; William Armstrong, Napoleon, Arkansas, to William Medill, January 24, 1847, N.A., O.I.A., Choctaw Emigration, Letters Received, Microcopy 234, Roll 186.

[18] Ann J. Marshall, *The Autobiography of Mrs. A. J. Marshall*, 31.

[19] Armstrong, Vicksburg, to Medill, March 10, 1846, N.A., O.I.A., Choctaw Emigration, Letters Received, Microcopy 234, Roll 186.

pay the scrip outside of Mississippi radically altered Pitchlynn's situation. It was important to his associates that, when the land warrants were paid, Peter should be on hand to influence their sale to the organization. In April, 1847, after meeting at Vicksburg with Saffarans and Arnold Harris, two of the principals in the removal contract, Pitchlynn returned to the Nation to guard the group's interests.[20] Thus, after more than a year in Mississippi, Peter appeared in Indian Territory in May, 1847, still in pursuit of the speculator's fortune.

The success of the program as envisioned by Saffarans required a vigorous removal policy. By late 1847, however, emigration slowed to a trickle, though less than half of the six thousand Mississippi Indians had been removed. The Indian agent attributed the disappointing results to the "guardians" who thwarted removal as long as they were denied their "fee." Finally, to speed up the process, the government decided to assume the physical responsibility of emigration itself, but this altered the situation little. As the flow of emigrants ebbed, few scrip payments occurred that Pitchlynn could influence, and the expected fortune never materialized. Although Saffarans owed Peter $1,200, if he ever made more than expenses, the records do not show it.[21]

While Pitchlynn was working with organizations he also operated as a private speculator. On his second trip to Washington in 1842 he urged recognition of a number of individual fourteenth article claims, expecting a contingent fee. On another occasion he secured bounty warrants for his mother which had been issued for John Pitchlynn's service during the War of 1812. For a fee he also agreed to collect a debt owed by his sister's husband to a Mississippi merchant. During the

[20] A. Harris, Vicksburg, to Pitchlynn, April 6, 1847, and W. B. Stone, Washington, Arkansas, to Pitchlynn, May 21, 1847, Pitchlynn MSS, G.M.
[21] *Report of the Commissioner of Indian Affairs, 1847*, 735; Pitchlynn to A. A. Halsey, July 27, 1846, and Will of Peter Pitchlynn, Choctaw Nation, March 4, 1848, Pitchlynn MSS, G.M.

1850's, when he spent even more time in Washington, he represented tribes other than the Choctaws, interesting himself in claims of the Pawnee Indians in 1857 and in 1860 in those of the Chippewa tribe. But this private practice as a claims representative never really succeeded.[22]

The era, however, seemed to offer rewards in matters not related to Indian affairs. In 1842 possibilities of a silver mine in the Choctaw country excited Pitchlynn, as did a practice of "botanic medicine" four years later. In 1845 he hoped to make something as an agent for the Van Buren *Arkansas Intelligencer*, while ten years later he and R. M. Jones attempted to start a local newspaper with N. A. Hartley, the editor of the *Chickasaw Intelligencer*. More as a donation than as an investment, in 1852 he purchased a bond from the Hungarian Count Louis Kossuth, while in 1857, through a company controlled by William H. Russell, of Majors and Russell, he bought one lot and one block of land in Leavenworth, Kansas, for $3,000 and an interest in the companies developing Ogden City and Lecompton. Furthermore, like other investors of the period, the Choctaw purchased two hundred shares of common stock in the Cairo and Fulton (Arkansas) Railroad Company, paying $250 down on the total purchase price of $2,500.[23]

None of these "investments" proved profitable. There was no silver in Indian Territory and no profit in herbs. The paper

[22] Pitchlynn, Washington, to Mother, September 11, 1854, William Garrett, Mobile, to Pitchlynn, May 15, 1847, S. G. Kearney, St. Louis, to Pitchlynn, May 14, 1857, and M. D. Bourassa, Arenac, Michigan, to Pitchlynn, May 9, 1860, *ibid*.

[23] David Folsom, Doaksville, to Pitchlynn, 1842, Folder 42–52, William Jenks, New York, to Pitchlynn, June 13, 1846, Agreement to practice Botanic Medicine, September, 1846, Folder 46–25, H. A. Hartley, Doaksville, to Pitchlynn, August 29, 1855, Hungarian Bond, February 2, 1852, Smoot, Russell and Company, Leavenworth, Kansas, to Pitchlynn, May 18, 1857, and Stock Certificate, June 9, 1857, *ibid*.; Van Buren *Arkansas Intelligencer*, February 22, 1845.

died unborn, the Hapsburgs retained their crown, the Leavenworth lands nearly sold for taxes, and the balance on the stock remained unpaid. Yet they all represented legitimate speculations and honest efforts to live by one's wits rather than by one's hand. Some of Pitchlynn's endeavors were not so honorable.

In 1848 he had assumed the role of guardian for Choctaw students at school in the East. The Educational Act of 1853 further confirmed his authority as general superintendent of schools, gave him supervision of students at home and abroad, and granted him unlimited powers of the purse. At first Pitchlynn made every effort to administer the funds properly, arranging for the commissioner of Indian affairs to distribute directly the tribal annuities allotted to the various students. Though on occasion he used educational funds for side trips, once visiting Niagara Falls, the Choctaws at first received full value for the money spent.[24] But in 1855, rather than have the Office of Indian Affairs pay individual student accounts, Pitchlynn elected to draw on the $6,000 fund himself and personally allocate the money.[25] He at once experienced difficulties in making a proper account. For example, in November, 1856, he reported to the Choctaw council that he had spent only $3,900 of the total funds available when in fact he had spent $650 above the reported figure.[26]

In April, 1858, Peter ceased trying to meet demands on the educational fund. On the fifteenth he requested from the Indian Office a requisition for $3,854.58 to cover the annual expenses of the students. The office foolishly issued the requisition on

[24] Pitchlynn et al., Washington, to C. E. Mix, August 22, 1854, N.A., O.I.A., Choctaw Agency, Letters Received, Microcopy 234, Roll 173; Pitchlynn et al., Washington, to G. W. Manypenny, Commissioner of Indian Affairs, February 13, 1855, N.A., O.I.A., Schools, Letters Received, Microcopy 234, Roll 788.

[25] Pitchlynn et al., to Manypenny, February 13, 1855, Pitchlynn MSS, G.M.

[26] Educational Report, Fort Towson, November 10, 1856, Folder 56–153, *ibid.*

April 19, 1858,[27] and five days later Pitchlynn deposited a draft for the very same amount with the banking firm of Sutter, Lea and Company, Washington, D.C. Drafts on the "Choctaw School account" were issued between April 26 and November 22, 1858, for the following purposes:[28]

Israel Folsom	April 26	$120.00
Colonel Ready	April 26	745.00
John H. Savage	April 26	104.00
(illegible)	May 1	900.00
Self	May 24	100.00
William Cash	July 10	450.00
Thomas B. Cannon	July 22	250.00
Self	July 24	450.00
Sampson Folsom	July 27	350.00
Self	November 22	385.00

Some of the money probably got to the students, but not much. Pitchlynn deposited the last withdrawal to his personal account.[29]

Reports of peculation from the education fund made their way back to the Choctaw Nation. Israel Folsom, Peter's brother-in-law who had been in Washington with him, defended the superintendent of schools, denied all charges of misconduct, and attributed the rumors to political detractors.[30] Despite a moderate investigation, with such support Pitchlynn covered up his misappropriation of school funds. To be sure, this type of conduct occurs occasionally when a product of a less developed society assumes the values and expectations of a more mature, perhaps more corrupt one. Also, the Age of Jackson

[27] Pitchlynn, Washington, to Mix, April 15, 1858, N.A., O.I.A., Schools, Letters Received, Microcopy 234, Roll 791.

[28] Account of Choctaw Schools with Sutter, Lea and Company, Washington, November 22, 1858, Pitchlynn MSS, G.M.

[29] Account of Peter Pitchlynn with Sutter, Lea and Company, Washington, 1858, Folder 58–143, *ibid.*

[30] Israel Folsom, Choctaw Nation, to Pitchlynn, January 2, 1860, *ibid.*

with which Peter increasingly identified made a practice of exploiting the Indian. No manner of rationalization, however, can excuse Pitchlynn for this shameful act.

Several things drove him to taking tribal monies, the most important of which was his profitless farm. In 1845 the cotton crop on his plantation had netted only $256.[31] Four years later, when he returned unrewarded from the speculative wars, he had devoted full time to his farm on Mountain Fork River. At this well-watered and extremely fertile site he collected about him his slaves, constructed a small cabin, cleared new land, planted extensive crops, purchased blooded horses, built a cotton gin, and planned for a new house. Indeed, Pitchlynn demonstrated a touch for farming, and the failure to devote himself to agriculture was truly the tragedy of his business life.

But Peter had quit his revived plantation in late 1853, leaving in charge G. L. Taylor, a professional overseer and capable administrator. By mid-March, 1854, Taylor had ginned eighty-seven bales of cotton with prospects of ten or twelve more. That same spring he had planted 180 to 190 acres of cotton, sowed 125 acres in corn, and moved into a new house. In the fall the overseer harvested one bale of cotton an acre. Yet even with this energetic activity the plantation had still failed to pay. The cotton sold in the spring of 1854 brought only $500, and by December, 1855, an account of $4,000 at the local merchant's had to be paid from sources other than agriculture. Taylor left in 1855 because of his family's ill health and some unrecorded trouble with the neighbors, whereupon the plantation reverted to the administration of the Pitchlynn family.[32]

Leonidas Pitchlynn, Peter's second son, assumed management. The most enterprising of the children, he cleared addi-

---

[31] D. S. Folsom, Doaksville, to Pitchlynn, December 17, 1845, *ibid.*

[32] George Hudson, Eagletown, to Pitchlynn, July 14, 1854; J. M. Skelton, Lukefahtah, to Pitchlynn, February 23, 1854, Pitchlynn Account with J. M. Skelton, Lukefahtah, December, 1855, Folder 55–141, and Taylor, Eagletown, to Pitchlynn, March 10, 1854, August 22, 1854, and November 15, 1854, *ibid.*

tional lands in early 1856 and, besides cotton, planted eighty acres of corn and thirty acres of oats. He fenced off pasture for calves, registered a cattle brand, and provided meat for the plantation. The emphasis upon cattle suggested a little-recognized economic trend among the Indians. In the late 1850's several Choctaws moved farther west to the prairies to raise beef, which they sold to buyers in Arkansas, Texas, and frontier forts. Pitchlynn had intended to emphasize cattle in his farming operations because of the high freight rate on cotton —five dollars a bale—but the Civil War prevented the transition. Yet for all of Leonidas' efforts the plantation had continued unprofitable. The cotton crop in 1856 brought only $2,500 and drove Peter to malfeasance in public office.[33]

The real burden on Pitchlynn's agricultural effort was slavery. The Negroes were seldom profitably employed but always adequately maintained. For example, in 1841 as few as 4 slaves worked on the farm, and then only at pulling corn. Yet, a few years later, the overseer had purchased 38 pairs of shoes and 450 yards of different textured materials for the plantation hands.[34] This purchase suggested large slave holdings. In fact, a census taken after 1866 revealed that 135 freedmen had once belonged to Pitchlynn, 32 of whom had also taken his family name.[35] With diminishing cotton profits and an increasing emphasis upon cattle, Peter had far too much invested in slaves in the late 1850's. In fact, he never found slavery profitable unless he hired his Negroes out to others.

Leonidas continued to manage the farm until 1859, after

[33] Eagle County, 1857, Volumes from the Choctaw Nation 72, Indian Archives, O.H.S.; Lanman, "Peter Pitchlynn," *Atlantic Monthly* (April, 1870), 490; Leonidas, Eagletown, to Pitchlynn, March 7, 1856, R. M. Jones, Kiamechie, to Pitchlynn, April 5, 1854, and J. M. Skelton, Lukefahtah, to Pitchlynn, December 18, 1857, Pitchlynn MSS, G.M.

[34] Rhoda Pitchlynn, Choctaw Nation, to Peter, September 26, 1841, and G. L. Taylor, Eagletown, to J. M. Skelton, October 24, 1854, *ibid*.

[35] Names of Ex-slaves Admitted to Citizenship, n.d., Volumes from the Choctaw Nation 361, Indian Archives, O.H.S.

which he began his own farming operations. The plantation then passed to the care of Peter, Jr., who cleared additional land, planted some tobacco, harvested a crop of peas, and urged his father to build a new mansion.[36] The new home never materialized nor did the plantation ever really prosper. In 1861, when the Civil War began, Pitchlynn moved his family into the vacant buildings of a nearby school. After the war, the plantation existed in name only.

The Age of Jackson held out great promises to Pitchlynn, but the promises proved fragile and frequently costly. This was certainly true financially, but also personally. Whatever he gained as a Jackson man, and it was not much, he lost as a family man. His speculative interests deprived his wife of a husband and his family of a father, a condition for which he paid with heartache and tragedy. Peter's wife, Rhoda, was a woman of education, pride, and strength. She loved her husband deeply, never complained, and always accepted his patriarchial admonitions with grace. "I hope you will bear my absence . . . like a good Christian woman," he once wrote to her. "Trust in God and all will be right. Thank God for all his mercies and be contented."[37] She also understood the purpose of his absences and shared in his hope of profit. "If you make anything I want you to buy heap things," Rhoda wrote, but added ruefully, "that is if you should make anything."[38] She raised his children with tenderness and bestowed upon them that affection and direction which in the eyes of the missionary Cyrus Byington made her a "good woman."

Rhoda gave birth to at least eight children. Those born prior to removal were Lavina in late 1825, Malvina on April 7, 1828, Lycurgus in July, 1830, and a baby who died at birth in 1832.

---

[36] S. H. Webb, Little Rock, to Pitchlynn, February 12, 1860, Pitchlynn MSS, G.M.

[37] Pitchlynn, Choctaw Academy, to Rhoda, July 26, 1841, *ibid*.

[38] Rhoda, Eagletown, to Peter, December 22, 1841, *ibid*.

Those born in Indian Territory included Leonidas in the mid-1830's, Peter, Jr., in 1837, Rhoda in 1839, and Israel about 1843. The youngest child died at the age of three. As a mother, Mrs. Pitchlynn was without peer, instructing her children in things religious, guarding them in her husband's absence, teaching them to love their father, and instilling in them a character that in later life sustained at least the older children. Frequently ill, she expected an early death. "I was born to die," she wrote, but then added, "I hate to leave my children too young."[39] Unfortunately, she did leave her children young. Pregnancy after Peter's return in 1842 sapped her strength and hastened her death in mid-March, 1844. She was buried near Wheelock Mission. Peter exhibited deep grief after her death and was moved to join the Presbyterian church formally, something that Rhoda had encouraged. But in April, 1845, he placed his children with relatives and missionaries and left the country for two years in pursuit of his business interests.[40]

Pitchlynn always justified his absences from home as duty and opportunity: opportunity to make a fortune and duty to country and family. Generally his family accepted such an explanation but not always with resignation. "Yes, dear father," his daughter Lavina once wrote, "while I am writing these few lines the tears are fast falling."[41] His relatives were not always as generous. Israel Folsom declared:

> I am truly astonished at the course you have taken in leaving your little children to be absent from them several months. But I do not pretend to pronounce a sentence of censure on you. I am only astonished. I do not know how in the world you can stand it to endure the idea of separation from your children. But

[39] Rhoda to Peter, September 10, 1841, *ibid.*

[40] Carolyn Thomas Foreman, ed., "Journal of a Tour in the Indian Country," *The Chronicles of Oklahoma*, Vol. X (June, 1932), 224.

[41] Lavina and Malvina Pitchlynn, Dividing Ridge, to Father, November 22, 1845, Pitchlynn MSS, G.M.

you are a political man, engaged in matters of the world and for money—it don't sound so well after all.[42]

To say that Pitchlynn deserted his children is grossly unfair. He loved them deeply. He arranged an education for them, sending his older daughters to the missionary schools in both old and new Nations. Lycurgus and Leonidas both attended Spencer Academy, and at the expense of the tribe Lycurgus enrolled in colleges at Newark, New Jersey, and Lebanon, Tennessee. Rhoda and Peter, Jr., attended tribal schools at home as well as private institutions at Covington, Georgia, and Staunton, Virginia. Actually Pitchlynn overindulged his family. The children all incurred expenses beyond their father's capacity to pay; and in matters concerning school he frequently accepted their judgment rather than that of their teachers. But overindulgence expressed Pitchlynn's affection, as did also his admonitions. "Do the best you can, aim high, and don't miss the mark," he wrote to Lycurgus. "Keep up the name of Pitchlynn. I look forward to the day when my dear son will stand by my side in the councils of the Nation and in all that is noble, good and praiseworthy. What a blessing this will be to me."[43]

In the main, though, Peter's family sorely disappointed him. The inattention of their father and lack of parental guidance told in their characters. Of Lycurgus his teacher at Delaware College wrote: "He is of good abilities and perhaps the best scholar of them all but utterly destitute of stability or principle."[44] Lycurgus made debts that he never paid,[45] and he failed to cope with alcohol, a weakness that prevented him from

[42] Israel Folsom, New Hope, to Pitchlynn, March 4, 1845, *ibid.*

[43] Peter, Baltimore, to Lycurgus, May 28, 1848, *ibid.*

[44] James P. Wilson, Delaware College, to Orlando Brown, Commissioner of Indian Affairs, February 21, 1851, N.A., O.I.A., Schools, Letters Received, Microcopy 234, Roll 785.

[45] D. Lowrey, Lebanon, Tennessee, to Pitchlynn, February 10, 1854, Lycurgus, Lebanon, to Pitchlynn, April 17, 1854, and John S. Dashhull, Nashville, to Pitchlynn, January 21, 1855, Pitchlynn MSS, G.M.

completing law school. His youngest brother had the same problem with strong drink; yet Leonidas seems to have overcome it. All three sons had violent tempers. In 1857, the federal court in Van Buren, Arkansas, convicted Leonidas and Lycurgus on accounts of assault and battery. The conviction stemmed from an argument during which Lycurgus shot off another man's finger. The most serious display of temper occurred when Peter, Jr., in 1860, became so enraged about a dispute regarding the use of a blacksmith that he killed his uncle, Lorenzo Harris. In both incidents Pitchlynn's position prevented any significant punishment.[46]

Peter did not attend the weddings of any of his children. His oldest daughter, Lavina, married Richard Harkins in 1846. Malvina, during the early 1850's, won as her husband a first cousin, Loring S. W. Folsom. Leonidas eloped with his cousin, Sophia Harris, in April, 1856, while Lycurgus married a New Orleans girl in 1858, and Peter, Jr., wed the daughter of an Arkansas family in 1859. During the Civil War Rhoda eloped with John Arnold, but her father had the marriage annulled by the tribal courts because he questioned the legality of Arnold's divorce from a former wife. In 1873, Rhoda married one of the plantation's tenant farmers, a man named Kennedy.

Pitchlynn survived all of the children born to his first wife except Malvina. Lavina passed a grossly unhappy life, losing most of her children and witnessing first her husband's murder by a deranged Negro and finally her daughter's insanity. Malvina and her husband provided a home for orphaned relatives and became Peter's staunchest political allies in the Choctaw Nation. Rhoda had little to do with her father after the annulment, and both Peter and Leonidas died during the Civil War. Lycurgus served in the Choctaw government during the same

---

[46] Pitchlynn, Washington, to President Buchanan, July 23, 1857, and Sam Garland, Choctaw Nation, to Pitchlynn, July 17, 1860, *ibid*.

conflict, but died of fever in 1866, continuing to the end to make excuses for his personal weaknesses.

The Age of Jackson found Pitchlynn in the prime of life. He weighed two hundred pounds, stood six feet tall, and measured forty inches in the waist. His hazel eyes, brunette hair, and erect posture commanded attention. He moved with grace, spoke with deliberation, and manifested many admirable characteristics. He aspired to lead the Pitchlynn family as his father had done before him. "May the Lord bless your soul and your dear children is the prayer of your affectionate brother," he wrote to a relative.[47] Yet he never quite achieved the status of his father. The families of his four sisters—the Howells, the Garlands, and the two Harris families—frequently rejected his leadership. Peter responded with periods of depression and self-pity. "I feel I am persecuted, hated, and much despised by my own kindred and relations," he once wrote. "The ancient union of our house is broken. Were it not that brother Thomas were true and faithful to me I should say that I was alone. . . . There is nothing true but heaven."[48]

Obviously, Pitchlynn was a man of deep emotions, emotions that were shaped in the main by his Indian heritage. Increasingly influenced by the era in which he lived and at times almost entirely given over to materialism, he never lost a sense of oneness with nature. He saw a bird in its nest, a sunset on the western prairies, the morning haze over the Blue Ridge Mountains, and his own soul as but different manifestations of the same infinite spirit. Such sensitivity, such empathy with mother earth always made him an alien in the mainstream of the white culture he so much admired. Few white men, for example, could issue the following invitation:

[47] Pitchlynn, Choctaw Nation, to Lorenzo Harris, [1842], H–44, J. L. Hargett Collection, Western History Collection, U.O.L.
[48] Statement of Peter Pitchlynn, Choctaw Nation, October 29, 1842, Pitchlynn MSS, G.M.

Will you go with me
To my home in the West,
To the land of the mountains,
To the land of the prairies,
To the land of the setting sun,
Far away toward the setting sun?

I say will you go with me,
And be mine for me to love,
For me to protect, cherish and love,
To be mine in heart and soul,
For me to love among the flowers,
Love among the songs of birds?

Will you go with me
To my home in the forest,
To my home that's far away,
Far beyond the Mississippi,
In a pleasant valley is my home,
And, Oh will you go with me?

I would not have thee to go
To my home in the forest,
If I loved thee not as a man,
If I could not protect thee as a man
If I could not make thee as a man,
My loving, my dear, my happy wife.
Will you go with me?[49]

Perhaps Pitchlynn best demonstrated the source of his sensitivity in lines written when his daughter, Rhoda, visited him in Washington during summer vacation from her Virginia school. He captured her anxiety to return to the West in his "Song of the Choctaw Girl."

I'm looking on the mountain,
I'm gazing o'er the plain;

49 "Poem," n.d., Folder Un–350, *ibid.*

I love the friends around me,
  But wish for home again!

I hear their tones of kindness,
  They soothe my every pain;
I know they love me truly—
  I wish for home again!

My mother's grave is yonder,
  And there it must remain;
My Father's care is tender,
  I wish for home again!

My sisters and my brothers—
  Alas! it may be vain,
This longing for beloved ones—
  I wish for home again!

O, take me to my Nation,
  And let me there remain;
This other world is strange, strange—
  I wish for home again!

Give me the western forest—
  The mountain, stream and plain.
The shaded lawns of childhood—
  Give me my home again!

The free breeze of the prairie
  The wild bird's joyous strain,
The tree my father planted—
  O, take me home again!

The sunshine and the flowers,
  My mother's grave again,
Give me my race and kindred—
  O, take me home again![50]

Peter undoubtedly wanted these sentiments attributed to
Rhoda only, but poems reveal much about the poet. Surely the

[50] Pitchlynn, "Song of the Choctaw Girl," n.d., Folder 49-19, *ibid.*

lines also suggest his sense of alienation in white society and his yearning for a tribal fellowship that was not really his to enjoy.

Pitchlynn also had sensitivity of taste. He frequented art galleries and theaters in Washington, enjoyed the poetry of Sir Walter Scott, read Shakespeare and Milton, and included in his library such volumes as A. B. Meeks's *Red Eagle: A Poem of The South* and Comte Emmanuel de las Casas' *Journal of the Private Life and Conversations of Emperor Napoleon at St. Helena*.[51] He adopted the use of calling cards, enjoyed the company of the famous, and was recognized as the intellectual of the tribe. He aided the erudite Cyrus Byington in compiling a Choctaw grammar, translated into Choctaw "Nearer My God to Thee," and furnished cultural information to the government on western Indian tribes.

But Pitchlynn also had many ungracious qualities. He could be obstinate, determined, and vindictive. He occasionally lost complete control of his temper and frequently was egotistical and vain. The last qualities account for his frequenting doctors of phrenology in 1846 and 1857. Peter's boundless ambition and capacity for revenge were noted, but in the main both "professional" reports were extremely flattering.[52] He was proud of the Catlin portrait and often posed for other pictures. As prominent men belonged to many organizations, he joined the Union Tract Society, the Masonic Order, the Temperance Union, and the Eagletown Debating Society.[53] His concept of the fullblood Choctaw and the "wild" Indians of the West also evidenced his egotistical, almost ethnocentric, nature. To him both were ignorant, the only difference being that the latter was more curiously dressed and the former more easily educated.

[51] See Rare Book Section, G.M.
[52] Phrenological Report of Dr. J. L. Berthollet, April 15, 1846, Folder 46–1 and February 11, 1857, Folder 57–178, Pitchlynn MSS, G.M.
[53] *Choctaw Telegraph*, May 17, August 9, August 23, 1849.

Pitchlynn prized his oratorical talent. He never refused an opportunity to address organizations on temperance, religion, or Indian history. At one Indian temperance meeting in 1842 he depicted the bad effects of whisky in language anticipatory of the Woman's Christian Temperance Union. With the use of alcohol, he declared, tribal farms would grow up in weeds, schools destroyed, Choctaw wives and daughters forced to prostitution, and churches cease to ring with the songs of praise. He more than once addressed the President of the United States, and he had so much confidence in his speaking ability that he went out of his way to engage in public debate. In 1840 he reportedly opposed and defeated Henry Clay in a shipboard contest.[54]

Peter had other qualities that he did not make so public. He habitually procrastinated, never paying a bill unless dunned at least twice. Abhoring whisky, he more than once succumbed to its temptation, though this was more a problem of the age than of the man. His religious professions early in life lacked sincerity, and his expressions of grief often were more for effect than from sorrow. Brass knuckles and a brace of dueling pistols, now in the Oklahoma Historical Society, detracted from his pretentions to peacemaking. Ambitious to the point of dishonor and shrewd to the point of disaster, Pitchlynn also fancied himself as a connoisseur of women. He enjoyed feminine associations and sought them out soon after his wife's death. His assessment of his own prowess was confirmed in April, 1846, when a doctor of phrenology declared that he had "the highest order of attachment to women, was admirably sexed, naturally gallant, and a most devoted lover."[55] Miss N. A. Nold's thanks for his "thrillingly interesting letter" helped too.[56]

[54] Lanman, "Peter Pitchlynn," *Atlantic Monthly* (April, 1870), 487, 489.
[55] Phrenological Report, Washington, April 15, 1846, Folder 46–1, Pitchlynn MSS, G.M.
[56] Nold, Frankfort, Kentucky, to Pitchlynn, March 16, 1846, *ibid.*

In 1850 friends and family began to look for possible mates for Pitchlynn. Peter, Jr., wrote from his school in Georgia that he had his eye on two or three widows who might suit his father.[57] Another friend advised that he had taken the matter up with his sister-in-law, but as she had rejected the proposal, he highly recommended the daughter of his cousin who was as beautiful as any woman of the West. The young lady had a "good education, knew how to weave any kind of double cloth, cut out and make coats, pants, and other wear for men or women and was uncommon nice on bed quilts."[58] By 1855, Pitchlynn had pretty well determined upon the woman of his dreams. He courted Mrs. Carolyn Eckloff Lombardi, the widowed daughter of a Washington boardinghouse proprietor, during 1856 and 1857, and, after several excursions into the Virginia countryside, won her. But he did not marry her at that time; Mrs. Lombardi simply became his common-law wife. Five children were born of this liaison: Sampson in November, 1857, dying within the year, Tommy in 1859, Edward Everette in 1860, Sophia in 1864, and Lee in 1866. All were born in Washington except Sophia, who was born in the Choctaw Nation. On October 21, 1869, after Pitchlynn became seriously ill and felt an increasing interest in religion, he and Mrs. Lombardi were legally married.[59] The marriage, along with his speculative activities, signaled Peter's increasing commitment to that part of his heritage which was white.

[57] Pitchlynn, Jr., to Father, February 6, 1854, *ibid*.

[58] S. L. Westmoreland, Williamston, South Carolina, to Pitchlynn, March 8, 1854, *ibid*.

[59] Marriage Index No. 4, Old Marriage Records M–Z, September 1, 1858 to June 16, 1870, Supreme Court of the District of Columbia.

CHAPTER V

Establishing the Net Proceeds

By 1850, Peter Pitchlynn's taste for public life and speculative investment seemed satiated. He had spent years outside of the Choctaw Nation in an unsuccessful quest for profit, and he had assisted in the organization of tribal government in Indian Territory. Tired of it all, Peter turned to his plantation and his family, which gave him some of the joy, success, and remuneration he sought so vigorously elsewhere. Yet the rural life proved only an interlude, for in December, 1853, he again journeyed to Washington in pursuit of that elusive pot of gold.

Several things prompted Pitchlynn to abandon his nominal political retirement. Since his last mission to the federal capital in 1848 other Choctaw delegations had pressed tribal and individual claims upon the government. Of these, the one composed of Thompson McKenney and Forbis LeFlore, two prominent mixed-bloods, was the most important. In 1853, these two men secured a $600,000 payment to fourteenth article claimants in full satisfaction of claims under that article of the treaty of 1830. McKenney and LeFlore received 5 per cent of the appropriation for their services to the tribe. Pitchlynn resented the prestige and financial reward that accrued to these men, so

95

much so that he even tried to thwart the congressional appropriation redeeming the $600,000 in land scrip. Suddenly private life became too confining for him, and he decided that the Choctaw Nation still needed his strong leadership.[1]

The Choctaws did indeed require vigorous direction as conflict at home and policy from Washington threatened their sovereignty. Relations with the Chickasaws represented the most difficult local problem. This brother tribe complained about bearing the administrative expenses of their own district, about the lack of participation in the benefits of the money they had paid to the Choctaws in 1837, and about the common boundary. They desired total independence from the Choctaws and employed Luke Lea, a former commissioner of Indian affairs, to represent them. Lea influenced his old office to bring the two tribes together for negotiations that would effect a political separation. Pitchlynn served as the chief spokesman for the Choctaws in the discussions which began at Doaksville on November 5 and continued until November 17, 1853. The commissioners of both tribes ultimately submitted to the United States for arbitration all questions arising out of differing interpretations of the Treaty of 1837, such as the boundary lines, but made little progress in the Chickasaw objective of separation. That the Choctaws should oppose the political divorce displeased Commissioner of Indian Affairs George W. Manypenny. It was "much to be regretted," he wrote, "that the Choctaws, to whom the union is of no advantage whatever, still continue indisposed to yield to the natural and reasonable wishes of their brethren." Hoping to capitalize on this official sentiment, Luke Lea advised the Chickasaws to appoint a delegation to go to Washington and in that favorable climate negotiate a separation with the Choctaws. He, of course, would accompany the delegates.[2]

[1] John B. Luce, Washington, to G. W. Manypenny, April 15, 1853, N.A., O.I.A., Choctaw Agency, Letters Received, Microcopy 234, Roll 172; Sampson Folsom, Washington, to Pitchlynn, July 26, 1852, Pitchlynn MSS, G.M.

[2] Proceedings between the Choctaw and Chickasaw Commissioners, Doaks-

The Chickasaw efforts coincided with a growing Choctaw desire to settle finally with the federal government all claims growing out of removal inequities during the 1830's and non-fulfillment of treaty obligations. To produce such a result obviously required the efforts and skill of one familiar with Washington procedure and acquainted with government officials. Thompson McKenney recommended Pitchlynn for the job as early as October, 1852, but the Choctaw council did not concur until November 9, 1853. It appointed Pitchlynn, Dickson W. Lewis, Israel Folsom, and Samuel Garland as delegates with full power to settle by treaty or otherwise "all and every claim and interest of the Choctaw people against the United States."[3]

Peter and Samuel Garland arrived in Washington on January 20, 1854, well before the other delegates even left the Nation. The two first called on John T. Cochrane, an attorney familiar with Choctaw affairs, and Robert W. Johnson, United States senator from Arkansas. Both of these gentlemen urged the delegates first to present their credentials to the Office of Indian Affairs and then to employ a man of influence who could advise them on fact and protocol. Some weeks later, on March 13, they thus contracted with Albert Pike, the notable Arkansas poet and attorney who was also a friend of Johnson's, to represent the tribe in its negotiations with the United States.

Pike was already acquainted with the Choctaw claims and two years earlier had sent a representative into Indian country to persuade the tribe to retain him. Now, possessing a contract calling for a contingent fee of 25 per cent of any financial settlement with the government, he moved quickly to advance

ville, November 5–17, 1853, and Charles E. Mix, Commissioner of Indian Affairs, to Douglas H. Cooper and Andrew J. Smith, June 29, 1853, N.A., O.I.A., Choctaw Agency, Letters Received, Microcopy 234, Roll 172; Thompson McKenney, Washington, to Pitchlynn, April 21, 1853, Pitchlynn MSS, G.M.; *Report of the Commissioner of Indian Affairs, 1853*, 255.

[3] Folsom, *Constitution and Laws of the Choctaw Nation, 1869*, 123–25 (hereinafter *Laws of the Choctaw Nation*).

the claims. His first action was to involve other men of influence in the project. Assigning to each an equal share of the prospective fee, Pike gained the aid of John T. Cochrane, included at the insistence of Pitchlynn but already associated with Pike in a Creek claim; Luke Lea, the Chickasaw attorney and a man of many contacts in Washington; and Douglas H. Cooper, the Choctaw agent who had accompanied the Indians to the capital. A native of Mississippi, Cooper received his appointment as agent in 1853 upon the recommendation of Jefferson Davis, with whom he had served in the Mexican War. Pike also secretly assigned or, more accurately, rebated to Peter Pitchlynn, who was never unmindful of an opportunity for profit, a one-fifth interest in the attorney fee. The Arkansan, therefore, divided the 25 per cent contract five ways, arranging it so that he, Cochrane, Lea, Cooper, and Pitchlynn would each get 5 per cent of any settlement with the United States.[4]

To open negotiations the Choctaw team, with all delegates now present, presented a memorial to Commissioner of Indian Affairs Manypenny on April 5. "It is the fixed sentiment of our people," the delegation wrote, "that scarcely one executive stipulation has been carried out in a manner to do justice and according to its intent." The Choctaws requested the adjudication of all claims and suggested that Agent Cooper be delegated to "investigate" their demands. Despite Cooper's participation in the attorney contract, they assured the commissioner that since they had carefully abstained from consulting him, he was therefore free to make an "objective" determination. Manypenny saw merit in the desire to settle all outstanding differences and accordingly instructed the agent to ascertain the character and the extent of the tribal complaints. With the case

[4] Pitchlynn, Washington, to Friend, January 20, 1854, H–44, J. L. Hargett Collection, Western History Collection, U.O.L.; 49 Cong., 2 sess., *Senate Report 1978*, 33; *Court of Claims Report 59*, 769; Albert Pike, "Letter to the Choctaw People," Washington, February 21, 1872, Folder 72–14A, Pitchlynn MSS, G.M.; 42 Cong., 3 sess., *House Report 98*, 496.

referred to Cooper, whose conclusion certainly was foregone, Pike left Washington in late April to return to Arkansas, entrusting the management of further negotiations to Cochrane.[5]

On May 1, during Cooper's investigation, the Choctaws admitted that most tribal claims could not be adequately proved although they were just. Pitchlynn and his co-delegates proposed a specific method whereby the individual claimants could obtain justice. After 1830, they argued, the tribe had removed to lands previously guaranteed to them in the treaty of 1820 and thus had relinquished the ten million Mississippi acres without any substantial consideration. The government sold these lands, and even after deducting survey and administrative expenses, it had reaped a huge profit. The "net proceeds" of this sale, the Choctaws maintained, were part of the tribal estate, for the eighteenth article of the treaty of 1830 provided that "the lands hereby ceded are to remain a fund pledged to the fulfillment of the treaty provisions." The government had not met its treaty commitments, and in lieu thereof the Choctaws would take the net proceeds and settle privately with the individual claimants. To put it another way, Pitchlynn and his co-delegates wanted to combine all the individual claims against the United States into one large demand with any financial settlement being administered locally by the tribe. Accordingly, they requested that a new treaty be written encompassing such a proposal.[6]

Predictably, Cooper reported to the commissioner that article eighteen had indeed assigned the profits of the Mississippi

[5] Choctaw Delegates, Washington, to G. W. Manypenny, April 5, 1847, N.A., O.I.A., Choctaw Agency, Letters Received, Microcopy 234, Roll 173; Manypenny, Washington, to the Hon. R. McClelland, Secretary of the Interior, April 13, 1854, Box 2, Letters Received, Office of Indian Affairs, Records of the Department of Interior, N.A.
[6] Choctaw Delegation, Washington, to Agent Douglas Cooper, May 1, 1854, N.A., O.I.A., Choctaw Agency, Letters Received, Microcopy 234, Roll 173.

land sale to the Choctaws. The ceded lands were pledged as collateral to the fulfillment of treaty provisions, provisions that clearly had not been executed. Furthermore, he considered it impossible to settle the tribal claims on the basis of treaty stipulations alone and recommended that the government instead grant either the proceeds of the land sale, a procedure permitted the Wyandots and the Chickasaws, or a reasonable sum in lieu of individual claims.[7] The report showed Pike's wisdom in including Cooper on the Choctaw team.

Pitchlynn and his associates were principally interested in the recognition of what they called the net proceeds claim, but the Office of Indian Affairs was more concerned about other matters. It wanted to locate reservations for the Wichitas and other Plains Indian tribes in the western reaches of the Choctaw cession and to ease the troubled relations between the Chickasaws and the Choctaws. Led by Sampson Folsom, a nephew of Pitchlynn's, and Edmund Pickens, the Chickasaw delegation came to Washington dedicated to tribal independence. Luke Lea advised them on procedure, but his inclusion in the Pike contract suggested less than complete devotion. Furthermore, the Choctaws nearly ignored the Chickasaws during the negotiations since the paramount question for them was the "disposition of the government" toward their own demands. "Let the government first answer and answer liberally the appeal of the Choctaws for justice," they wrote, and then they would "be disposed to discuss in an equally liberal spirit the Chickasaw question."[8]

The government negotiators matched the Choctaw obstinancy. Not only did the commissioner insist upon some kind of accommodation with the Chickasaws, but Secretary of Interior R. L. McClelland concluded on June 20 that the Choctaws had no claim against the government because the removal treaty

[7] D. H. Cooper, Washington, to G. W. Manypenny, May 25, 1854, *ibid.*
[8] Choctaw Delegation, Washington, to Manypenny, May 30, 1854, *ibid.*

in 1830 had provided for an unqualified land cession. Further-more, the Secretary deemed it inexpedient to reopen the whole subject of nonfulfillment of treaty provisions and suggested that the tribe approach Congress instead once the Chickasaw question was settled.[9]

McClelland's ruling elicited a belligerent response from the Choctaws. In a statement prepared by Cochrane, the delegates maintained that Congress was wholly inaccessible to the Indians, that it was the executive's responsibility to execute treaties, and that they were denied justice because they represented a Southern tribe. They declared that the position of the government left them no alternative but to terminate discussions with the Chickasaws. Furthermore, the Choctaws threatened to remove those alien tribes like the Wichitas who had settled within their borders and to occupy that land between 100 and 103 degrees west longitude guaranteed to them in the 1820 treaty.[10] The land in question fell within the state boundaries of Texas. The Secretary, however, was not intimidated and simply reiterated that the Choctaws should go to Congress.[11]

Negotiations languished during the remainder of 1854. Still directed by Cochrane, the Choctaw delegation considered appealing to the Senate, hoping to force the Office of Indian Affairs to receive the Indian proposals for a new treaty more favorably. Cochrane wrote to Pike in September asking him to present the matter to Congress, but for some reason the attorney failed to return to Washington. Left on its own, the Choctaw

[9] R. L. McClelland, Secretary of Interior, to Charles E. Mix, June 20, 1854, *ibid.*

[10] The borders of the Choctaw reservation as described by Jackson in the treaty of 1820 set its western limit at a north–south line beginning at the headwaters of the Canadian River and terminating on Red River. This language gave the Choctaws territory beyond the 100th meridian, at the time part of the Spanish Empire and in 1854 part of Texas.

[11] Choctaw Delegation, Washington, to C. E. Mix, July 11, 1854, Pitchlynn MSS, G.M.; R. McClelland, Washington, to C. E. Mix, September 25, 1854, in 34 Cong., 1 sess., *Sen. Misc. Doc. 31*, 44.

team then decided to appeal directly to the President. Before the appeal they obtained affidavits supporting their proposal for an equitable adjustment of the net proceeds claim from John H. Eaton, Senator J. J. McRae of Mississippi, and others, and through the influence of Cooper met with Secretary of War Jefferson Davis to impress upon him the justice of their cause.[12]

On February 3, 1855, in a ceremony at the White House, Pitchlynn presented the Choctaw appeal to President Franklin Pierce. "As representatives of a once powerful, but now weak and dependent people," he told the President, "we come today to the White House . . . to ask for justice at the hands of our political 'great father.'" The Washington *Union* considered it a "most touching and elegant address." It may have been touching, but it was not effective. The President refused to intervene, and the discussions with the Office of Indian Affairs continued at a stalemate.[13]

This situation and Pike's absence from Washington resulted in an adjustment in the management of the Choctaw claim. To the delegates it appeared that Pike had abandoned them, and on February 13, 1855, they made an agreement with Cochrane which granted him 30 per cent of any sum obtained from the government. The next day the new attorney, as Pike had done, rebated to Pitchlynn one-sixth of the contingent fee, still 5 per cent of any final settlement, and assigned equal interests to both

---

[12] J. T. Cochrane, Washington, to Pike, September 14, 1854, in Albert Pike, "Letter to the Choctaw People," Washington, February 20, 1872, Folder 72–14A, Choctaw Delegation, Washington, to John H. Eaton, May 1, 1854, Delegation, Washington, to J. J. McRae, December 26, 1854, Delegation, Washington, to David W. Haley, December 27, 1854, and Memorandum, n.d., Folder 53–49, Pitchlynn MSS, G.M.

[13] Papers Respecting the Rights and Interests of the Choctaw Nation, Washington, 1855, Folder 55–17, *ibid.*; Choctaw Delegation, Washington, to President Franklin Pierce, February 3, 1855, Box 29h, Letters Received, Private Sources, Indian Division, Records of the Secretary of Interior, N.A.; McClelland to Manypenny, March 28, 1855, N.A., O.I.A., Choctaw Agency, Letters Received, Microcopy 234, Roll 174.

Luke Lea and Douglas Cooper.[14] A new indenture seemed necessary for several reasons, but Cochrane wanted principally the additional assistance and influence which were impossible to procure from his subordinate position. Cochrane advised Pike that nothing had changed except the substitution of names and the increase in fee, but he failed to tell the Arkansas attorney that he stood charged with abandoning the case.[15]

Despite its displeasure with the Choctaw demands, the United States could ill afford to break off negotiations. The matters of the Chickasaw desire for political independence and the location of a permanent home for the "strolling Indians" of the West demanded a solution. The government's commitment to solve these problems worked to the advantage of the Choctaws, who by May 3, 1855, had also assumed a more flexible position on the questions at issue. If the Department would agree to refer to the United States Senate the right of the tribe to the net proceeds, the Choctaws offered to quitclaim their title to land west of the 100th meridian for $400,000 and for another $400,000 to lease to the United States the portion of their country west of 98 degrees west longitude which the government envisioned as a home for some of the Plains Indians. Furthermore, though they could not give a complete and unencumbered land title to the Chickasaws, they would agree to some kind of separate jurisdiction. The adoption of such a proposal, of course, depended upon a moderated Chickasaw demand and the generosity of the federal government. In this regard, including Luke Lea in the attorney's contract paid dividends as did Pitchlynn's kinship with Sampson Folsom. Both encour-

[14] Contract between the Choctaw Delegation and John T. Cochrane, Washington, February 13, 1855, Folder 55–23, Contract between John Cochrane and Peter Pitchlynn, February 14, 1855, Folder 55–20, Pitchlynn MSS, G.M.; *Court of Claims Report 59*, 771.

[15] Pike, "Letter to the Choctaw People," Washington, February 21, 1872, Folder 72–14A, Pitchlynn MSS, G.M.; "Report of the Choctaw Delegation," Washington, August, 1856, H10.55, Hargrett Pamphlet Collection, G.M.

aged the Chickasaws to accept just a separate political jurisdiction instead of total independence.

Government generosity, however, did not match Chickasaw moderation. It offered only $600,000 for both a quitclaim to the lands located in Texas and a lease to the land between 98 and 100 degrees west longitude. The negotiations threatened to break up over the question of compensation, but after a timely intervention by Jefferson Davis with President Pierce, the United States agreed to pay the Choctaws and the Chickasaws $800,000 at a ratio of three to one for the lease and quitclaim, to sanction only a separate political jurisdiction for the Chickasaws, and to send the question of the net proceeds to the Senate for determination. The United States, the Choctaws, and the Chickasaws formally signed the concordat on June 22, 1855.[16]

As finally written, the treaty represented the labor and effort of many. Albert Pike envisioned combining the many individual demands into one large claim against the government, while Cochrane conducted all of the correspondence and Pitchlynn and his associates provided the information and made the oral presentations. Douglas Cooper's role proved as crucial as it was impartial; he had remembered the Choctaw claim to the Texas territory and had secured the timely influence of Jefferson Davis. But all the labor had been worth it. The Choctaws had obtained a reasonably equitable treaty, and Pitchlynn had gained partial recognition of existing tribal claims against the government.

During the period of the negotiations other matters frequently concerned the delegation. Senator Johnson introduced

16 Choctaw Delegation, Washington, to Cooper, April 24, 1855, Manypenny to George C. Whiting, Acting Secretary of Interior, June 7, 1855, and Choctaw Delegation to Manypenny, June 14, 1855, N.A., O.I.A., Choctaw Agency, Letters Received, Microcopy 234, Roll 174; D. H. Cooper, "Address and Memorial to the Choctaw Council," October, 1873, Folder 73–108, Pitchlynn MSS, G.M.; Kappler, *Indian Affairs: Laws and Treaties*, II, 706–14.

legislation to provide the Choctaws with a territorial form of government. The measure favorably impressed Pitchlynn, and he sent copies of it to influential Choctaws. Both R. M. Jones and Thompson McKenney agreed that the bill's provisions were enticing and obtained an endorsement for the measure from the tribal council's special committee on territories.[17] Johnson's measure ultimately came to naught, but it was a milestone in Pitchlynn's career, for he never again wholeheartedly supported any form of territorial government. It also reflected one of Pitchlynn's political techniques. He kept friends at home advised of the developments in Washington in the same way that any member of Congress did. The practice always impressed the less sophisticated Choctaws.

Throughout the treaty discussions Peter worked on Capitol Hill urging an appropriation to cover arrearages in tribal annuities guaranteed in past treaties. Other Choctaws had initiated the claim in 1852, at which time they had employed Cochrane. On March 3, 1855, Congress finally appropriated $92,238.30 and ordered the funds paid "as may be requested by the authorized delegates now in Washington." Seventeen days later, Cochrane drafted a letter for Pitchlynn and his colleagues directing that the money be paid to them immediately to prevent starvation among the Choctaws. The demand did not impress Commissioner Manypenny, who asked how the funds would be distributed and, when the Choctaws were imprecise and vague, expressed doubt that Congress had given the delegation a blank check to distribute the money without restrictions. "Permit us to say, Sir," responded the Choctaws, "while you are doubting, our people are starving." Ultimately, in June, the

---

[17] Pitchlynn, Washington, to Friend, January 20, 1854, and Pitchlynn to Hampton, March 2, 1854, H–44, J. L. Hargett Collection, Western History Collection, U.O.L.; R. M. Jones, Kiamechie, to Pitchlynn, April 5, 1854, Thompson McKenney, Choctaw Agency, to Pitchlynn, March 29, 1854, and Report of the Committee on Territories, Choctaw Nation, 1854, Folder 54–185, Pitchlynn MSS, G.M.

Commissioner released the money to Agent Cooper, whom the delegation then directed to pay $40,000 to the "starving" Indians, about $3 each, $28,000 to Pitchlynn as superintendent of schools, and the remainder to the tribal treasury. Peter then released all but $323 of the money he had received to Cochrane as his fee of 30 per cent for collecting the sum. Doubtless Cochrane rebated part of the fee to Pitchlynn as his share of the attorney's contract.[18]

The implementation of the Treaty of 1855 required ratification by the Choctaw council. Pitchlynn and his co-delegates hurried home to attend personally to the politically delicate maneuver. He quickly learned that reaction to the treaty was less than enthusiastic, that heading the opposition were his brother, Thomas, R. M. Jones, and Thompson McKenney, and that they objected principally to the political separation of the Chickasaws. Jones later cynically congratulated Peter upon his work and wished him long life to enjoy the gratitude of a grateful people. "Gratitude, did I say? Rumor with her thousand and one tongues have it already that our country has been sold!" Furthermore, Jones expressed the opinion that nothing had been accomplished on the net proceeds; the Senate might decide against the claim, in which case "the Choctaws will be fairly outwitted." "So brother," he advised his friend, "you must go to Washington, pick your flint and try again. Make a treaty which will sacrifice no right of our people and if you make a million in the transaction you will never find me opposing it on that account." Jones, obviously knowing Pitchlynn's motives, curiously made no moral indictment.[19]

18 Manypenny to Choctaw Delegation, March 27, 1855, and Delegation to Manypenny, April 6, 1855, N.A., O.I.A., Choctaw Agency, Letters Received, Microcopy 234, Roll 174; Delegation to Manypenny, March 20, 1855, Manypenny to Choctaw Delegates, April 5, 1855, Choctaw Delegation to Cooper, June 22, 1855, Delegation to Pitchlynn, June 22, 1855, and Receipt of John T. Cochrane, New Orleans, July 2, 1855, Pitchlynn MSS, G.M.

19 Jones, Choctaw Nation, to Pitchlynn, August 1, 1855, August 20, 1855, and March 19, 1856, *ibid.*

But Jones's objection to the treaty carried little weight in the Choctaw council. Both Cooper, who had a personal stake in the matter, and George W. Harkins, the chief of Pitchlynn's home district, joined Peter in the ratification fight in early September. Harkins expected Pitchlynn "to do something for me if it turns out to be profitable," but in the meantime he wanted a share of the arrearages money. "When I go into this treaty," he declared, "I don't want to go in with the harness pinching me." The delegates arranged for a comfortable harness and at the same time ensured the support of the district chief. On November 2, 1855, before the ratification convention, they agreed to give him an equal share of whatever sum they might realize out of the net proceeds claim. The delegates having taken the proper precautions, the Choctaw council ratified the treaty and directed Pitchlynn and his colleagues to return to Washington to prosecute the claim before the Senate. Furthermore, the chiefs approved a contract assigning to the 1853 delegation 20 per cent of all they collected on "claims arising or accruing to the Nation, or to individuals under the Treaty of June 22, 1855." Taken together with his cut from the Cochrane contract, this measure guaranteed Pitchlynn 10 per cent of whatever he recovered.[20]

The Chickasaws had not yet ratified the treaty. Many members of the tribe opposed the new concordat because it provided only political separation, and they accused Sampson Folsom of having sold out to the Choctaws. So pressed, Folsom appealed to his uncle, Peter, to testify that the Chickasaws had very shrewdly forced the larger tribe to grant a measure of independence when such a concession had not seemed possible. Pitchlynn wrote the desired testimonial and also attended the

[20] Cooper, Fort Towson, to Pitchlynn, August 20, 1855, Harkins, Choctaw Nation, to Pitchlynn, September 7, 1855, and October 13, 1855, and Agreement between Harkins and the Choctaw Delegation, Fort Towson, November 2, 1855, *ibid.*; Acts of the Choctaw Council, November 21, 1855, 17635, Choctaw Nation–Federal Relations, Indian Archives, O.H.S.

Chickasaw ratifying convention at Tishomingo in mid-December. His efforts, combined with those of Folsom and Agent Cooper secured the desired ratification and the appointment of Folsom to lead a delegation to Washington to consummate the treaty.[21]

In late December, 1855, Pitchlynn returned to the capital to guide the treaty through the United States Senate. Unaware of the charges of abandonment, Albert Pike also appeared there early in February, 1856, to assist with the congressional lobbying. He secured the support of the Arkansas senators, William Sebastian, the chairman of the committee on Indian affairs, and Robert Johnson, both of whom were influenced by the lease provisions and by the tribal quitclaim to the region west of the 100th meridian. These features also impressed the Senate, which approved the treaty on February 21, 1856.[22]

With the treaty ratified by all parties, the Indians looked to the implementation of those provisions which called for the payment of large sums to both tribes. The Choctaws received $600,000 as their share of the lease and quitclaim payments. Of this sum, however, only $250,000 came directly to Indian Territory; the rest the government placed in a trust fund. Part of this money was slated for the attorney, and after a quick trip to Niagara Falls, Pitchlynn traveled home in October to collect his share. The tribal agent delivered the money in November, and Cochrane, who had come from Washington with Peter, claimed $120,000 (30 per cent of the compensation granted the tribe for the quitclaim) as due him under his contract.

The division of the $120,000 attorney fee created no little difficulty. Cochrane felt that Pike did not deserve a full 5 per cent of the net fee, but the Arkansan objected so vigorously that he was sent $10,000 as a "full and equal share." According to

[21] Israel Folsom, Mineral Bayou, to Pitchlynn, August 26, 1855, August 30, 1855, and December 19, 1855, Pitchlynn MSS, G.M.

[22] Manypenny to the Hon. A. G. Brown, February 11, 1856, 34B–C4, Records of the United States Senate, N.A.

Peter P. Pitchlynn, member of delegation of 1853. Painting by Charles Fenderich, 1842. (Courtesy Library of Congress, Washington, D.C.)

Samuel Garland, member of the delegation of 1853. (Courtesy Smithsonian Institution National Anthropological Archives, Bureau of American Ethnology Collection, Washington, D.C.)

Israel Folsom, member of the delegation of 1853. (Courtesy Smithsonian Institution National Anthropological Archives, Bureau of American Ethnology Collection, Washington, D.C.)

Dickson Lewis, member of the delegation of 1853. (Courtesy Gilcrease Institute, Tulsa, Oklahoma)

Peter Folsom, who replaced Dickson Lewis as a member of the delegation of 1853. (Courtesy Smithsonian Institution National Anthropological Archives, Bureau of American Ethnology Collection, Washington, D.C.)

Albert Pike, Arkansas attorney representing Choctaws in negotiations for the Treaty of 1855. (Courtesy Brady Collection,
National Archives, Washington, D.C.)

Douglas H. Cooper, Choctaw agent with delegation of 1853, later Confederate general in charge of Indian troops. (Courtesy Library of Congress, Washington, D.C.)

William K. Sebastian, United States senator from Arkansas, 1848–61. (Courtesy National Archives, Washington, D.C.)

Cochrane, Douglas Cooper received the largest cut of the fee for his service in discovering the Choctaw claim to land west of the 100th meridian. Luke Lea, of course, was compensated for his part in moderating Chickasaw demands, and Pitchlynn took at least $18,000 as his share, a fee that he undoubtedly divided with other prominent Choctaws. The division of the money was Peter's first big dividend from his speculative interests and only whetted his appetite.[23]

His hunger abated somewhat after another financial division, this time among the Chickasaws. To grant the smaller tribe a separate political jurisdiction required a major concession on the part of the Choctaws and liberal compensation of tribal leaders. The government, knowing this, provided $150,000 in the treaty for the smaller tribe to use as an "attorney" fee, money that George Harkins believed had been "set apart for Tom, Dick and Harry." The Chickasaws could "well afford to pay us $10,000 each and never grunt at it," he wrote to Pitchlynn. Sampson Folsom controlled the distribution of the money and had promised Pitchlynn, Harkins, and others a portion of the attorney stipend for their support of the political separation. But Luke Lea claimed the largest share for his services, despite his earlier sellout to Pike and Cochrane. Lea's claim endangered the size of the cut for Pitchlynn, who declared that the Choctaws had dealt directly with the able Chickasaw delegates during the negotiation rather than with Lea. The Chickasaw council nevertheless awarded Lea $75,000, but they permitted the balance of the money to be distributed to Choctaw friends who had supported the treaty, including Pitchlynn.[24]

[23] Pike, "Letter to the Choctaw People," Washington, February 21, 1872, Folder 72–14A, Cooper, "Address and Memorial," October, 1873, Folder 73–108, Pitchlynn MSS, G.M.; Answer of the Defendant, *John D. McPherson v. Albert Pike*, September, 1872, Supreme Court of the District of Columbia, in Albert Pike MSS, Scottish Rite Library.

[24] Harkins, Doaksville, to Pitchlynn, January 20, 1856, and n.d., Folder 16–180, Pitchlynn, Eagletown, to Sir, December 26, 1856, Robert Nail, Choctaw

Well rewarded for his several months' work in Indian Territory, in January, 1857, Peter returned to Washington to present the net proceeds case to the Senate and to implement the different provisions of the new concordat. He and his co-delegates first demanded a stay of the United States Attorney General's decision upholding the Chickasaw practice of excluding Choctaws from public office in their new tribal government. They also requested that the Indian office appoint Captain Randolph B. Marcy, the eminent military explorer, to survey the three Choctaw boundaries as described in the 1855 agreement.

The government responded favorably to only a part of the delegation's proposals. The Bureau of Indian Affairs recognized the decision of the attorney general as binding and found impractical the suggestion that Marcy delineate the tribal borders. But in October, 1857, it did award a surveying contract to Alfred H. Jones and Henry M. C. Brown. In the following January, these two gentlemen began their survey at Fort Smith and quickly determined that the historic border with Arkansas, a supposedly due south line one hundred paces east of old Fort Smith, was inaccurate. Tending southwestward ever so slightly, the boundary deprived the Indians of an estimated 161,280 acres. But rather than permit the survey team to mark a border conforming to the treaty language the Office of Indian Affairs issued new instructions to simply re-mark the old line. The delegates vigorously protested this course of events, but their opposition carried little weight, and the boundary with Arkansas remained as it had been erroneously drawn in 1825.[25] On

Nation, to Pitchlynn, February 20, 1857, Thomas Pitchlynn, Choctaw Nation, to Peter, February 22, 1857, and Daniel Folsom, Boggy, to Pitchlynn, March 30, 1857, Pitchlynn MSS, G.M.

[25] Caleb Cushing, Attorney General, to R. McClelland, January 7, 1857, Choctaw Delegation, Washington, to Manypenny, April 4, 1857, Pitchlynn et al., Washington, to C. E. Mix, March 21, 1856, and September 3, 1856, J. W. Denver, Commissioner of Indian Affairs, to Pitchlynn, October 27, 1857, and Mix to Jones and Brown, January 8, 1858, *ibid*.

the other hand, the limits of the Chickasaw Nation were surveyed with little difficulty.

Actually, the attorney general's decision and the boundary survey were incidental to the real interests of the Choctaw delegation. In the Treaty of 1855 the tribe was directed to submit to the United States Senate for adjudication claims relating to the removal from Mississippi. If that body found the demands just, then it should award the Choctaws either the net proceeds of their ceded land or a gross sum in satisfaction of their individual claims. In any event, the decision of the Senate would be final. The burden of the delegation, then, was to secure some kind of Senate action.

Since Albert Pike was absent from Washington again, Cochrane planned the strategy of the Choctaw team. He wanted the Senate to award the net proceeds rather than the gross sum, not because the amount was larger but because its justice seemed to him more easily demonstrated. He hoped to persuade the upper chamber by reverse psychology. The team gathered facts throughout 1856 and illustrated at least to its own satisfaction that the total of unfulfilled treaty obligations amounted to more than three million dollars. Thus, if the Senate decided upon a gross award, an appropriation at least that large would be necessary. Cochrane believed that the thought of making such a huge award would encourage the Senate to turn to the net proceeds. In the meantime the Senate leadership referred the whole matter to the committee on Indian affairs.[26]

The membership of the Choctaw team altered a great deal with the congressional session which began in December, 1856. Albert Pike left his law practice, now in New Orleans, to direct the presentation of the case before the Senate. In addition to Cochrane, Lea, and Cooper, John B. Luce, an attorney and former secretary to the Choctaw agent; Edward Hanrick, an

[26] Report of the Choctaw Delegation, Washington, August, 1856, H10.55, Hargrett Pamphlet Collection, G.M.

Alabaman with many friends in Washington; and Benjamin J. Jacoway, an Arkansas speculator long involved in Choctaw affairs, joined the group. Pike prepared his monumental "Notes Upon the Choctaw Question" to demonstrate that the Choctaws were entitled to the net proceeds of their land, an argument positive in its approach but somewhat at odds with Cochrane's reverse psychology. Pike believed that the Choctaws should enter the front door unashamed and unafraid and secure as large an award as possible. But even Pike's masterful appeal and the additional influence of the new members failed to move the United States Senate.[27]

After three months in the capital, in March, 1857, Pike returned to New Orleans, leaving Cochrane once again to manage the claim. But the following May when the two men collected a $200,000 legal fee from the Creek Indians, Cochrane turned nominal control of Choctaw affairs over to John B. Luce. He thought the transition of leadership would have several advantages. First, his and Pike's success with the Creek claim might prejudice the Senate against the net proceeds claim. With Luce appearing to control the team, that possibility was minimized. Second, since Luce was a prominent Fort Smith attorney, the claim would take on the aspect of an Arkansas project.

Two things, though, took the edge off Cochrane's tactics. First, Pitchlynn and his associates obtained a statement from the Indian Bureau that the federal government had realized three million dollars in net profits from the sale of the tribal domain in Mississippi. Such a figure ruined Cochrane's reverse psychology approach; he could not very well stampede the Senate from an excessively large gross award for individual

[27] Pike, "Letter to Choctaw People," Washington, February 21, 1872 Folder 72–14A, and Cooper, Choctaw Agency, to Pitchlynn, December 29 1856, Pitchlynn MSS, G.M.; Answer of the Defendant, *John D. McPherson* v. *Albert Pike*, September, 1872, Supreme Court of the District of Columbia in Pike MSS, Scottish Rite Library; 42 Cong., 3 sess., *House Report 98*, 497–504

claims when the net proceeds equaled it. Second, Pike returned to Washington in February, 1858, and immediately objected to Luce's management of the claim, a course he considered devious. Instead, he insisted on a straightforward presentation to Congress. But the Senate paid little attention to Pike, to Cochrane's strategy, or to Pitchlynn's report and adjourned in June unconvinced of the Choctaws' right to the net proceeds.[28]

When the Thirty-fifth Congress met for its second session in December, 1858, Pitchlynn and his associates were on hand. After it appeared that Pike's forthright presentation had only confused the situation, the team unanimously returned to Cochrane's original approach. E. B. Grayson, a government clerk, provided a quantity of material from the Indian Office files which Pike incorporated into a forty-two page "Memorandum of Particulars." This document demonstrated that the government owed the Choctaws over three and one-half million dollars on the basis of broken treaty promises alone, a sum considerably more than the net proceeds as earlier estimated by the Indian Bureau and one that would have to be matched if the Senate awarded a gross sum. Luce prepared a written statement for Senator Sebastian setting forth the obvious arguments in favor of the net proceeds and then for some unexplained reason retired from the case and returned to Arkansas. Pitchlynn, Pike, Hanrick, and Cochrane continued to press the matter and obtained pledges to support the Choctaw claim from Senators Johnson of Arkansas, Daniel Clark of New Hampshire, James R. Doolittle of Wisconsin, and Henry D. Anthony of Rhode Island.[29]

The elaborate strategy and careful arguments paid off on February 15, 1859, when the committee on Indian affairs

[28] Cochrane, Washington, to E. Hanrick, February 3, 1858, Hanrick MSS, University of Texas Library (hereinafter U.T.L.); Mix, Washington, to Hon. J. Thompson, Secretary of Interior, May 15, 1858, 34A–E5, Records of the United States Senate, N.A.

[29] 42 Cong., 3 sess., *House Report 98*, 505–28.

chaired by Senator Sebastian issued a report largely written by Pike but based upon Luce's statement. The committee found that the Choctaws were not entitled in law and strict right to the profits of lands ceded in 1830, but because the United States had not fulfilled its many treaty commitments the Senators recommended that the net proceeds of the land sale devolve upon the tribe. The committee then suggested that the secretary of the interior calculate the actual amount of the net proceeds, in the computation of which he should value the land scrip issued during the 1840's at $1.25 per acre and the lands yet unsold as worthless. The last recommendation was wholly unsolicited; and since it would deprive the tribe of thousands of dollars, Pitchlynn and his colleagues pressured Sebastian to amend the measure on the Senate floor so that it would give the Choctaws credit of twelve and one-half cents an acre for unsold lands.[30]

On March 9, 1859, during a special session of the Senate, Sebastian called up the committee report and then moved the adoption of the amendment suggested by Pitchlynn. Finding no opposition to his proposal, he asked for approval of the bill. In a debate lasting no more than ten minutes and involving only two people, the Arkansas senator declared that the net proceeds was a just claim and would amount to only $800,000, a sum substantially less than that previously established by Pitchlynn. Either Sebastian had ignored the 1857 report or, more likely, did not know of it. With little fanfare the Senate adopted the measure and awarded the Choctaws the net proceeds of their Mississippi lands in satisfaction of all claims against the United States. It also directed the secretary of the interior to make an account along the guidelines set forth in the legislation.[31]

In securing the Senate award many people made significant contributions. Albert Pike later declared that he alone won the

[30] 35 Cong., 2 sess., *Senate Report 374*, 15.
[31] 35 Cong., 2 sess., *Congressional Globe*, March 9, 1859, p. 1691.

adjudication. Though Luce had helped some, he insisted that Cochrane had played no part and did not give any credit to Pitchlynn.[32] Such a conclusion was absolutely unfair and characteristically self-centered. Cochrane's strategy of emphasizing the large number and amount of individual claims to encourage the Senate to accept the supposedly smaller net proceeds award had been the key to the congressional decision. Furthermore, Pitchlynn had resided in Washington during the whole of the Senate presentation and had taken a vigorous part in the lobbying efforts. He usually left his room in the early morning, walked the mile to the Capitol, haunted the cloak and committee rooms, and returned to his home in the late afternoon. He rested an hour, ate dinner, and then visited members of Congress in their private quarters, not returning to his own until eleven o'clock. In contrast to his energetic schedule, his fellow delegate, Israel Folsom, was "discouraged and ready to fall back and to give up the ship." Pitchlynn symbolized the Choctaw claim and inspired the group who worked to collect it. To be sure, he seldom wrote an official paper and even occasionally weakened the total effort. Yet, when others faltered, he remained confident, and more than once his attitude alone ensured continued action.[33]

Once the Senate made the award and the secretary of the interior began his account, Pitchlynn returned to the Choctaw Nation. Peter found the tribe deeply divided over the question of one chief or three, a weak executive or a strong one. During his absence, in January, 1857, a new constitution had been adopted at Skullyville that abolished the office of district chief and created a single governor for the Nation. Objection to the new document came primarily from fullblood citizens; they

---

[32] Pike, "Letter to the Choctaw People," Washington, February 21, 1872, Folder 72–14A, Pitchlynn MSS, G.M.

[33] Pitchlynn, Washington, to Friend, May 30, 1860, and Folsom, Choctaw Nation, to Pitchlynn, January 18, 1860, *ibid.*

had met at Doaksville in May, 1858, adopting another constitution and electing a rival set of officers that included district chiefs. Prudently supporting both sides, Pitchlynn occupied himself by serving as constable, school trustee of Eagle County, and district senator. Of course he received pay for all three posts, as well as for his service in Washington. Ultimately the tribal factions reconciled their political positions and, in a constitution adopted at Doaksville in January, 1860, accepted an executive composed of a principal chief assisted by three district chiefs, all of whom were elected for two year terms. Other national offices were established, but the nature of the legislative and judicial departments remained similar to that provided by earlier documents. The 1860 constitution continued in full force until the Choctaw Nation was abolished in 1907.[34]

Through the whole controversy, Pitchlynn did not forget his primary reason for being in Indian Territory. The United States Senate had now agreed that the Choctaws deserved the net proceeds derived from the sale of their Mississippi lands, and according to Peter's best preliminary information the sum in question would amount to nearly three million dollars. The tribe had already guaranteed him 5 per cent of the total sum reclaimed from the government, and he was assured of another 5 per cent from the attorney contract. Altogether he would receive 10 per cent, or nearly $300,000. No wonder Peter was, according to one missionary, "full of visions of self-aggrandizement, constantly and laboriously at work building splendid castles in the air for the Pitchlynns to inhabit at no distant day." To realize the anticipated fortune he and his co-delegates needed the continued support of friends at home. They spent most of their time reaffirming their agreement with George Harkins and maintaining political rapport with all tribal fac-

---

[34] Records of the National Treasurer, Volumes from the Choctaw Nation 379, Indian Archives, O.H.S.

tions. Peter returned to Washington in early November, 1859, for the new session of Congress.[35]

After much delay the secretary of the interior rendered his account as directed by the Senate on March 22, 1860. The Choctaws had ceded over ten million acres of land, he reported, nearly six million of which were sold by January, 1859. Adding to the actual sum received the twelve and one-half cents for each acre remaining unsold, the United States had grossed over $8,000,000 on the land cession. The secretary deducted from this sum the cost of survey, all removal and other expenses incurred under the treaty of 1830, and the value of the scrip issued in the 1840's. He thereby concluded that $2,981,247.30 was the net profit of the transaction. The secretary also observed that the Choctaws had been paid an additional $1,130,000 for lands controlled by the Chickasaws and leased to the United States but made no recommendation as to further deductions.[36]

The account having been rendered, the Choctaw team acted. Returning from New Orleans, Albert Pike appeared before the committee on Indian affairs and argued that the Senate had made the award in accordance with the Treaty of 1855, the secretary had made the account, and now Congress had to appropriate the $3,000,000. Under his influence the committee agreed to reject an additional $1,130,000 deduction and to adopt a report drafted by him calling for payment of the entire amount realized by the government. Issued on June 19, 1860, the completed document, much to Pike's dismay, recommended deducting first the commission paid to the state of Mississippi on the land sale and second the value of those lands granted to the state for railroads, school purposes, and swamps.

[35] Thoburn and Wright, *Oklahoma*, I, 233–34; Agreement between the Delegation and Harkins, Boggy Depot, October 21, 1859, Pitchlynn MSS, G.M.; Alexander Reid, Spencer, to Walter Lowrie, January 9, 1854, Box 12, Vol. I, American Indian Correspondence, Presbyterian Historical Society.

[36] 36 Cong., 1 sess., *House Exec. Doc. 82*, 23–25.

The charge amounted to $648,686.45 and, according to the committee, left $2,332,560.85 due the tribe. The report concluded that "every charge against the Choctaws and every deduction has been made that any equity would warrant."[37]

Surprisingly, Senator Sebastian attempted to secure an appropriation of the recommended amount even before the final report was written. On June 13, he sought to attach a rider to the Legislative Appropriation Act, in the process of which both he and Senator Clark of New Hampshire made an able defense of the award. A powerful opposition consisting of Robert Toombs of Georgia, R. M. T. Hunter of Virginia, and Jefferson Davis of Mississippi countered their efforts. Both Toombs and Davis acknowledged that something was due the Choctaws but maintained that the Senate should deduct the $1,130,000 mentioned by the secretary of interior. Other senators argued that the question had not been investigated thoroughly and that the award had been made hastily the previous year. The opposition carried the debate, and the Senate defeated Sebastian's amendment by a vote of twenty-two to twenty-four.[38] Albert Pike later proudly declared that he had been solely responsible for the defeat of the rider because its passage would have reflected upon the righteousness of the Choctaw claim. But he also said that he had gained Robert Toombs's "support." His memory failed him utterly in regard to the Georgia senator and probably in regard to the vote as well. If he did defeat the measure, he rendered the Choctaws a great disservice and had cause to regret it within the year.[39]

If the defeat pleased Pike, it certainly did not please Pitchlynn. He maintained that Hunter and Toombs had opposed Sebastian's amendment because of its immensity, a conclusion

---

[37] 36 Cong., 1 sess., *Senate Report 283.*

[38] 36 Cong., 1 sess., *Congressional Globe,* June 14, 1860, pp. 2959–65.

[39] Pike, "Letter to the Choctaw People," Washington, February 21, 1872, Folder 72–14A, Pitchlynn MSS, G.M.

completely opposite Pike's opinion. Peter reported to his people that he got revenge, though, for he and his friends defeated a favorite project of Senator Hunter's. Yet the Senate rejection failed to discourage Pitchlynn. "If I live the Choctaw business will be driven through next session," he wrote to his nephew. "Your old uncle is on the warpath and sees in the distance the snake of the enemy's campfires and will be certain to extinguish them."[40]

In December, 1860, the Choctaw team prepared to present its case again to a new congressional session. Great obstacles faced them, for the election of Abraham Lincoln the previous November had brought the secession of some Southern states and the prospect of civil war. Pike prepared a memorandum objecting to the Senate committee's proposed deductions from the $3,000,000 award; and to influence the chairman of the House committee on ways and means, John Sherman, the team brought the former commissioner of Indian affairs, George W. Manypenny, to Washington from Ohio.[41] All efforts culminated on February 2, 1861, when Sebastian offered in the Senate a Pitchlynn-endorsed amendment to the Indian appropriation bill already passed by the House. He proposed that Congress authorize payment to the Choctaws of $1,202,560, a sum derived by deducting both the $1,130,000 questioned by Toombs in the earlier debate and the amount suggested by the committee in 1859.

In the Senate debate that followed, William P. Fessenden of Maine led the opposition, which cited the unsettled conditions of the Union, the seeming lack of investigation, and the hastiness of the original award as reasons for not funding the claim. Senator Johnson responded vigorously, declaring his support

[40] Pitchlynn, Washington, to Nephew, July 13, 1860, *ibid.*
[41] Pitchlynn, "Memorial," Washington, December 28, 1860, Folder 60–32, Manypenny, Columbus, to Pitchlynn, February 9, 1861, and February 13, 1860, and J. T. Cochrane, Washington, to Pitchlynn, n.d., Folder Un–25, *ibid.*

for the entire $3,000,000 award. "They may say they will take two and three pence, but for my part I will never consent to any compromise that is simply palatable and bare faced robbery inflicted on the weak by the strong. . . . My God!" he exclaimed, "what kind of respect can we have for ourself when we seek to break our obligations." Johnson's position was strongly influenced by his friend, Albert Pike, who remained critical of any reduction in the appropriation and who opposed Pitchlynn's tendency to compromise. But Peter had a more realistic grasp of the situation than Pike; to push for the total award might mean another Senate rejection. The upper chamber vindicated his judgment when on February 9, 1861, it voted twenty-nine to fifteen to allow the Choctaws $1,200,000, with the remainder of the claim to be held pending further investigation.[42]

To secure similar action by the House of Representatives, Pitchlynn and his colleagues had major prejudices to overcome. On February 7, 1861, the tribal council had resolved that the destiny of the Choctaws lay with the South in its dispute with the Union, word of which reached Washington through the Memphis newspapers. With the House largely Northern after the secession of some Southern states, this alignment meant that something more than reason would be required to push the amendment through. Therefore, the Choctaw delegation padded the able arguments of Representatives Horace Maynard of Tennessee and John Stevenson of Kentucky with liberal promises to key congressmen of financial reward contingent upon payment of the net proceeds claim, which totaled $70,000. Notwithstanding these offers, opposition to the Senate-passed measure remained vigorous. John Phelps of Missouri verbalized the dissent, but John Sherman actually directed it. This Ohio representative, little influenced by the presence

[42] 36 Cong., 2 sess., *Congressional Globe*, February 6 and 9, 1861, pp. 704–709, 824–31.

of George Manypenny, led his colleagues in rejecting the Senate proposal on February 28.[43]

The nonconcurrence of the two chambers in amendments of the Indian Appropriation Act forced the measure to a conference committee. The members from the Senate, whom Albert Pike later declared he influenced Sebastian to select, stood firm in demanding the Choctaw amendment, and the conference report adopted the upper chamber's version of the bill. The Senate agreed to the report on March 2, but in the House Sherman declared that he would rather see the whole bill die than agree to the Choctaw appropriation. Accordingly, the House asked for another conference, and to this committee the Senate, or Pike, named Senators Doolittle of Wisconsin, Nicholson of Tennessee (a schoolmate of Pitchlynn's), and Pugh of Ohio. The very day of its appointment the committee rewrote the language of the amendment entirely and awarded to the Choctaws $500,000, one half to be paid in cash and the other half in United States bonds. Moments later the Senate accepted the report, and the House, with Sherman still objecting, did the same by a vote of seventy to sixty-one.[44]

Thus, forty-eight hours before Lincoln entered Washington, Pitchlynn and his associates were awarded $500,000 in partial satisfaction of tribal claims. The congressional action fittingly concluded a co-operative effort, an effort that Pike forgot when he later declared that he "alone" secured the appropriation. Pike always thought of himself as the key to the Choctaw team, but in doing so he overlooked the contributions of Cochrane, Lea, Cooper, Hanrick, and especially Pitchlynn. Though Pike's

---

[43] D. H. Cooper, Washington, to John H. B. Latrobe, February 28, 1861, in John E. Semmes, *John H. B. Latrobe, and His Times* (Baltimore, 1917), 535; 36 Cong., 2 sess., *Congressional Globe*, February 28, 1861, p. 1291, and March 2, 1861, pp. 1341, 1357, 1362, 1414, 1419, 1427; Cochrane, Washington, to John B. Luce, June 1, 1861, Cochrane MSS, G.M.

[44] *Ibid.*

role was important, it was never as crucial as he later maintained and certainly not in March, 1861.

Pike and Hanrick left Washington immediately after the congressional action, but the Choctaw delegation remained and appealed to the commissioner of Indian affairs to issue a warrant for the allotted funds. Supported by the new senator from Arkansas, Charles B. Mitchell, and Congressman Thomas Corwin of Ohio, they asked that a portion of the $250,000 in cash be paid to Agent Cooper so he could purchase corn for the starving Choctaws, who always seemed to be ill-fed when funds were available.[45] But the Republican administration had not yet decided to retain Cooper, a Southern man, as tribal agent and hesitated to put him in charge of so much money. Aware of the government's suspicions, the delegation sought an interview with President Lincoln to urge the reappointment of Cooper.[46] This demonstration of faith in the agent encouraged the government to release $134,512.55 to him, on March 22 and April 5, to buy corn.[47] Cooper, of course, had already decided for the South and later, when his handling of the money was questioned, conveniently produced "evidence" to show he had so advised the federal executive. Yet it is incredible that the government would release so much money to a man whose patriotism was in doubt.[48]

On April 5, Secretary of the Treasury Salmon P. Chase told

[45] J. T. Cochrane, Washington, to Albert Pike, April 15, 1861, and Pitchlynn, Washington, to Thomas Corwin, March 8, 1861, *ibid.*; Pitchlynn et al., Washington, to W. P. Dole, Commissioner of Indian Affairs, March 15, 1861, Papers Relating to Claims, Trust Fund, Indian Division, Records of the Secretary of Interior, N.A.

[46] Letter draft from Chickasaw and Choctaw Delegates, Washington, to Sir, March 12, 1861, Pitchlynn MSS, G.M.

[47] Payments to the Choctaw Nation on Account of their Claims, Vol. II, Index to Appropriation Ledgers, Division of Finance, Records of the Office of the Secretary of Interior, N.A.

[48] Cooper, "Reply to Charges Made by J. P. C. Shanks," Washington, August, 1873, Folder 73–108, Pitchlynn MSS, G.M.

the Choctaws he would pay them the portion of the cash not given Cooper, or $115,000, if they would wait two weeks to demand the $250,000 in bonds. He pointed out that the $250,000 in bonds could be cashed only at great sacrifice, and after the government floated its first bond issue, he would redeem the bonds either in cash or in 6 per cent treasury notes. The Choctaws agreed, and on April 12, as shells fell on Fort Sumter, the Treasury handed Pitchlynn $3,187.45 in cash and a draft on a New York bank for $112,000. Pitchlynn elected not to cash the draft immediately, but from money paid to Cooper he transferred $5,600 to Cochrane who then passed $4,000 on to Senator Mitchell for services rendered. Mitchell then left the city intending to call upon President Jefferson Davis on his way back to Arkansas about enlisting the Indians in the Southern cause. In this instance at least, the federal government contributed directly to the Confederacy.[49]

On April 20, Pitchlynn went to the Treasury to pick up the notes that Secretary Chase had promised to issue in lieu of the $250,000 in bonds. Administrative complications developed, and the notes were not immediately paid. Cooper and Cochrane, tense about the situation because the attorney fee depended on the treasury notes, suggested that Pitchlynn see Commissioner of Indian Affairs William P. Dole that evening at his home. As a result of the after-hours interview with Dole, Peter and his two co-delegates, Israel and Peter Folsom, made an appointment to meet Secretary Chase the following morning, April 21.[50]

At the Sunday conference Chase and Dole apparently took

[49] Cochrane to E. Hanrick, April 8, 1861, and April 22, 1861, Hanrick MSS, U.T.L.; Payments to the Choctaw Nation, Vol. II, Index to Appropriation Ledgers, Division of Finance, Records of the Office of the Secretary of Interior, N.A.; Cochrane to Choctaw Delegates, April 12, 1861, and Cochrane to Pike, April 15, 1861, Pitchlynn MSS, G.M.
[50] Cochrane to Pike, April 23 and 25, 1861, and Cochrane to J. B. Luce, June 1, 1861, Cochrane MSS, G.M.

the Choctaws into their confidence. They explained that the government suspected Cooper of Southern sympathies and feared that the agent would not use the funds placed in his hands for the benefit of the tribe. Ample evidence supported their suspicion. Earlier in the week Cooper had written a pro-Southern letter to Tandy Walker, a chief under the Skullyville constitution, but failed to place a stamp on it. The letter was opened by the post office and returned to the Office of Indian Affairs, which relayed the contents of the letter to the Treasury. Furthermore, Chase and Dole told the delegates that the tribal council needed to requisition the $250,000 in notes directly before the government could release them. The two therefore recommended that Pitchlynn and his associates return to the Nation, see that Cooper spent the "corn money" for the benefit of the tribe, secure a requisition directly from the council for the notes, and ensure the loyalty of the Choctaws to the United States.[51]

Flattered by the confidence of such high officials—Pitchlynn later said that he had talked to President Lincoln—the Choctaw delegation left almost immediately for home. On Sunday afternoon, Israel and Peter Folsom took the $112,000 draft and crossed the Potomac to Alexandria, Virginia, while Pitchlynn went to his residence to gather his family. On Monday morning, Cochrane visited Peter, finding him intoxicated and the family packing to move. He was "inexpressably pained" when he learned that the Secretary had refused to deliver the treasury notes and that the Folsoms had already left with the $112,000 bank draft. The course of events left Cochrane without compensation for his work on the Choctaw claim.[52]

That afternoon Pitchlynn met his co-delegates in Alexandria and started immediately for Indian Territory. He left behind

[51] *Ibid.*
[52] *Ibid.*

him eight years of concentrated effort, but with his share of the $112,000 he did not feel wholly uncompensated. Furthermore, if the Choctaws retained their senses in the critical days to follow, another $250,000 would also be paid.

CHAPTER VI

The Civil War Years

Peter Pitchlynn left Washington in April, 1861, convinced that the Choctaws must remain loyal to the Union. Years of residence in the capital, wide travel in the North, a wife with family connections in the same region, and lack of emotional attachment to slavery partially accounted for his commitment to the federal government. But, more important, Peter had a financial interest in a continued alliance with the Union. Lincoln's administration would not pay the balance of the net proceeds if the Choctaws sided with the Confederacy.

Pitchlynn arrived with his family at Eagletown in early May and immediately expressed his opposition to the predominant Southern influence within the tribe. He conferred with George Hudson, the first principal chief of the Nation elected under the compromise constitution of 1860, and sold him on the advantages of maintaining the Washington alliance. Hudson had already called a special session of the council to meet at Doaksville, the tribal capital, in mid-June and with the advice of Pitchlynn prepared an address recommending neutrality in the conflict between North and South.[1]

[1] Speech Draft, n.d., Folder Un–321, Pitchlynn MSS, G.M.; John Edwards, "My Escape," *The Chronicles of Oklahoma*, Vol. XLIII (Spring, 1955), 71.

But before Hudson gave his speech several events occurred
that forced the chief and Peter to alter their course at the last
moment. First, a Texas vigilance committee crossed Red River
and surrounded Pitchlynn's home, calling him an abolitionist
and threatening him with dire consequences if he persisted in
his Union sympathies. Second, R. M. Jones, who anticipated
the chief's position, addressed the assembled council before
Hudson, declaring that anyone who opposed southern secession ought to be hanged. Finally, white men from Texas and
Arkansas descended upon the tribal meeting and lobbied for a
Confederate alliance. Under these pressures, the chief threw
away his Pitchlynn-prepared speech and declared instead that
the United States no longer existed as a government, that it had
refused to pay money awarded by Congress to the tribe, that
it had abandoned its military posts in the Choctaw country, and
that it now planned an invasion. He stated that the Choctaws
ought to ally with the Confederacy and recommended that
the tribe select commissioners to meet with the proper authorities to negotiate a treaty of alliance and annuity with the
South.[2]

Thoroughly intimidated by the presence of so many Southern sympathizers, on June 10 the council declared the Choctaw
Nation free and independent of the United States and appointed delegates to make an alliance with the Confederate
States of America. R. M. Jones headed the delegation that proceeded to North Fork Village in the Creek Nation where it
met other representatives from the Creek and Choctaw tribes,
drew up articles of confederation, formed a Grand Council,
and on July 12 signed a treaty of alliance with the Confederacy, which was represented by Albert Pike.

[2] Orlando Lee, Huntington, Long Island, to W. P. Dole, March 15, 1862,
in Annie Abel, *The American Indian As Slave Holder and Secessionist*, I, 75–79
(hereinafter *The Indian as Slaveholder*); Speech of James Hudson, Doaksville, n.d., Folder 64-1, Pitchlynn MSS, G.M.

Earlier that summer Pike's colleagues in the net proceeds case had been astonished when he accepted a commission to treat with the western Indians. "I think he is too hard up for money to undertake such a proceedings," John Cochrane had written, "when he knows that if the Choctaws will only remain quiet and uncommitted they can get the balance of the appropriation and we our fee."[3] But Pike had other plans. In the new concordat he signed with the Choctaws the Southern government guaranteed the tribe not only a large measure of independence but also assumed the old obligations of the United States, including the net proceeds. Obviously, Pike expected to get from the Confederacy what he had been unable to secure from the United States. Furthermore, he undermined any Choctaw opposition which assumed that support for the South would mean loss of tribal annuity funds. Even Pitchlynn's loyalty to the Union decreased when the language of the treaty became known.[4]

At the very time Peter suffered insult at the hands of white men and political defeat in the tribal council, he and his co-delegates delivered the $112,000 draft to the Choctaw treasurer. Efforts to realize the face amount of the draft set in motion an incredible chain of events. The tribal treasurer turned the order over to a local mercantile company owned by John P. Kingsbury and Sampson Folsom who, for a 20 per cent commission, promised to secure its payment. The firm sent two Presbyterian missionaries, Ebenezer Hotchkins and O. P. Stark, behind the Union lines to New York City where they exchanged the draft for gold. The missionaries succeeded in moving the coin to St. Louis, but found they could not recross the lines to Indian Territory with all of the money in their possession. There-

---

[3] John T. Cochrane, Washington, to Pike, April 25, 1861, and Cochrane to J. B. Luce, June 1, 1861, Cochrane MSS, G.M.

[4] Debo, *Rise and Fall*, 82; Convention Records, June, 1861, Folders 61–38, 61–39, 61–40, Pitchlynn MSS, G.M.

fore, they left $33,000 in gold at St. Louis in the care of John C. Johnson, a representative of Lehman and Company. The remainder they successfully smuggled into the Choctaw Nation and handed over to Folsom in October, 1861, at Doaksville.[5]

After deducting his fee Folsom paid $59,100 to a tribal committee specially created to investigate Pitchlynn's accounts. The committee, headed by R. M. Jones, awarded the whole amount to Pitchlynn and his four co-delegates, who immediately loaned $20,260 back to the Nation, paid $3,000 to Forbis LeFlore, and divided the remaining $35,840, according to the 1855 agreement, among themselves and the heirs of George W. Harkins. Altogether, Pitchlynn received $7,168.10. After the transaction Jones's committee issued a report that defied interpretation but clearly declared that, in addition to the $59,100, the tribe still owed the delegation of 1853 over $70,000.[6]

By the terms of their 20 per cent contract, Pitchlynn and his associates certainly were due $50,000 of the $250,000 collected on the Senate award. But they had received that amount and more from the committee, and still the tribe owed them! The indebtedness resulted from Peter's charging the tribe as if his contract applied 20 per cent of the $400,000 received for the quitclaim according to the Treaty of 1855 and the more than $90,000 paid in arrearages the same year. Such a charge was absolutely improper; the old district chiefs had agreed to the 1855 contract with the delegation after the payment of the arrearages and the ratification of the treaty. The committee

---

[5] Receipt of S. M. Folsom, Doaksville, June 12, 1861, Pitchlynn MSS, G.M.; Sampson Folsom, Horse Prairie, to Sam Garland, August 10, 1863, N.A., O.I.A., Choctaw Agency, Letters Received, Microcopy 234, Roll 181; Plaintiff's Final Reply Brief, *Sophia Pitchlynn* v. *Choctaw Nation*, Court of Claims, H10.79, Hargrett Pamphlet Collection, G.M.

[6] R. M. Jones, Doaksville, to Choctaw Council, October 23, 1861, N.A., O.I.A., Choctaw Agency, Letters Received, Microcopy 234, Roll 179; Israel Folsom, Elm Grove, to Pitchlynn, November 13, 1861, and Pitchlynn, Washington, to J. P. C. Shanks, April, 1873, Folder 73-18, Pitchlynn MSS, G.M.

report suggested embezzlement and did little credit to either Pitchlynn or Jones.

Efforts to collect the $33,000 left in St. Louis by the two missionaries were equally incredible. In May, 1862, Sampson Folsom sold the gold for $44,000 in Confederate currency to Frank Williams of Heald and Company, a Fort Smith firm with offices at Skullyville. From the money realized, on August 11, 1862, Folsom paid the delegation $25,000, of which Pitchlynn received $6,354.18. All parties kept the transaction secret, for Williams feared he might be charged with treason for dealing behind enemy lines. He paid for the money in advance and sent to St. Louis a man with an order for the gold to present to Lehman and Company. Unfortunately, parties at both St. Louis and Philadelphia refused to honor the draft since Johnson had ended his association with Lehman and moved the gold to Memphis. All of Williams' efforts to collect proved futile and, since the Choctaws refused to refund the money he had paid to them, Heald and Company ceased to function. Pitchlynn permanently forgot the whole incident, but not the gold.[7]

The $33,000 remained with Johnson until the summer of 1863, when he came to the Nation to acquire legal control of the money entrusted to him. Dealing surreptitiously with Samuel Garland and Peter Pitchlynn, he purchased the gold for $26,515.84 in Confederate money, all parties apparently undisturbed that it had been sold the year before to Williams. The delegation realized nearly $15,000 from this impossible deal, $3,800 of which accrued to Pitchlynn.[8] Thus, after selling part of the money twice the delegates realized $76,461.20 from the

[7] F. E. Williams, Choctaw Agency, to Sampson Folsom, May 26, 1862, HR 40A–F11.5, Records of the House of Representatives, N.A.; Receipt, August 11, 1862, 17642, Choctaw Nation–Federal Relations, Indian Archives, O.H.S.; 42 Cong., 3 sess., *House Report 98*, 125.

[8] Sampson Folsom, Horse Prairie, to Samuel Garland, August 10, 1863, N.A., O.I.A., Choctaw Agency, Letters Received, Microcopy 234, Roll 181; Account, n.d., Folder Un–149, Pitchlynn MSS, G.M.

initial draft, not including the money "loaned" to the Nation or paid to LeFlore. Of this amount Pitchlynn and his colleagues had secured over $17,000 each, and after the sale to Johnson were still on the books to receive an additional $55,000 for services rendered. The entire transaction illustrates amply the resourcefulness of Peter Pitchlynn.

An equally dubious manipulation involved the $134,000 the United States turned over to Douglas Cooper for the purchase of corn. The agent used part of the funds, about $40,000, to buy grain in the Ohio Valley which he had shipped down the river. At Cairo, Illinois, Union army officers intercepted the barges and confiscated some of the grain but ultimately permitted the vessels to continue. At Skullyville Cooper distributed a portion of the corn that arrived in Indian Territory by way of the Arkansas River; he sold the remainder, transferring the proceeds of $4,500 to the Choctaw treasury. The agent had shipped most of the corn up the Red River, but low waters detained it at the "raft," an obstruction near Shreveport, Louisiana. When the shipment began to spoil, Cooper sent Sampson Folsom and an equally resourceful mixed-blood, Eastman Loman, to sell the grain, the proceeds of which they were to return to the Nation. Exactly how much the Choctaws realized from this sale was not recorded.[9]

Obviously most of the "corn" money was not spent for corn. Cooper had left in New York at least $50,000 of the funds he had received in Washington in March, 1861. Some sixty days later he sent William Wilson, a former agent of the Choctaws, to collect that part of the gold. Wilson took the money as far as St. Louis, where he, like Hotchkins and Stark before him, was unable to go any farther. He returned to New Hampshire where he buried the money. The gold remained in New Eng-

[9] Cooper, "Reply to Charges made by J. P. C. Shanks," Washington, 1875, Folder 73-108, Pitchlynn MSS, G.M.; Accounts, 1861, Volumes from the Choctaw Nation 397, Indian Archives, O.H.S.

land until early 1862 when the Nation used it to satisfy attorney fees.[10]

After Pitchlynn left Washington in April, 1861, without paying the contingent attorney fee, Cochrane looked to Albert Pike to satisfy the charge by collecting 30 per cent of the $250,000 turned over to the Choctaws by the United States. Short of money, Pike took the first opportunity to demand $75,000 from the Nation, and in order to get Pitchlynn's support may well have threatened to reveal Peter's surreptitious 5 per cent contract with the attorneys. He met with no immediate success; in January, 1862, when he encountered Folsom and Loman in Richmond, Virginia, he again demanded his fee. Finally Folsom wrote out an order to Douglas Cooper to pay Pike $40,075.60, "being the balance of money placed in your hands by the Choctaw nation for the purchase of corn." The "corn money" was that part of the $250,000 specifically reserved to relieve the "suffering" of individual Choctaws, but Pike was anxious for his pay and for the moment the morality of the transaction did not disturb him. When it did later he insisted that the money he received came from the draft originally issued to Pitchlynn. Pike knew better; two months after the Richmond meeting he had written of the $112,000, "I never received a dollar of it, I know."[11]

Nonetheless, Sampson Folsom considered the use of the corn money to pay the attorneys as "good financiering" and ar-

[10] Answer of the Defendant, *John D. McPherson* v. *Albert Pike*, Supreme Court of the District of Columbia, September, 1872, in Pike MSS, Scottish Rite Library.

[11] Cochrane to Pike, April 25, 1862, Cochrane MSS, G.M.; Folsom and Loman, Richmond, to D. H. Cooper, January 2, 1862, Pike, North Fork of the Canadian, to Sir, March 23, 1862, Sampson Folsom, Richmond, to George Hudson, January 20, 1862, and Pike, Washington, to Pitchlynn, September 12, 1873, N.A., O.I.A., Choctaw Agency, Letters Received, Microcopy 234, Roll 181; F. E. Williams, Richmond, January 2, 1862, to Heald and Company, HR 40A–F11.5, Records of the House of Representatives, N.A.; *McPherson* v. *Pike*, September, 1872, Pike MSS, Scottish Rite Library.

ranged for Pike to deposit the draft with Frank Williams of Heald and Company. Williams agreed to pay the attorney $20,000 in gold and $20,000 in Confederate currency, presented the note to Cooper, and received an order for the gold in New England from the former agent. On this occasion Williams was able to secure the gold, although he could not in the deal that later ruined his firm. Of the $40,000 initially placed to his credit Pike retained all but $2,000 paid to the Choctaw treasurer, $2,000 to John B. Luce, and $15,000 to Douglas Cooper. Later, when he learned that there was more than $40,000 in New England, Pike demanded and received $10,000 more in Confederate currency from Williams, most of which he paid to Edward Hanrick.[12]

Thus, of the $250,000 obtained in 1861 as partial payment of the net proceeds claim, little if any was used to benefit the fullblood Indians. The funds realized from the draft issued to Pitchlynn were either paid to the delegation or placed to its ultimate credit. Of money entrusted to Cooper, at least $50,000 was given to Albert Pike and some was used for grain, but most of it was obscurely applied.[13] The whole chaotic transaction illustrated the basic immaturity of the Choctaw governmental system and the disastrous consequence of channeling large sums of money into an under-developed society without proper controls. As no organized group existed within the tribe with experience sufficient to force a careful accounting, those with knowledge and skill acquired in a different community took advantage of the situation. This role of shyster was taken by the principal parties—Pitchlynn, Pike, Cooper, and Folsom.

A part yet coincidental to the distribution of the $250,000 were efforts to obtain the $250,000 in bonds held by the United States Treasury. In 1863, at the time Johnson purchased the

---

[12] *Ibid.*
[13] Account of Douglas H. Cooper, April, 1861, to January, 1862, N.A., O.I.A., Choctaw Agency, Letters Received, Microcopy 234, Roll 181.

gold from Pitchlynn and Garland, he offered to collect the bonds for a commission of $60,000. Eager for more funds, the net proceeds delegation signed an order upon the Treasury antedated April 27, 1861, to obscure the obvious attempt to transfer money from the United States Treasury to the Rebel Indians. The scheme failed, and the United States retained the bonds, but the order remained to haunt Pitchlynn in the postwar period.[14]

In spite of the favorable accounting rendered in October, 1861, most Choctaws considered Peter a Union man. Such a concept forced him to curtail his political activities and to turn to his family and farm. Despite one historian's account, Pitchlynn did not return to Washington after the tribe allied with the Confederacy but moved his family into the defunct female seminary, Iyunabi, near his home at Eagletown.[15] Several reasons prompted the move, the most important being that the plantation already housed members of his first family who were highly critical of Peter's early support of the Union. Pitchlynn and his wife (who some people thought was Abraham Lincoln's sister), their two young sons, Tommy and Everette, and Mrs. Pitchlynn's son, Charles Lombardi, found the vacant buildings commodious and hospitable throughout the war. Reestablished on Mountain Fork, the Colonel, as most Choctaws referred to him, devoted time and attention to both of his families, all of whom lived comfortably throughout most of the war. Pitchlynn even fed hundreds of indigent families in his own area.

But the Colonel did not altogether retire from public life. He served as senator in the called council session in 1862, as national auditor from January to April, 1862, and as Confed-

[14] 42 Cong., 3 sess., *House Report 98*, 65, 554; Statement Relative to Lehman Claim, n.d., Folder Un–82, Pitchlynn MSS, G.M.

[15] Thoburn and Wright, *Oklahoma*, I, 318; Mrs. S. H. Byington, Belpere, Ohio, to Sue McBeth, n.d., Sue McBeth Papers, Section X, Indian Archives, O.H.S.

erate postmaster at Eagletown in 1864. In 1863, Pitchlynn recorded individual claims for spoliation committed by Confederate troops; the Choctaws expected to be prepared if they should have to present a claim to the Southern congress after the war.[16]

Despite the acts of public service and the feeding of indigent Choctaws, Pitchlynn still suffered from the taint of Yankeeism. To establish his sympathies and protect himself from "jayhawking raids" Pitchlynn wrote in 1863 to the Washington (Arkansas) *Telegraph* that he was a Southern man by "birth, education, association, and interest." He might not have been blatant for Southern rights, he said, but he had remained consistent and hopeful, furnished sons for the battle, and a free table for the Southern soldiers. His image improved further in May, 1863, when his neighbors elected him captain of the home guard. In July, 1864, he offered his company for regular service in the Second Choctaw Regiment. Pitchlynn did not see military action, but he did see an increase in popularity.[17]

This flurry of military and political activity on Pitchlynn's part in 1863 and 1864 coincided with a Union invasion of the Choctaw Nation. In February, 1864, Colonel William A. Phillips led a federal force almost to Fort Washita, distributing along the way copies of Lincoln's Amnesty Proclamation. He sent a message to the Choctaw council inviting them to "choose between peace and mercy and destruction." Pitchlynn served in the council which Colonel Phillips addressed and was appointed by it along with R. M. Jones, Sampson Folsom, and

[16] Journal of the Senate, 1857–1867, February 7, 1862, Volumes from the Choctaw Nation 297, Indian Archives, O.H.S.; George H. Shirk, "The Confederate Postal System in the Indian Territory," *The Chronicles of Oklahoma*, Vol. XLI (Summer, 1963), 199; Account Book 10, Pitchlynn MSS, G.M.

[17] E. G. Corder, Sand Springs, Arkansas, to Pitchlynn, October 31, 1863, Pitchlynn, Eagletown, to Editor, October 21, 1863, in Washington (Arkansas) *Telegraph*, and Lieut. Colonel D. H. Hurray, Lukefahtah, to Pitchlynn, July 20, 1864, Pitchlynn MSS, G.M.; The Diary of Cyrus Byington, May 24, 1863, Box 21, Vol. II, Foreman Collection, G.M.

others to meet with representatives from the different tribes to discuss the proclamation. The convention met at Tishomingo on March 16, where some delegates argued for immediate submission and others urged continued loyalty to the South. Finally, under the influence of Confederate Generals Samuel Bell Maxey and D. H. Cooper, the tribes decided to make one last stand for the Confederacy on Red River.[18]

Despite the continued influence of Maxey and Cooper and the vigorous patriotism of the First Choctaw Regiment, enthusiasm for the Confederacy among the full bloods waned in the early months of 1864. Undoubtedly the tribe would soon have to make its peace with the Union, and to many, including Pitchlynn, it seemed advisable that someone serve as chief who might achieve a rapprochement with Lincoln's administration. As the Colonel knew the Washington officials, desired the position, and had gained the confidence of Southern sympathizers, he agreed to run for the executive office.[19]

In the election that followed, Peter's unique position stood him in good stead. On October 6, 1864, the council met to count the ballots cast by the tribe, some of which, on the motion of Lycurgus Pitchlynn, they destroyed for voting irregularities. A clerk counted the remaining ballots, and the speaker of the house announced that Pitchlynn had received 294 votes, Franceway Battice, 284, and Jerry Wade, 265. It was a close vote, so close that the council recorded that Pitchlynn was "declared" chief rather than elected. Nonetheless, he was chief.[20]

The new chief addressed the council on October 7 in a message designed to clarify the international and domestic situa-

18 Angie Debo, *Rise and Fall,* 83; Minutes of the Senate at the Called Session, February, 1864, 18308, Choctaw Nation–National Council, Indian Archives, O.H.S.; Abel, *The Indian as Slaveholder,* III, 27, 28.

19 John B. Meserve, "The McCurtains," *The Chronicles of Oklahoma,* Vol. XIII (September, 1935), 302.

20 House Records, October 6, 1864, Records from the Choctaw Nation 294, Indian Archives, O.H.S.

tion. He declared that the force of circumstances had compelled the tribe to participate in the Civil War, but having committed themselves to the South the Choctaws should stand as firm as the eternal mountains. Pitchlynn assured the council that he would enforce the civil laws, uphold the Confederate treaty stipulations, and co-operate with the military authorities. The chief urged the appointment of a special agent to care for tribal refugees and the creation of a local police force to prevent rampant thieving and robbing. Pitchlynn's general theme was commitment and steadfastness, counsel he later reinforced by issuing a proclamation setting aside the third Friday in November as a day of fasting and prayer for the Confederate cause. The Washington (Arkansas) *Telegraph* saw the address as suggestive of "the true spirit of devoted patriotism," but at the moment the chief had no other practical alternative.[21]

Great public misfortune confronted Pitchlynn when he took office. The war had little affected the Choctaws until the late summer of 1863, when Union forces captured Fort Smith, Arkansas, and penetrated to Perryville. With these defeats, destitute Indian refugees and Confederate forces flowed over the Kiamichi Mountains to Red River and created a distressing food shortage. To alleviate the problem the chief induced the council to establish a roll of needy families and to supply provisions for those so enrolled. In two separate acts, the council also appropriated $30,000 to purchase "cards" to prepare cotton and wool fibers for spinning and directed the district chiefs to supply wagons for food distribution. When scarcity of food continued, the chief decided that food consumption by non-Choctaw soldiers contributed to the famine. He demanded that the troops stationed at Shawneetown, one of R. M. Jones's Red River plantations, be removed and the corn stored there re-

[21] The Inaugural Address of Peter Pitchlynn, October 18, 1864, Pitchlynn MSS, G.M.; Washington (Arkansas) *Telegraph*, February 8, 1865, and October 26, 1864, p. 2.

served for the families of Choctaw soldiers. Even though Confederate forces withdrew, food continued to be scarce until the end of the war.[22]

During wartime criminal activity always increases, but reports of murder and robbery among the Choctaws in 1865 were unusually frequent. This deeply disturbed Chief Pitchlynn, and he recommended concerted efforts by both civil and military authorities to control the destitute refugees and unprincipled gangs that perpetrated the crimes. But he gained no satisfactory response, and the conditions of near-anarchy lingered throughout the war and ended only with the appearance of the Union cavalry after the Confederate capitulation.[23]

The continued destitution, social disorder, military deterioration, and economic instability prompted the Colonel to convene an extraordinary session of the national council at Goodwater Seminary in January, 1865. In his address Pitchlynn noted the lack of food and the civil disorder, but, more important, he raised several questions with regard to the continued depreciation of the Confederate currency. Should the tribe receive money at par when it was negotiable only at ruinous rates of discount? Could the Choctaws afford to make such a sacrifice just to exhibit loyalty? Did depreciation not constitute a tax in direct contradiction to the treaty? Pitchlynn also questioned the wisdom of an emergency plan that called all male Choctaws to the Confederate service; he believed a sufficient number should always remain at home to carry on

[22] Acts of the Choctaw Council, October, 1864, 18308, Choctaw Nation–National Council, Indian Archives, O.H.S.; Pitchlynn, Eagletown, to Major General Samuel Bell Maxey, December 29, 1864, in *War of Rebellion: A Compilation of the Official Records of the Union and Confederate Armies* (hereinafter *War of Rebellion*), LIII, 1035; Maxey, Fort Towson, to Samuel F. Mosley, December 9, 1864, and General D. H. Cooper, Choctaw Nation, to Pitchlynn, April 14, 1865, Pitchlynn MSS, G.M.

[23] Proclamation of Pitchlynn, Choctaw Nation, n.d., Folder Un–240, Pitchlynn MSS, G.M.

agricultural endeavors. The chief also made some specific recommendations. Among other things he proposed that the troops elect their officers, that an agent be appointed to register property stolen by Confederate soldiers, and that the common schools be reopened. Pitchlynn continued to declare his faith in the Confederacy and urged the Choctaws to stand united in reverence of the Bible, in obedience to the laws, and facing the future.[24]

The council considered Pitchlynn's recommendations but took little action other than authorizing an agent to procure supplies and authorizing the chief to negotiate the money question. But the Colonel had convened the council not because he desired action but because he hoped to test the temper of the Nation. Interestingly enough, few seriously objected to the questions he asked or the doubts he instilled. In this sense the called council had been a great success.

In the final days of the Civil War, the importance of Indian Territory to the Confederacy increased. If the military effort in Virginia should collapse, General Kirby Smith believed that the South could continue the struggle west of the Mississippi. Such a plan made control of Indian Territory essential, and General Douglas Cooper, now in command, sought to ensure that control by concentrating his Indian troops on the Little Boggy River. But as Cooper's dependence on the Choctaws increased, Chief Pitchlynn's allegiance to Jefferson Davis decreased. After Appomattox he spoke openly of the futility of continued resistance and expressed his increasing disenchantment by naming a delegation headed by Israel Folsom to attend a combined council of civilized and Plains Indian tribes scheduled to meet at Council Grove on the North Canadian River, west of present Oklahoma City.

Because of a threatened federal invasion, the meeting ulti-

[24] Address of Chief Pitchlynn, Goodwater, January, 1865, Folder 65-30, *ibid.*

mately took place in mid-May at an improvised location, known as Camp Napoleon, on the Washita River, near present Verden, Oklahoma. The sentiment expressed by the different delegations confirmed that Pitchlynn was not alone in his assessment of the future of the Confederacy. The tribes agreed that the South was doomed and on the twenty-sixth entered into a compact of perpetual peace and friendship promising unity of action in future contacts with the Union. With the collapse of the Confederate military effort in the East and the denial of additional troops by the Indians, Cooper realized that he could not continue alone. Even while the delegates met at Camp Napoleon he recommended that the grand council of tribes allied with the Confederate States, which convened annually in the Choctaw Nation at Armstrong Academy, or Chahta Tamaha, meet again to assess the future.[25]

The suggested council gathered at Armstrong on June 12, 1865, two weeks after General Kirby Smith surrendered all Confederate forces in the West. Illness prevented Pitchlynn's attendance, but he sent a delegation that included Samuel Garland, Israel Folsom, and Sampson Folsom. The conclave continued the discussions begun at Camp Napoleon and reaffirmed the Indian intention to act in unison in the envisioned negotiations with the federal government, even inviting Union-allied Indians to co-operate with them. The convention suggested that the tribes each appoint no more than five commissioners to go to Washington to enter into treaty negotiations.[26]

In the meantime the United States Army moved to secure the military surrender of the various Indian tribes. On June 9, Major General F. J. Herron, commander of Union forces in

[25] Minutes of the Grand Council, Camp Napoleon, May 13 to 26, 1865, Folder 65–18, and Compact, May 26, 1865, Folder 65–19, Pitchlynn MSS, G.M.; Cooper, Fort Washita, to Scott, May 14, 1865, *War of Rebellion*, XLVIII, 1304; Abel, *The Indian as Slaveholder*, III, 121, 130, 141.

[26] Minutes of the Grand Council, Chahta Tamaha, June 12, 1865, and Resolution of the Grand Council, June 15, 1865, Pitchlynn MSS, G.M.

Louisiana, ordered Lieutenant Colonel A. C. Matthews, of the Ninety-ninth Illinois Volunteer Infantry, to go to Armstrong Academy to enter into a temporary treaty or alliance with the Indians. He directed Matthews also to convene another grand council in early August where commissioners from Washington would meet with the Indians. If the tribes agreed to a temporary peace and to calling such a meeting, the cavalry forces Herron had prepared for operation among the Indians would not be sent.[27]

Unfortunately arriving after the grand council at Armstrong had adjourned, Matthews called on Chief Pitchlynn and revealed the nature of his mission. Anxious to prevent further military operations and to demonstrate his cooperation, on June 18, 1865, the Colonel issued a call to reconvene the grand council at Armstrong Academy on September 1 when the tribes would meet with the federal peace commissioners. In the interim he called upon all tribes to cease hostilities, close ranks, and face the future with unity. Having demonstrated his sincerity, the next day at Doaksville Pitchlynn signed terms of surrender with the United States far more generous than those of Appomattox. Matthews simply directed the Choctaws to return home, and instead of treating the Indians as paroled Confederate soldiers he granted them the protection of the United States.[28]

Confusion followed in the wake of Matthews' visit and Pitchlynn's proclamation. The Chickasaws, as agreed upon at Armstrong, prepared to send delegates to Washington to negotiate a peace treaty with representatives of the United States, while Chief Pitchlynn called a special session of the Choctaw council to meet co-ordinately with the grand council scheduled for September. In other words, the American peace commis-

[27] Copy of Major General F. J. Herron, Shreveport, to Colonel A. C. Matthews, June 9, 1865, *ibid.*

[28] Proclamation, Executive Department, June 18, 1865, and Surrender Agreement, Doaksville, June 19, 1865, *ibid.*

sioners were scheduled to be in two places at once. To compound the confusion the Department of the Interior, the only agency authorized to treat with the tribes, directed the Indians to assemble at Fort Smith the first of September. As this date coincided with the Matthews-Pitchlynn-arranged conference and the scheduled special session of the Choctaw council, Pitchlynn protested the Interior directive. He pointed to the impossibility of altering the arrangements made with the Army and, since the Choctaws could not be in two places at once, requested the United States to keep the appointment at Armstrong. Yet he agreed to hasten on to Fort Smith if his suggestion was denied.[29]

As scheduled the chief met with both the grand council of the confederated tribes and the Choctaw council at Armstrong Academy on September 1, 1865. Pitchlynn announced that the Interior Department had refused to alter its stated course and thus had not sent peace commissioners. He recommended that the convention adjourn and reconvene at Fort Smith to seek a new relationship with the United States. "I have every reason to believe and to trust," he stated, "that our advance will be received cordially, kindly, and liberally." At the same time he declared to his own council that the Choctaws as a sovereign nation had joined the South largely because they had been abandoned by the North. Their course had been proper but unfortunate. Now the tribe had to face its defeat and build a permanent peace by re-opening schools, encouraging manufacturing, enacting good laws, and establishing a printing press.[30] Obviously, Chief Pitchlynn spoke as one charting the future instead of one lamenting the past. But the Choctaw council, more concerned with the present, ignored the chief's

---

[29] Proclamation of Chief Pitchlynn, Chahta Tamaha, July 15, 1865, *ibid.*; Pitchlynn, Eagletown, to Cyrus Bussey, August 9, 1865, in Abel, *The Indian as Slaveholder*, III, 169.

[30] Address to the Grand Council, n.d., Folder 65–63, Pitchlynn MSS, G.M.

reconstruction measures and devoted itself to the forthcoming peace conference. It selected twenty-one commissioners, seven from each district, to make up the delegation that would meet with representatives of the United States at Fort Smith. Pitchlynn thought the deputation too large to be effective, but "owing to the disordered and demoralized state of the people" acquiesced in the decision. The council selected Robert M. Jones to lead the group, directing the principal chief to accompany them, and provided for a fifty-three man escort.[31]

As the Choctaws gathered at Armstrong the United States peace commissioners to the Indian tribes arrived at Fort Smith. The ten to fifteen thousand "dusky children of the plains" expected by the New Era had not yet appeared when the chief commissioner, D. N. Cooley, called the meeting to order on September 8. Cooley set forth his belief that the Confederate Indians had violated their treaties with the United States, thereby forfeiting all rights, and thus were "at the mercy of the government." He announced on the following day that the tribes must accept treaties that contained provisions for permanent peace with the United States, the abolition of slavery, the adoption of the freedmen, and peace with the Plains Indians. The commissioner insisted that the rebellious Indians must cede a part of their territory for the settlement of tribes from Kansas and other areas and that they must accept some form of territorial government. His proposals shocked even the loyal Indians.[32]

The Choctaw delegation arrived from Armstrong on September 15 unconcerned about tardiness and unrepentant of past sins. Cooley's terms upon which new treaties might be

[31] Washington (Arkansas) Telegraph, November 1 and 2, 1865, p. 1; Account Book 11, Pitchlynn MSS, G.M.; Folsom, Laws of the Choctaw Nation, 1869, 405–406.
[32] Fort Smith New Era, August 19, 1865, p. 2; Report of the Commissioner of Indian Affairs, 1865, 34.

made somewhat startled them, and R. M. Jones refused to accept the guidelines until Chief Pitchlynn arrived. On September 18, having conferred with the Chief, Jones agreed to the proposed terms but only with the understanding that the Choctaws continue to control their local affairs. Further, he valiantly denied that the Southern states had surreptitiously induced the Choctaws to join them, insisting instead that the tribe had embraced the South as a sovereign and independent entity. And if that were not enough, Jones stated that the Southern states had had the right to secede.[33]

Upon reflection Jones and Pitchlynn realized that harsh language reaped only harsher language. They asked to withdraw Jones's previous forthright statement and submit instead a response that deleted references to sovereignty and states' rights. The modified language encouraged Cooley to submit to the Choctaws and the Chickasaws a draft of a permanent treaty. Cooley suggested that the Choctaws abolish slavery, relinquish one-third of the tribal lands *east* of 98 degrees west longitude, open their country to other Indians, abandon all rights to the Leased District as delineated in the Treaty of 1855, agree to territorial government, and accept any treaty modification ordered by the Senate. In return, the United States guaranteed to protect the tribe against white emigration and to restore all annuities, except those expended for loyal Indians, and other monies, presumably even the net proceeds.[34]

Cooley had badly misread the moderated Choctaw statement. Pitchlynn and the delegation were not about to sign an agreement that resulted in the loss of any settled tribal lands. And when the commissioner insisted upon his draft the Choctaws broke off negotiations and deferred the question of a final treaty until they could discuss the matter with Cooley's superiors in the Department of the Interior. But the experience at

[33] *Ibid.*, 337, 345, 349.
[34] *Ibid.*, 349; Folsom, *Laws of the Choctaw Nation, 1869*, 410–13.

Fort Smith certainly subdued the delegates and made them realize that the United States would not treat the tribe as prodigal sons. Yet they did not believe that the decision there was final or that ruin was imminent. For the Choctaws justice generally came only after continued petitions to Washington. Pitchlynn and his associates left Fort Smith determined to appeal the matter there.

As the chief made his way home he contemplated the composition of a Washington delegation. Since the group would deal not only with matters of state but also the net proceeds claim, he needed men he could manage. Consequently, even before the council discussed the question of a delegation, he recommended nine men he believed he could influence: Robert M. Jones, Sampson Folsom, Israel Folsom, Alfred Wade, Samuel Garland, Lycurgus Pitchlynn, Peter Folsom, Jackson McCurtain, and John Page.[35] But the recommendation did not deter the council from its chosen course.

Meeting in early October, the Choctaws first provided for the emancipation of slaves and repealed all laws enacted between February, 1861, and September, 1865, that were repugnant to the federal constitution. The council then dealt with some of the reconstruction measures proposed by the chief at earlier sessions: establishment of tribal schools, punishment of crime and robbery, and management of war refugees. Finally, on October 16, it authorized five commissioners to enter into treaty negotiations at Washington. Pitchlynn responded to this act of independence by vetoing the measure on the grounds that he should appoint the delegates instead of the council. But the veto impressed no one, and both houses repassed the measure unanimously the following day, condescending only to permit the chief to "commission" the delegates. On Friday, October 19, the council agreed to the appointment of three of

[35] Pitchlynn, Choctaw Nation, to Senate, September 18, 1865, Pitchlynn MSS, G.M.

the nine men Pitchlynn had initially suggested, R. M. Jones, Alfred Wade, and John Page, but it forced him to accept two delegates he had tried to avoid, Allen Wright and James Riley.[36]

On October 19 the council met in executive session to write instructions for the five commissioners. It clothed the new delegation with plenary powers for "negotiating a treaty," directed it to work closely with the Chickasaws, and commanded it not to sell, bargain, or exchange any of the tribal estate east of 98 degrees west longitude. Rather than sacrifice any land the tribe preferred to yield all claims to any money due the Nation, even the net proceeds. The Choctaws agreed to the permanent settlement of other Indians only in the Leased District and not even there unless the tribe received a reasonable compensation. The council authorized the commissioners to demand remuneration for emancipated slaves and modification of proposed territorial legislation.[37] From the nature of the instructions to the commissioners, the Choctaws did not expect their delegates to sit down at a love feast in Washington, but they certainly anticipated no wake. This attitude proved important in the light of future events.

On November 10, 1865, the chief formally confirmed the appointment of the "new delegates," as contrasted to the "old delegation" of 1853 of which Pitchlynn was a part, and three days later ordered them to proceed to Washington. At the same time he decided to return to the capital himself. At Fort Smith Commissioner Cooley had asked him to accompany the negotiators, and friends at home urged him to accept the invitation. Since Pitchlynn wanted to participate in any discussions that might relate to the net proceeds claim, late the same month he and his family left Eagletown to resume their residence in

[36] House Records, 1865–66, Volumes from the Choctaw Nation 294, Indian Archives, O.H.S.; Folsom, *Laws of the Choctaw Nation, 1869*, 413–29.

[37] Resolutions of the General Council in Executive Session, October 19, 1865, HR 40A–F11.5, Records of the House of Representatives, N.A.

Washington. John Wilkin, president of the tribal senate, assumed the office of chief.[38]

Pitchlynn, Robert M. Jones, and Allen Wright journeyed to Washington independently. The other three commissioners, Alfred Wade, James Riley, and John Page, traveled with General Douglas Cooper who expected to fish in the troubled waters of Choctaw–United States relations. The former agent's party stopped in Baltimore where Cooper introduced them to John H. B. Latrobe, his brother-in-law. Latrobe was a man of considerable prestige and stature. The son of the architect of the national Capitol building, he graduated from West Point, illustrated *Horse Shoe Robinson*, wrote novels, had led the American Colonization Society and served as attorney for the Baltimore and Ohio Railroad.[39] Cooper convinced the delegates that Latrobe, a Union man, could provide the guidance and the appearance of patriotism the tribe needed during negotiations with the government. When all the Choctaw commissioners met in Washington this opinion prevailed, and the whole delegation, perhaps including Pitchlynn, agreed to Latrobe's employment and the association with him of both Cooper and John T. Cochrane, who had remained in Washington throughout the war.[40]

In late January, 1866, the five commissioners and Latrobe, Cooper, Cochrane, and Pitchlynn composed the new Choctaw team. In the initial presentation to the Department of the Interior, the delegates denied that their Southern alliance revoked all previous treaties with the United States. To be sure,

[38] Proclamation of Chief Pitchlynn, Choctaw Nation, November 10, 1865, Pitchlynn MSS, G.M.; Pitchlynn, Washington, to Commissioner of Indian Affairs, April 11, 1866, *Choctaw Nation* v. *United States*, Court of Claims, in Phillips Collection, U.O.L.; D. N. Cooley, Commissioner of Indian Affairs, to Pitchlynn, July 17, 1866, N.A., O.I.A., Letters Sent, Microcopy 21, Roll 80.

[39] See Semmes, *John H. B. Latrobe and His Times.*

[40] 42 Cong., 3 sess., *House Report 98*, 613; Latrobe, "Address of John H. B. Latrobe," Baltimore, June 19, 1873, Box 42h, Letters Received, Private Sources, Indian Division, Records of the Secretary of Interior, N.A.

in July, 1862, Congress had authorized the abrogation of Indian treaties by presidential proclamation, but Lincoln had made no such proclamation, and thus treaties with the Choctaws, and particularly that of 1855, still bound the United States. Latrobe later maintained that he made this happy discovery and that it proved crucial to the negotiations. Yet all of February and most of March, 1866, passed without real accomplishment, during which time Latrobe returned to Baltimore, leaving matters to Cooper.[41]

As negotiations languished, Chief Pitchlynn turned his attention to other matters. News of reconstruction excesses among the Indians reached Washington in the early spring of 1866. For example, after Robert Jones left the Nation federal authorities confiscated his cotton valued at thousands of dollars. He appealed to President Andrew Johnson for assistance and immediately left Washington to return to his plantation. Pitchlynn appealed to old government acquaintances in his friend's behalf and on March 8 gained the release of the impounded goods.[42] On other occasions deputy marshals operating out of Arkansas arrested some Choctaws for offenses committed during the war. Pitchlynn and his colleagues protested these arrests and obtained from the attorney general a promise not to prosecute the Indians who were incarcerated.[43]

Also, the destitution of his fellow tribesmen continued to disturb the chief during the early months in Washington. He and the delegation petitioned the government for relief and in

[41] John H. B. Latrobe, Baltimore, to D. N. Cooley, January 30, 1866, N.A., O.I.A., Choctaw Agency, Letters Received, Microcopy 234, Roll 176; Baltimore *Gazette*, August 5, 1872, p. 1.

[42] Affidavit of Pitchlynn, n.d., Folder Un-336, and Jones, Washington, to President Andrew Johnson, January 18, 1866, Pitchlynn MSS, G.M.; Pitchlynn et al., Washington, to D. N. Cooley, February 28, 1866, N.A., O.I.A., Choctaw Agency, Letters Received, Microcopy 234, Roll 176.

[43] D. F. Harkins, Doaksville, to Pitchlynn, February 25, 1866, Pitchlynn MSS, G.M.; Pitchlynn et al., to Cooley, May 14, 1866, N.A., O.I.A., Choctaw Agency, Letters Received, Microcopy 234, Roll 176.

January submitted a list of farm implements and garden seeds needed to supply the Choctaws for 1867. Among other things, they requested 1,500 one-horse plows, 500 two-horse plows, 3,000 weeding hoes, 3,000 chop axes, 600 bushels of Irish potatoes, and 300 papers each of cabbage, onion, turnip, English pea, tomato, and mustard seeds. In a separate requisition the chief ordered 90,000 yards of brown domestic, 84,000 yards of print, and 72,000 yards of blue plaid cloth, as well as 6,000 pairs of boys' shoes, 3,000 pairs of Mackinaw blankets, and 250 dozen men's hats.[44] These orders suggested compassion on Pitchlynn's part, but also a good deal of brashness. The past was forgotten, and the chief expected to receive what he requested from the federal government.

Yet all of these services remained incidental to the Colonel's principal interest—a treaty that would reaffirm the net proceeds claim. Later when the negotiations fell under the cloud of scandal Pitchlynn would deny that he participated in the discussions with the federal government, but in fact he worked with the delegation in drafting the language of the proposed treaty, interviewing government officials, and lobbying for favorable provisions. The co-operative effort culminated in a treaty agreeable to the three parties—the Choctaws, the Chickasaws, and the United States. Appropriate officials signed the document on April 28 in a ceremony witnessed by Latrobe, Pitchlynn, and Cooper. And on June 29, after an effort supervised largely by Cooper and Cochrane, the United States Senate ratified the treaty with certain amendments by a vote of nineteen to six. The Choctaw delegates, clothed as they were with plenary powers, sanctioned the amendments and President Johnson approved the concordat on July 10.[45]

[44] Pitchlynn to Cooley, January 29, 1866, N.A., O.I.A., Choctaw Agency, Letters Received, Microcopy 234, Roll 176.
[45] Pitchlynn, "Reply to Libellous Pamphlet," Washington, 1873, in Pike MSS, Scottish Rite Library; 42 Cong., 3 sess., *House Report 98*, 470; see Book

Considering the temper of the times the Choctaws secured a favorable treaty. It combined the question of the Leased District with the problem of the freedmen. The United States, hoping to induce the Choctaws and Chickasaws to adopt their former slaves, promised to pay $300,000 at a three to one ratio for relinquishment of any title to the Leased District if the Negroes were integrated into the tribes. But if they made no provision for the former slaves within two years, the $300,000 would be used to remove the freedmen from among the tribes. The treaty also granted the right of way to north–south and east–west railroads, set up an elaborate structure for an Indian "Territory of Oklahoma," and sought to induce the Indians to accept land allotments in severalty. By the treaty the tribes consented to the settlement among them of not more than 10,000 Kansas Indians and the establishment of a United States court. In turn, the government restored to the Choctaws and the Chickasaws their pre-1861 trust funds and promised to resume payment of regular annuities on June 30, 1866.[46] For Pitchlynn the latter provision reaffirmed the net proceeds claim.

In evaluating the Treaty of 1866, historians generally contrast what the Choctaws could have lost with what the treaty supposedly secured. It is stated that the tribe faced total ruin after Fort Smith, subject to loss of land and treaty payments, but ultimately relinquished only the Leased District while winning the restoration of all annuities. The tribe certainly did save its lands east of 98 degrees west longitude, a success materially aided by Latrobe's contention that past treaties remained in effect. But the "salvation" of the annuities, so pride-

---

11, Pitchlynn MSS, G.M.; Latrobe, "An Address to the Choctaw and Chickasaw Nations," Baltimore, June 19, 1873, Box 42h, Letters Received, Private Sources, Indian Division, Records of the Secretary of Interior, N.A.; Tally Sheet, United States Senate, June 28, 1866, 39B–C14, Records of the United States Senate, N.A.

46 Kappler, *Indian Affairs: Laws and Treaties*, II, 918–31.

fully remembered by the negotiators to justify their fee, simply did not occur at Washington. The Fort Smith treaty draft generally considered so ruinous had called for the restoration of all past treaty commitments. Thus, the annuities were "saved" even before the delegation went to Washington. Without question the Choctaw commissioners secured a favorable treaty, but it was not as brilliant as some suggest, and certainly it was no diplomatic coup.[47]

The contribution of the negotiators even further was diminished as the result of an unpleasant financial transaction. When the three Choctaw commissioners first met with Latrobe in Baltimore, they arranged to secure his services without any real understanding as to compensation. Latrobe left the matter of a fee to his associate and brother-in-law, Douglas Cooper, the moving spirit of the whole arrangement. In January, after all the delegates had arrived in Washington, Cooper proposed to Robert Jones that the Choctaws "advance" $100,000 to Latrobe for negotiating the treaty. He also suggested that the Choctaws retain the Baltimore attorney to redeem the nearly $2,000,000 in tribal funds presumably confiscated by the United States during the war. Upon collection of these back annuities and other monies, he proposed that Latrobe and his associates, Cooper and Cochrane, receive 50 per cent as a contingent fee, out of which they would return the $100,000 advanced to negotiate the Treaty of 1866. Furthermore, Cooper agreed to rebate to the delegates of 1866 one-half of everything paid to Latrobe. Jones reported the proposition to his companions who accepted the arrangement but who did not commit it to writing until May 16, 1866.[48]

[47] See Debo, *Rise and Fall*, 87, 90; Latrobe, "An Address to the Choctaw and Chickasaw Nations," Baltimore, June 19, 1873, Box 42h, Letters Received, Private Sources, Indian Division, Records of the Secretary of Interior, N.A.; Folsom, *Laws of the Choctaw Nation, 1869*, 410–13.

[48] 42 Cong., 3 sess., *House Report 98*, 569–72, 613–15; Memorandum of Agreement between John H. B. Latrobe and Choctaw Delegates, Washington, May 16, 1866, Pitchlynn MSS, G.M.

Money to activate the contract depended upon the payment of funds provided in the Treaty of 1866. The forty-eighth article granted $25,000 to the delegates to discharge financial obligations incurred while in the city and the forty-ninth article loaned $150,000 to the tribe for no stated purpose. To hasten the release of funds, the delegates used Pitchlynn's old ploy. They pointed to the destitution of the Choctaws at home and the need of immediate funds to prevent starvation. Allen Wright, one of the Choctaw commissioners, was the treasurer of the Choctaw Nation, and they asked that the money be paid to him. But James Harlan, secretary of the interior, fearing that most of it would go to their attorney, refused to pay even the $25,000 until the delegates advised how they expected to dispose of the funds. Cooper insisted that the money would go for expenses, and Latrobe wrote that he anticipated a fee of only $5,000 or $6,000. On August 8 the delegates compounded falsehood when they denied any formal agreement with their attorney as to compensation. Surprisingly, these disclaimers plus a brief statement as to possible distribution of the money in late August, 1866, assuaged the Secretary's fear and prompted him to order the release of all the funds. The $25,000 plus the additional consideration of three dollars a day above travel expenses, authorized by the Nation and paid by the government, provided the delegation with adequate remuneration.[49] Or at least it should have.

But it did not. On September 5, the government issued a

[49] Draft of a letter from the Choctaw Delegates, Washington, to D. N. Cooley, August, 1866, Folder 66–48, Harlan, Washington, to Cooley, July 28, 1866, and Draft of a letter from the Choctaw Delegation, Washington, to James Harlan, August 8, 1866, Pitchlynn MSS, G.M.; Cooper, Washington, to Cooley, August 2, 1866, Latrobe, Newport, to Cooley, August 10, 1866, Pitchlynn et al., to Commissioner of Indian Affairs, August 22, 1866, Elijah Sells, Superintendent of Indian Affairs, to D. N. Cooley, April 13, 1866, and Letter Fragment, Washington, to D. N. Cooley, June 13, 1866, N.A., O.I.A., Choctaw Agency, Letters Received, Microcopy 234, Roll 176.

draft to Treasurer Wright for the other $150,000.[50] After exchanging the order for crisp treasury notes, Wright hurried down Pennsylvania Avenue to the Lempreux home where, in an upstairs room, he met the other three remaining delegates of 1866, as well as Pitchlynn, Cooper, and Cochrane. Wright counted out $100,000 and passed it to Cochrane, who receipted the tribe in full for its payment of the attorney fee and then returned one-half of the money to Wright as prescribed by the earlier oral agreement. The Choctaw treasurer divided the $50,000 rebate among the three commissioners, Pitchlynn, and himself, each of whom received nearly $10,000. And despite Latrobe's pious statements thirty days earlier Cooper, Cochrane, and Latrobe divided their $50,000 equally.[51]

Pitchlynn's role in the transaction was somewhat ambivalent. He had not pushed for the adoption of Cooper's original proposal that a contingent fee be paid the attorneys, but he did participate in the pay-off. He denied knowing of the $100,000 payment until two or three days before, yet some weeks earlier he had arranged to buy publishing company stock in anticipation of money he would receive.[52] The difficulty lay in the fact that the rebate was destined for the delegation of 1866 of which Pitchlynn was not officially a member. Thus, the $10,000 really belonged to Robert M. Jones, whose share Pitchlynn demanded for having acted in his place. Yet when the whole transaction was exposed Pitchlynn insisted he had received the money as an advance for his work in prosecuting the net proceeds, an explanation that Jones accepted. Allen Wright always maintained that he took the money for services to Latrobe and to

[50] Index to Appropriation Ledgers, III, 208, Division of Finance, Records of the Secretary of Interior, N.A.

[51] 42 Cong., 3 sess., *House Report 98*, 569–70; *Court of Claims Reports*, LIX, 776.

[52] R. M. McCurdy, New York City, to Pitchlynn, August 27, 1866, Pitchlynn MSS, G.M.

pay his personal expenses. Considering that the tribe paid three dollars a day and the United States $25,000, this explanation seemed weak to the Choctaws, weaker even than Pitchlynn's.[53]

The money having been divided, the Choctaw commissioners prepared to return home to push for the ratification of the treaty by the tribal council. Before leaving Washington, Pitchlynn joined with Winchester Colbert, governor of the Chickasaw Nation, in signing a printed address commending the delegates, their attorneys, and the treaty. The report gave birth to the myth that the brilliant efforts of the delegates and attorneys had saved the Choctaws from sure disaster. These marvelous men, the message stated, had preserved the national boundaries, gained the establishment of post offices, secured funds from the federal government to meet "present liabilities," and won the right to have their lands surveyed and allotted. The document urged the acceptance of the Territory of Oklahoma and the adoption of Negroes into the tribes. "Let us be wise and guard the future," it declared, "and ratify the treaty."[54] Pitchlynn later asserted that he did not write the address, but for the moment with copies of it in hand he left for home to push the treaty through the tribal council.

The delegates had expected to report to the regular session of the council in early October, 1866, but delay in getting the money prevented it. The assembly met as scheduled, however, and elected Allen Wright chief, but then adjourned to reconvene in mid-November. On the seventeenth it gathered again to receive the treaty and to hear former chief Pitchlynn deliver a final address and Chief Wright give his inaugural. His term of office over, Pitchlynn then took a seat as a member of the house of representatives.[55]

[53] Statement of Allen Wright, Rocky Comfort, December 14, 1867, Robert M. Jones MSS, Section X, Indian Archives, O.H.S.; 42 Cong., 3 sess., *House Report 98*, 617.

[54] Peter Pitchlynn and Winchester Colbert, "Address," Washington, July 12, 1866, H10.38, Hargrett Pamphlet Collection, G.M.

On November 27 the council met to hear Chief Wright report the course and results of the recent negotiations. Wright urged ratification of the treaty as written and approval of the delegation's acts, particularly the one employing Latrobe and the one paying him $100,000. He did not mention, however, the rebate to the Choctaw commissioners. The council proved somewhat hostile and at first appeared more interested in the acts of the commissioners than in the provisions of the treaty. A committee headed by David Harkins, a son of George, objected to Wright's division of the $25,000 and to Latrobe's fee, but finally got down to the question of the treaty. After some serious dissent about the loss of the Leased District, the council ratified the concordat on December 21 with the exception of the optional provisions regarding the adoption of the freedmen, participation in the intertribal council, and the allotment of lands in severalty. It deferred decisions on these questions until after the next general election. Also on the same day, the council passed a resolution approving "all the acts" of the delegation of 1866, a blanket endorsement the tribe lived to regret.[56]

The war over, the treaty ratified, and his office term expired, Pitchlynn busied himself again in the net proceeds claim, a claim he and his recent colleagues believed had been preserved. On December 14, Chief Wright authorized the Colonel and his co-delegates of 1853 to return to Washington and directed them to work with John H. B. Latrobe to secure the three-million-dollar award.[57] Wright obviously issued his instructions in the shadow of his own agreement with the Baltimore

[55] Inaugural address of Chief Allen Wright, November 17, 1866, Letters of the Chiefs, Volumes from the Choctaw Nation 415, and House Records, 1865–66, Volumes from the Choctaw Nation 294, Indian Archives, O.H.S.

[56] Report of the Committee, Chahta Tamaha, December 18, 1866, 18312, Choctaw Nation–National Council, Indian Archives, O.H.S.; Debo, *Rise and Fall*, 90–91.

[57] Wright, Choctaw Nation, to Pitchlynn et al., December 14, 1866, Letters of the Chiefs, Volumes from the Choctaw Nation 415, Indian Archives, O.H.S.

attorney, but for the moment Pitchlynn accepted the orders without question and within weeks had returned to the Potomac. He fully expected to collect the net proceeds within the next year.

CHAPTER VII

The Postwar Period

Chief Allen Wright's instructions to Pitchlynn directing him to work with John H. B. Latrobe reflected the confused leadership of the net proceeds claim in 1867. John T. Cochrane, holder of an earlier contract with Pitchlynn, had participated with Latrobe in the negotiations surrounding the Treaty of 1866 and had shared in his $100,000 fee, in return for which he apparently assigned to the Baltimore attorney an interest in his own 30 per cent contract on the net proceeds claim. But on October 21, 1866, before the assignment to Latrobe was committed to writing and while Pitchlynn was in Indian Territory, Cochrane died. Douglas Cooper, acting as an associate of Latrobe, advised Pitchlynn of the attorney's death and sought to protect the unwritten agreement. "I was interested with Cochrane in the Chickasaw-Choctaw claims," he wrote, "and know all about your interest. Do not take any steps or listen to overtures from any quarter without consultation," lest a misunderstanding prove fatal to the claim.[1]

Unknown to Cooper, before Cochrane died he repented of

[1] D. H. Cooper, Washington, to Pitchlynn, October 22, 1866, Pitchlynn MSS, G.M.

his agreement with Latrobe and attempted to make other arrangements to secure to his heirs an interest in the net proceeds claim. He negotiated with Jeremiah Black, attorney general in President James Buchanan's administration and a prominent Democratic politician, to purchase his 30 per cent contract with the Choctaws. Cochrane died before reaching a final agreement and left to John D. McPherson, his executor and a Washington attorney, the implementation of his scheme.[2] As envisioned by his deceased friend, on November 8, 1866, McPherson transferred to Black the 30 per cent contract with the Choctaws.

The whole transaction, of course, depended upon the approval of Pitchlynn and his co-delegates. Luke Lea, whom Cochrane named in his will as a copartner, wrote to the Colonel at Eagletown: "I can assure you that he [Cochrane] considered the value of the claim as depending in a great degree on the arrangements with Judge Black." Intimating that Pitchlynn knew all about it, he urged endorsement of the transfer and prompt return of the contract. Pitchlynn made no immediate response and on his way back to Washington in early 1867 stopped at Memphis to confer with Albert Pike. The Colonel asked him to prosecute the claim, but Pike declined the invitation because he believed his "Rebel" background would prejudice the claim in the eyes of the federal government. Unable to depend on Pike, when Pitchlynn and his co-delegates reached the capital city, they agreed to the arrangements already made with Judge Black.[3]

McPherson sold Cochrane's contract to Black for $150,000 with one half due immediately and the other upon the settlement of the claim. To finance the transaction Black approached a fellow Pennsylvanian, Thomas A. Scott, secretary of war

[2] Cochrane's Will, Washington, October, 1866, Folder 66–61, *ibid.*
[3] Luke Lea, Washington, to Pitchlynn, November 9, 1866, and Pitchlynn's History of the Net Proceeds Claim, Washington, July 28, 1880, *ibid.*; 42 Cong., 3 sess., *House Report 98*, 141.

under Lincoln and later president of the Pennsylvania Railroad, explaining the nature of the claim and assuring him that Congress would soon appropriate the money. Unable to resist such an opportunity, on February 14, 1867, Scott furnished $25,000 in cash and $50,000 in bonds of the Stubenville and Indiana Railroad, a sum divided equally between Cochrane's estate and his partner, Luke Lea. For Scott's speculative investment Black guaranteed him repayment of the initial contribution out of the first money received and an assignment of $150,000 from the final sum collected in satisfaction of the net proceeds claim.[4]

Rumors of the sale of Cochrane's contract deeply disturbed Chief Wright. He and his co-delegates of 1866 understood that Latrobe and Cochrane were equal partners in the attorney contract and considered any arrangement with Black subversive of the Baltimore attorney's interest: "It would not do to sell or transfer the net proceeds claim," the chief wrote to Pitchlynn early in March, 1867.[5] But Pitchlynn had everything to lose and nothing to gain by co-operating with Latrobe. Unlike Wright, he had no vested interest in the 1866 contract with the attorney. Obviously the value of the 20 per cent assigned to the delegation of 1853 and his own personal 5 per cent rebate hinged upon the success of the agreement in Black's hand. The Colonel, therefore, ignored his chief and joined the efforts directed by the former attorney general to fund the net proceeds award.

On February 5, 1867, Secretary of the Interior Orville H. Browning, as Black had predicted, independently asked Congress to appropriate the remainder of the net proceeds. On the basis of this request the House committee on appropriations included an allocation of $1,800,000 in the deficiency bill—

[4] Agreement between Black, McPherson, and Scott, Washington, February 14, 1867, Pitchlynn MSS, G.M.; 49 Cong., 2 sess., *Senate Report 1978*, 111.

[5] Wright, Boggy Depot, to Pitchlynn, March 2, 1867, Letters of the Chiefs, Volumes from the Choctaw Nation 415, Indian Archives, O.H.S.

$900,000 in cash and somewhat more in non-interest-bearing bonds—in "full satisfaction and discharge of all Choctaw claims against the United States existing prior to the twenty-eighth day of June, 1866." This reduced sum represented the amount considered absolutely "uncontested" by the Senate in 1861. John Kasson of Iowa, James Garfield of Ohio, and Thaddeus Stevens, chairman of the committee, supported the measure during the debate in the House. Stevens declared that the treaty awarding the net proceeds had to be honored despite the alliance of the tribe with the Confederacy, an argument which Charles Eldridge of Wisconsin found peculiar in view of the Pennsylvanian's philosophy that the South was a conquered province. But the distinguished support could not overcome the charges of treason leveled against the Choctaws because of their Southern sympathies, and the House struck the measure from the deficiency bill on March 2, 1867. An effort in the Senate to appropriate $250,000 in lieu of the confiscated bonds met a similar fate.[6]

The congressional action only aggravated the growing tension between Latrobe's associates and Pitchlynn. To Chief Wright not only had the Colonel refused to work with the Baltimore attorney, but he had very nearly sacrificed every other Choctaw claim, including the back annuities, in an effort to secure the net proceeds. The chief ordered Pitchlynn to co-operate with Latrobe or his commission as tribal delegate would be revoked. For his part, the Colonel denied sacrificing anything and charged Douglas Cooper with having defeated the appropriation. Furthermore, he declared that the "new delegation" of 1866 did not have the right to employ an attorney to aid in the net proceeds case; yet, as a contract did exist, he would grant Latrobe an interest in the $250,000 in bonds confiscated prior to the war as well as the back annuities. Wright

[6] 39 Cong., 2 sess., *Congressional Globe*, March 2, 1867, pp. 1747–51, and February 23, 1867, pp. 1811–14.

insisted, though, that the Baltimore attorney had a one-half share in the 30 per cent contract, according to the unwritten agreement with Cochrane, and summarily revoked Pitchlynn's credentials.[7]

The Colonel ignored the dismissal and resolved to present the matter to the October, 1867, session of the Choctaw council. Unable to attend personally, he sent E. S. Mitchell, a trader among the Indians, as his representative and promised to pay him $10,000 upon the payment of the claim if the tribe sustained the authority of the "old delegation." Not to be outdone, Cooper contracted with John Davis and Perry Fuller, both of whom had traded among the Choctaws, to represent Latrobe at the council. If the two secured exclusive control of the net proceeds claim for the attorney, Cooper promised to pay them one-fourth of all the money appropriated. With these pre-council maneuvers, the session promised excitement.[8]

In the meantime, the contesting parties in Washington had negotiated a compromise. Judge Black and McPherson, who still acted for the Cochrane heirs, were badgered by Cooper and Chief Wright into recognizing Latrobe's interest in the 30 per cent contract; they agreed to pay him $75,000 upon collection of the claim, two-thirds of which would come from Black and one-third from McPherson. Pitchlynn, however, had not been consulted and for the moment refused to accept the compromise offered.[9]

[7] Wright, Boggy Depot, to Pitchlynn and Folsom, March 28, 1867, Letters of the Chiefs, Volumes from the Choctaw Nation 415, Indian Archives, O.H.S.; Draft of a letter to Wright, Washington, April, 1867, Folder 67–10, Letter Fragment, Washington, May, 1867, Folder 67–16, and Wright, Boggy Depot, to Pitchlynn and Folsom, May 24, 1867, Pitchlynn MSS, G.M.

[8] Contract between Pitchlynn and Mitchell, Washington, May 4, 1867, *ibid.*; 49 Cong., 2 sess., *Senate Report 1978*, 121.

[9] John D. McPherson, Washington, to Jeremiah S. Black, n.d., Vol. XLVII, Black MSS, Library of Congress; 49 Cong., 2 sess., *Senate Report 1978*, 77; *H. E. McKee v. Ward H. Lamon*, Supreme Court of the United States, October Term, 1894, in Rare Book Section, G.M.

At the council which met at Armstrong Academy, now the capital of the Nation, Chief Wright announced that an agreement had been reached but, mindful of his own personal interests, he urged the tribe nonetheless to recognize Latrobe's contract alone. Mitchell and Israel Folsom, the latter just home from Washington, adopted Pitchlynn's view of the compromise and urged the council to sustain the "old delegation" which, if left alone, would undoubtedly secure an appropriation to fund the whole net proceeds claim the next session of Congress. The tribal legislators weighed both positions and ultimately enacted a law that reaffirmed Pitchlynn's authority and the Cochrane contract. Though it did not necessarily nullify the 1866 agreement with Latrobe, Chief Wright considered vetoing the measure because it did not directly sustain that accord, but after a forceful opinion by National Attorney Sampson Folsom in favor of the legislation, he reluctantly attached his signature. Folsom, of course, was Pitchlynn's old comrade in arms and himself a master of manipulation. He seldom acted from unselfish reasons, nor did he in this instance; for his decisive opinion the Colonel's associates promised him $100,000 upon payment of the net proceeds claim.[10]

The Latrobe interests received another rebuke when the council sent Folsom to Washington to defend the tribe against claims presented by the so-called loyal Indians and traders, heretofore within Latrobe's purview since any payment to them would come from the back annuities. The Treaty of 1866 had provided for a federal commission to adjudicate the claims of

[10] Mitchell, Armstrong Academy, to Pitchlynn, October 22, 1867, Opinion of Attorney General Folsom, Chahta Tamaha, November 16, 1867, and Pitchlynn's History of the Net Proceeds, Washington, July 28, 1880, Pitchlynn MSS, G.M.; Israel Folsom, Cottage Hill, to the Choctaw Council, October 14, 1867, N.A., O.I.A., Choctaw Agency, Letters Received, Microcopy 234, Roll 177; Folsom, *Laws of the Choctaw Nation, 1869*, 470; Message of Allen Wright, Choctaw Nation, October, 1867, and Allen Wright, Chahta Tamaha, to the General Council, November 18, 1867, Letters of the Chiefs, Volumes from the Choctaw Nation 415, Indian Archives, O.H.S.

those Choctaws and white men who had suffered for loyalty to the Union. The commissioners selected had held hearings at Fort Smith in September, 1866, and on the basis of the evidence presented awarded $109,742.08 plus interest to the loyal Choctaws, represented by the former Union general, James G. Blunt. The treaty directed the secretary of the interior to either confirm or deny the commission's finding, a decision he delayed for more than a year after an able protest by Latrobe and an inability to find enough Choctaw money to pay the award.[11]

As directed by the Choctaw council, Folsom appeared before the secretary in late 1867 to present additional arguments protesting the award to the loyalists. He made a vigorous initial statement but soon relaxed his opposition and on April 20, 1868, agreed to a compromise whereby the Choctaws would pay nearly the whole judgment out of funds held in trust for them by the United States. Several things prompted Folsom to compromise. Pitchlynn believed that speedy payment of the Choctaws who had remained loyal to the Union would increase congressional interest in the net proceeds; and General Blunt agreed to lend his influence in pushing the claim through. But even more important, Blunt promised Folsom $25,000 out of any award to the loyal Choctaws, an advance Pitchlynn agreed to refund Blunt and charge against Folsom's $100,000 contract upon the collection of the net proceeds.[12]

A similar chain of events occurred in relation to the claims of the "loyal" Indian traders. Reuben Wright, a white merchant at Boggy Depot, and Heald and Company, the Fort Smith firm

---

[11] Debo, *Rise and Fall*, 98; Latrobe, "Papers submitted to the Secretary of Interior," Washington, 1867, H10.85, Hargrett Pamphlet Collection, G.M.

[12] N. G. Taylor, Commissioner of Indian Affairs, to O. H. Browning, Secretary of Interior, April 27, 1868, Box 20, Letters Received, Office of Indian Affairs, Indian Division, Records of the Secretary of Interior, N.A.; Compromise Agreement, Washington, April 10, 1868, N.A., O.I.A., Choctaw Agency, Letters Received, Microcopy 234, Roll 177; Pitchlynn's History of the Net Proceeds, Washington, July 28, 1880, Pitchlynn MSS, G.M.

with operations at Skullyville, charged that the Choctaws confiscated their property during the war because of their declared loyalty to the Union. Joseph G. Heald based his claim largely upon Pitchlynn's sale of gold to Frank Williams in 1862 and Wright based his on equally questionable transactions; yet the Treaty of 1866 specifically provided for a payment of $90,000 to the traders. The Choctaws had agreed to the provision during the negotiations only because Heald threatened to defeat the treaty in the United States Senate unless it were included.[13]

The commission established by the concordat of 1866 adjudicated the demands of the traders, and it awarded them more than $90,000, a judgment in which the secretary of the interior concurred. When that officer attempted to pay the award, though, he found that legal restrictions prevented use of any available tribal funds. Furthermore, Pitchlynn and his co-delegates who did not deny the validity of the judgment requested that none of the tribal annuities be used to fund the claim since it would seriously damage the educational program of the tribe. Congress then undertook a discussion of possible methods of payment, but before a decision was made Sampson Folsom appeared to protest any payment at all.[14]

Folsom's hostility distressed Pitchlynn. It publicized his 1862 gold sale to Heald and Company and increased the possibility that Representative George Boutwell, Heald's powerful friend, might oppose a congressional appropriation for the net proceeds. Accordingly, he offered Folsom another slice of the net proceeds contingent upon its payment if he would tone down

13 House Records, 1865–67, November 18, 1867, Volumes from the Choctaw Nation 294, Indian Archives, O.H.S.; Choctaw Delegates, Washington, to Secretary James Harlan, May 12, 1866, HR 40A–F11.5, Records of the House of Representatives, N.A.

14 Pitchlynn and Israel Folsom, Washington, to N. G. Taylor, April 17, 1867, Papers Relating to Claims, Trust Funds of the Choctaws, Indian Division, Records of the Secretary of Interior, N.A.; "The Choctaws and Their Debts," 1868, Folder 67–27, Pitchlynn MSS, G.M.

his opposition to the award made to the traders. The Colonel secured Black's and McPherson's promises to pay Folsom $25,000 from the shares they would receive from the funded claim, and Pitchlynn himself agreed to add 5 per cent from the 30 per cent attorney fee. Peter, considering Folsom a blackmailer, undoubtedly did not expect to honor the contracts, but for the moment Folsom had performed a coup. He had milked Black and McPherson for a promise of $25,000, Pitchlynn for a part of the attorney fee, and Blunt for another $25,000, most of which was in addition to the $100,000 guaranteed him for the favorable opinion in October, 1867. The whole transaction proved that Folsom was a consummate extortionist and that for Pitchlynn the net proceeds took precedence over all other Choctaw claims.[15]

Folsom's visit coincided with additional efforts by the Colonel and his associates to secure a congressional appropriation for the net proceeds. In January, 1868, Thomas A. Scott reminded the secretary of the interior that the departmental budget as submitted to the Congress did not include the Choctaw claim. Secretary Browning took the hint of this powerful financier, presented the matter to the House of Representatives, and gained the inclusion of the "uncontested" $1,832,560.85 claim in the Indian appropriation bill. Scott thought that with this action he had secured the funding of the Senate award; he wrote to Judge Black, telling him to take possession of his share of the money. But the railroad tycoon had acted hastily. Members of the House protested that the appropriation would go to a "rotten Indian Ring" and during the floor debate suc-

---

[15] Report of Sampson Folsom to the Council, Chahta Tamaha, September 30, 1869, Vol. I, Acts of the Choctaw Nation, Western History Collection, U.O.L.; Heald, Washington, to E. C. Mitchell, March 5, 1870, and Contract between Folsom and Pitchlynn, Washington, September 11, 1868, Pitchlynn MSS, G.M.; Contract between Sampson Folsom and John D. McPherson, Washington, July 18, 1868, McPherson, Washington, to J. S. Black, July 18, 1868 and June 25, 1868, Vol. XLVIII, Black MSS, Library of Congress.

cessfully struck the measure from the bill in late May, 1868. Though the House committee on Indian affairs later moderated this rejection by reporting in favor of the net proceeds, the claim was dead for the rest of the year.[16]

The congressional defeat coincided with Pitchlynn's growing disenchantment with McPherson's and Black's leadership. Busy with ex parte Milligan, the veto of the first reconstruction act, and President Johnson's impeachment trial, Black was inaccessible to the Colonel and an anathema to the very Congress upon which the Choctaws relied for justice. Furthermore, Black's interest in the Choctaw claim had cooled considerably since his first involvement. Not only had efforts in Congress been unsuccessful, but he had been besieged by people claiming a share of the fee. Latrobe, Cooper, and Sampson Folsom had all demanded recognition, and after the strong showing of the claim in Congress, Albert Pike had suddenly decided that he could prosecute the case after all. The embarrassment of the lobby and the realization that his political beliefs hurt his clients prompted Black to retire. Contrary to his biographer's claim, he made nothing from the Choctaws, and after 1868 his only interest concerning them was the repayment of the money advanced by Scott.[17]

With Black leaving the case Pitchlynn looked elsewhere for leadership. But he could not see beyond Douglas Cooper, who

[16] Thomas A. Scott, Washington, to O. H. Browning, January 25, 1868, Box 35h, Letters Received, Private Sources, Indian Division, Records of the Secretary of Interior, N.A.; 40 Cong., 2 sess., *House Exec. Doc. 138*; R. D. Barclay, Philadelphia, to J. S. Black, May 12, 1868, Vol. XLVIII, Black MSS, Library of Congress; 40 Cong., 2 sess., *Congressional Globe*, May 30, 1868, pp. 2707–10; 40 Cong., 2 sess., *House Report 77*.

[17] C. William Brigance, *Jeremiah Sullivan Black*, 230; Pike, Memphis, to Black, April 4, 1868, Pitchlynn MSS, G.M.; Black, York, Penn., to Sir, March 27, 1883, in *Lamon v. McKee*, Supreme Court of the District of Columbia, September Term, 1888, in Rare Book Section, G.M.; Black, York, Penn., to Ward H. Lamon, March 7, 1869, Black MSS, Huntington Library.

continually asserted his right to control the claim by virtue of Latrobe's agreement with McPherson. Furthermore, at the Choctaw council in October, 1868, Pitchlynn's co-delegates and his stepson, Charles Lombardi, agreed to recognize Latrobe's management of the tribal claim for unpaid back annuities if the delegation of 1866 would acknowledge their right to control the net proceeds. Caught up in the harmony of the moment, Pitchlynn accepted Cooper's leadership of the Choctaw team, a post the former general retained until 1870.[18]

A serious illness—his enemies said it was mental—nearly incapacitated Pitchlynn in late 1868, but by the next January he had recovered sufficiently to present a memorial to Congress urging the funding of the balance of the Senate award. On February 3, 1869, for the second time during the Fortieth Congress, friends in the House attempted to secure an appropriation but failed as they had earlier. The Congress seemed more interested in the new Grant administration than in the net proceeds claim.[19]

Strenuous effort failing in the House, the Choctaw team turned its attention almost entirely to the Senate during the Forty-first Congress that met the first time in March, 1869. Influenced by Pitchlynn and a $10,000 contingent fee, former senator J. R. Doolittle of Wisconsin appeared before his old colleagues on the Indian affairs committee in support of the net proceeds. Doolittle maintained that the 1859 Senate award was final and that the tribe should receive both the uncontested $1,800,000 still due and the bonds authorized in 1861 but never

[18] Pitchlynn's History of the Net Proceeds, Washington, July 28, 1880, Lombardi, Choctaw Nation, to Pitchlynn, October 14, 1868, and October 19, 1868, Israel Folsom to Pitchlynn, November 28, 1868, and Agreement between Delegation and Cooper, Washington, March 24, 1869, Pitchlynn MSS, G.M.

[19] Cooper, "Address and Memorial," Boggy Depot, October, 1873, Folder 73-108, and "Brief of the Choctaws," Washington, January 30, 1869, *ibid.*; 40 Cong., 3 sess., *Congressional Globe*, February 3, 1869, pp. 837-38.

paid. Doolittle's reasoned argument gained only referral of the claim to the Senate judiciary committee for a determination of the legal questions involved.[20]

Congressional hesitancy resulted in part from the increasingly confused leadership of the Choctaw team. Chief Wright had visited Washington in February, 1869, to lend support to the independent authority of Cooper and Latrobe, and Pitchlynn had again agreed to Cooper's continued leadership, providing his efforts did not cost more than $100,000. Yet the Colonel was growing weary of Cooper's directions and increasingly protective of his own interest. Also, friends in Congress, particularly John P. C. Shanks of Indiana, were complaining about the influence of the former Rebel general on the Choctaw delegation. McPherson continued to assert his rights as executor of Cochrane's will, and Albert Pike belatedly declared that he alone represented the tribe. Luke Lea assigned his remaining interest in Cochrane's contract to John A. Rollins and James Gilfillan, two Washington claims agents, while Sampson Folsom independently contracted with the legal firm of Hughes, Denver, and Peck to secure the net proceeds and, with William P. Dole, a former commissioner of Indian affairs, and E. B. Grayson, a former employee of the Indian Office, to collect the back annuities.[21] And to top off the disorder, in March, 1870, Pitchlynn employed George W. Wright, a Republican and former member of Congress from California, to

[20] "Argument of the Hon. J. R. Doolittle," Washington, 1869, Folder 69–7A, Pitchlynn MSS, G.M.; 41 Cong., 1 sess., *Congressional Globe*, April 10, 1869, p. 718.

[21] Allen Wright, Washington, to E. S. Parker, May 1, 1869, N.A., O.I.A., Choctaw Agency, Letters Received, Microcopy 234, Roll 178; Journal of the Delegation, 1869, Folder 69–11, and Statement as to the Claim of Rollins and Gilfillan, n.d., Folder Un–79, Pitchlynn MSS, G.M.; Memorial of Albert Pike, Washington, 1869, in *Sophia Pitchlynn* v. *Choctaw Nation*, Court of Claims, Rare Book Collection, G.M.; Report of National Attorney Sampson Folsom, Chahta Tamaha, September 30, 1869, Vol. I, Acts of the Choctaw Nation, Western History Collection, U.O.L.

work for the release of the $250,000 in bonds still in the Treasury. Altogether the Choctaws had an enormous but confused lobby.

The addition of George Wright to Pitchlynn's team signaled a change in the prosecution of the claim. Heretofore all interest and energy had focused on the unfunded and uncontested Senate award, but when Wright offered to obtain the confiscated bonds without congressional action Pitchlynn jumped at the opportunity. Forgetting that he had once acknowledged Latrobe's right to petition for the bonds, he promised the Californian all of the interest paid or 25 per cent of the principal as a contingent fee, whichever was larger, provided that the certificates were released during the Forty-first Congress. At Wright's direction in April, 1870, Pitchlynn formally demanded the bonds from the secretary of the treasury. The carefully laid plans went awry, however, and instead of releasing the bonds, in September the secretary referred the request to the attorney general. This last officer rendered no opinion on the legality of Peter's requisition until December.[22]

Pitchlynn and his associates then had to return to Congress. Still concentrating on the Senate, the Colonel appeared before the committee on Indian affairs and asked that the secretary of the treasury be directed to issue the confiscated bonds. In response, Senator Garrett Davis of Kentucky on June 6, 1870, tried to amend the general appropriation bill on the Senate floor to cause the delivery of the bonds, but Senator John Sherman of Ohio remembered his doubts of 1861 and led the upper chamber in rejecting the proposal. Efforts on June 9 and July 13 to fund the whole $1.8 million claim in the Senate were equally unsuccessful. With this action, both houses of Congress had voted against the claim in the postwar period.[23]

[22] Agreement between Pitchlynn and Wright, March, 1870, Folder 70–121, Pitchlynn MSS, G.M.; Report of the Delegates, Washington, 1874, H10.99, Hargrett Pamphlet Collection, G.M.

[23] Pitchlynn, Washington, to the Senate Committee on Indian Affairs, May

This final congressional failure confirmed Pitchlynn's determination to get rid of the specter of Douglas Cooper and Rebel influence. In mid-July, 1870, he abandoned entirely the old Cochrane contract that the former agent claimed as his source of authority and entered into a new one with General James G. Blunt of Leavenworth, Kansas, and Henry McKee of Fort Smith, Arkansas, both of whom were Republicans and Union supporters. The contract with McKee and Blunt involved only the $1.8 million uncontested balance of the net proceeds upon the collection of which Pitchlynn guaranteed the historic fee of 30 per cent. The new attorneys agreed to adjust the claims of all parties who had been interested in the case, to pay Cochrane's heirs 5 per cent and, in another contract, to rebate the same amount to Pitchlynn.[24] With this agreement, non-Southern-sympathizers controlled both aspects of the net proceeds claim—the bonds and the unfunded Senate award.

Pitchlynn's independent action greatly irritated General Cooper. After George W. Wright appeared before the Treasury to demand the confiscated bonds, he decided to carry the matter of authority to the Choctaw council again. At the annual session which convened at Armstrong Academy in October, 1870, Cooper demanded a clear-cut endorsement of Latrobe's contract, a move that Pitchlynn's forces, led again by E. S. Mitchell, attempted to block. Sampson Folsom, however, complicated the already confused situation by proposing still another plan. He urged that the tribe appoint an entirely new delegation rather than confirm the credentials of either Pitch-

---

13, 1870, HR 41A–F2.20, Records of the House of Representatives, N.A.; 41 Cong., 2 sess., *Congressional Globe*, June 6, 1870, pp. 4136–41; Pitchlynn, "Report to the Council," Washington, 1870, H10.59. Hargrett Pamphlet Collection, G.M.; Pitchlynn, Washington, to Nephew, July 13, 1870, H–44, J. L. Hargett Collection, Western History Collection, U.O.L.

24 Agreement between Pitchlynn and Blunt and McKee, Washington, July 16, 1870, and Agreement between McKee and Blunt and Pitchlynn, Washington, July 16, 1870, Pitchlynn MSS, G.M.

lynn or Latrobe. Surprisingly, Mitchell agreed, but Loring Folsom (Pitchlynn's son-in-law), David Harkins, and even former chief Allen Wright joined to defeat the measure and retain the status quo. Wright considered Folsom's plan an effort to "decapitate" both delegations and kindly warned that Pitchlynn must not pride himself upon having many friends, including Mitchell, in the Choctaw Nation. Thus the conflict between Cooper and Pitchlynn reverted back to Washington.[25]

On the Potomac, the attorney general completed his investigation and in late December, 1870, ruled that the tribe or its designated representative was entitled to the $250,000 in bonds. But the opinion did not entirely persuade Secretary of the Treasury George Boutwell to release the disputed certificates, and he instead transmitted the matter to Congress, requesting a final decision. Cooper and Latrobe now vigorously reasserted their right to represent the Choctaws in all matters relating to the bonds. On January 9, in a Cooper-inspired letter, Latrobe requested a conference with Pitchlynn and indicated that he would regret taking any measures before the government which were not mutually approved. When the Colonel ignored this veiled threat, Latrobe publicly challenged the Choctaw delegate's authority to receive the bonds. Peter countered by having the incumbent Choctaw chief, William Bryant, prepare a statement reaffirming the validity of the credentials of the old delegation and asserting that Latrobe had no official contract with the tribe. Pitchlynn guaranteed the chief an interest in the net proceeds for his timely statement, while Cooper blistered him with a seventeen-page printed pamphlet remonstrating against the injustice done Latrobe.[26]

[25] E. S. Mitchell, Boggy Depot, to Pitchlynn, October 9, 1870, and October 13, 1870, Loring Folsom, Armstrong Academy, to Pitchlynn, October 24, 1870, and November 27, 1870, and Wright, Boggy Depot, to Pitchlynn, November 29, 1870, *ibid.*

[26] 41 Cong., 3 sess., *House Exec. Doc. 25*; Latrobe to Pitchlynn, January 9, 1871, and Latrobe to the Secretary of Treasury, January 10, 1871, in "Special

To further offset Cooper's attack on his credentials, Pitchlynn sought endorsements of his life's work from influential non-Choctaws. Through the agency of George Wright, Horace Greeley, editor of the New York *Tribune*, volunteered his opinion that the net proceeds claim was legitimate and intimated that the men who led the tribe into rebellion should be dismissed from their positions of influence. Armed with this testimony and that of Chief Bryant, Pitchlynn and his colleagues returned to Congress with a printed demand that the confiscated bonds be released to them as representatives of the tribe. On March 3, 1871, with some persuasive lobbying, this memorial won a congressional resolution that ordered the Treasury to deliver the bonds. Success seemed at hand.[27]

Only quick action could now preserve Cooper and Latrobe's "interest" in the $250,000. The very evening of the congressional action McPherson joined with the Baltimore attorney and the Rebel general in proposing to Pitchlynn that George Wright receive one-half of all the interest paid on the bonds, that McPherson accept for the estate of Cochrane somewhat more than $32,000, that over $41,000 of both principal and interest accrue to Latrobe, and that the Colonel control the

---

Report of Peter P. Pitchlynn and Peter Folsom," Washington, 1871, H10.45, Hargrett Pamphlet Collection, G.M.; William Bryant, Chahta Tamaha, to Pitchlynn, January 11, 1871, and March 11, 1871, in Letters of the Chiefs, Volumes from the Choctaw Nation 415, Indian Archives, O.H.S.; Bryant to Pitchlynn, February 7, 1871, Pitchlynn to Bryant, March 31, 1871, and Cooper, "Letter to William Bryant," Washington, 1872, Folder 74-147, Pitchlynn MSS, G.M.

[27] 41 Cong., 3 sess., *Sen. Misc. Doc. 65*; Typescript copy of a letter from Horace Greeley, New York, to Pitchlynn, February 3, 1871, Pitchlynn MSS, G.M.; Horace Greeley, New York, to George Washington Wright, January 9, 1871, Vol. I, George Washington Wright MSS, Library of Congress; 41 Cong., 3 sess., *Congressional Globe*, January 5, 1871, p. 310; "Special Report of Peter Pitchlynn and Peter Folsom," Washington, 1871, H10.45, Hargrett Pamphlet Collection, G.M.

Left, Allen Wright, Principal Chief of the Choctaws, 1866–70, member of the delegation of 1866. (Courtesy Smithsonian Institution National Anthropological Archives, Bureau of American Ethnology Collection, Washington, D.C.)

Right, Robert M. Jones, member of the delegation of 1866. (Courtesy Oklahoma Historical Society, Oklahoma City)

Left, Alfred Wade, member of the delegation of 1866. (Courtesy Smithsonian Institution National Anthropological Archives, Bureau of American Ethnology Collection, Washington, D.C.)

Right, John Page, member of the delegation of 1866. (Courtesy Gilcrease Institute, Tulsa, Oklahoma)

Left, James G. Blunt, former Union general who successfully represented loyal Choctaws at Fort Smith hearings in 1866. (Courtesy Gilcrease Institute, Tulsa, Oklahoma)

Right, John H. B. Latrobe, Baltimore attorney retained by the delegation of 1866. (Courtesy Library of Congress, Washington, D.C.)

Left, John P. C. Shanks, United States congressman from Indiana, 1861–65 and 1867–75. (Courtesy Indiana Historical Society, Indianapolis)

Right, Sampson Folsom, Peter Pitchlynn's nephew, Choctaw national attorney in 1866. (Courtesy Smithsonian Institution National Anthropological Archives, Bureau of American Ethnology Collection, Washington, D.C.)

Peter Perkins Pitchlynn, 1868. Photograph by A. Zeno Shindler. (Courtesy Smithsonian Institution National Anthropological Archives, Bureau of American Ethnology Collection, Washington, D.C.)

Photograph of Peter Pitchlynn, ca. 1879. (Courtesy Gilcrease
Institute, Tulsa, Oklahoma)

Tombstone of Peter Pitchlynn, Congressional Cemetery, Washington, D.C.

Sophia Pitchlynn, Peter Pitchlynn's youngest daughter by his second marriage. (Courtesy Gilcrease Institute, Tulsa, Oklahoma)

remainder. Genuinely fearful of a compromise with the former Confederate, Pitchlynn refused to accept the proposition.[28]

Latrobe immediately took revenge by formally declaring to the secretary of the treasury that Pitchlynn had absolutely no authority to receive the bonds ordered delivered by Congress and proposed as an alternative that they should be sent directly to the Choctaw Nation. Obviously, Cooper and Latrobe would rather have trusted the council than Pitchlynn to protect their share of the $250,000. The Colonel countered the accusation by having a thirty-page printed argument prepared for Secretary Boutwell supporting his credentials and by asking Horace Greeley to call upon that officer in his behalf. But neither measure completely mitigated Latrobe's challenge or secured the release of the bonds.[29]

Pitchlynn's secret arrangement with James Johnson during the Civil War to get the bonds across Union lines was now revealed, complicating the situation further. After Congress directed the release of the certificates, George E. West of Philadelphia, an agent for Lehman and Company with whom Johnson had been associated, presented Peter's old order to Secretary Boutwell and demanded the $250,000. When the money was not immediately forthcoming, West filed a petition for a writ of mandamus in the Supreme Court of the District of Columbia to compel the Secretary to release the bonds to him.[30]

Thus, with so many parties interested—the tribe even sent the United States Indian agent to pick up the bonds—with so

[28] Proposed Agreement between McPherson, Latrobe and Pitchlynn, Washington, March 3, 1871, and Latrobe, Baltimore, to Secretary of Treasury, March 14, 1871, in "Special Report," Washington, 1871, H10.45, Hargrett Pamphlet Collection, G.M.; John J. Weed and George W. Wright, "Arguments submitted to the Secretary of Treasury," Washington, 1871, Folder 71–98, Pitchlynn MSS, G.M.; Greeley to Wright, April 3, 1871, and June 10, 1872, Vol. I, George Washington Wright MSS, Library of Congress.

[29] *Ibid.*

[30] 42 Cong., 3 sess., *House Report 98*, 65.

many claims and counter-claims submitted, and with the Republican administration so financially embarrassed, Secretary Boutwell determined to investigate the claim himself before he complied with the congressional directive. He referred the matter to E. C. Banfield, solicitor of the treasury, and refused to consider it further until Banfield reported back.

Since the problem at the Treasury related largely to the question of authority, Pitchlynn resolved to have his authority sustained by the tribe and that of Latrobe and Cooper denied once and for all. He and his associates prepared a twenty-five-page "Special Report" for the Choctaw council explaining the progress of the bond transaction and accusing Cooper of preventing the delivery of the $250,000. The Colonel planned to have Chief Bryant call a special session and, on the strength of the report, push through a reaffirmation of his credentials; but when he learned that Cooper had returned to the Nation with the same objective in mind, he dropped this plan of attack. At any rate, Pitchlynn lacked the tribal support he once had. Robert Jones had cooled considerably to the Colonel after learning of the wartime bond sale to Johnson and the financial transaction in Washington following the Treaty of 1866. And Sampson Folsom, usually a reliable ally when paid, dismissed Pitchlynn's overtures with: "the less we know of each other's business the better for us." Furthermore, the Presbyterian missionary O. P. Stark, a champion of Lehman and Company among the Choctaws, everywhere planted seeds of doubt about Peter's honesty.[31]

Opposed by R. M. Jones, Sampson Folsom, Cooper, and Allen Wright, the Colonel decided that he should attend the regular session of the council himself. After making a new will

[31] "Special Report of Peter Pitchlynn and Peter Folsom," May 15, 1871, Washington, H10.45, Hargrett Pamphlet Collection, G.M.; D. F. Harkins, Wade County, to Pitchlynn, June, 1871, and Sampson Folsom, Horse Prairie, to Pitchlynn, September 13, 1871, Pitchlynn MSS, G.M.

he set out for Armstrong Academy with M. S. Temple, a member of a distinguished Tennessee family and an associate of George Wright, arriving at the tribal capital in early October, 1871. The ensuing meeting of the Choctaw legislature proved to be a great disappointment to the Colonel. He found that after five years' absence he had little influence within the tribe and even that was challenged by Cooper. He failed to secure any dramatic new confirmation of his authority to act for the Choctaws in Washington and had to satisfy himself with the endorsements given in past years. Yet the trip was not totally fruitless; Pitchlynn re-established a harmonious relationship with Sampson Folsom and regained the support of Jones by assuring his old friend that the $10,000 paid to him in 1866 by Allen Wright was an advance on the net proceeds claim and not money really belonging to Jones.[32]

Back on the Potomac, in November he learned from George Wright that an immediate new endorsement by the council of his authority to act for the tribe was absolutely necessary to prevent an adverse report by Solicitor Banfield. Physically unable to return, Pitchlynn and Wright sent M. S. Temple back to the Nation with a draft of the measure they wanted the council to adopt. In December, Temple worked with Sampson Folsom and R. M. Jones to get Chief Bryant to call the special session, which after many frustrating delays the Chief set for late January. But as that day arrived and passed without a council, Temple left the Nation in disgust. When the tribal representatives did assemble in early March, 1872, Pitchlynn depended upon the Chief, Robert Jones, Loring Folsom, and David Harkins to secure what he personally had failed to achieve five months earlier.[33]

[32] Pitchlynn, Armstrong Academy, to My Dear, October 29, 1871, *ibid.*
[33] Pitchlynn, Washington, to Folsom, December 9, 1871, Directions for Temple, n.d., Folder Un-222, M. S. Temple, Ultima Thule, Arkansas, to Pitchlynn, December 13, 1871, and Temple, Rose Hill, to Pitchlynn, January 8, 1872, *ibid.*

Fortunately, success attended their efforts. On March 18, the council passed the legislation recommended by Pitchlynn and Wright. The measure provided that any interest allowed by the government on the $250,000 in bonds be paid in Washington directly to Pitchlynn as the only surviving member of the delegation of 1853 and to his new colleague, Peter Folsom. The act, however, directed that the face value of the bonds be delivered to the Nation, where a tribal commission would adjudicate and pay any claims made against the United States by individuals and any demands made against the Choctaws by attorneys. The commission was not to recognize any contract for legal service made in 1866 by the "new delegation" or any assignment to Lehman and Company, nor was it to pay any attorney under the Cochrane contract unless authorized by Pitchlynn and his co-delegate. In other words, the "brush bill," as its opponents labeled it, gave the Colonel complete control of interest paid on the bonds, of attorney fees, and presumably of the 20 per cent due the delegates. Including interest, he controlled the distribution of over 50 per cent of everything realized upon the release of the bonds.[34]

Cooper, who was still in Indian Territory, and his associates were not about to accept legislation that rendered Latrobe's contract null and void. They conducted mass meetings of protest throughout the tribal domain and whenever possible obstructed the work of the commission that sought to adjudicate individual claims against the United States. Finally, they succeeded in getting the Choctaw supreme court to declare the "brush bill" unconstitutional. Though the Colonel agreed with R. M. Jones that the judicial decision as well as the opposition "amounted to just nothing," the ruling nonetheless dimmed the brilliance of his victory and the value of the endorsement of his authority.[35]

[34] Acts and Resolutions, 1865–72, Volumes from the Choctaw Nation 291, Indian Archives, O.H.S.

In Washington Pitchlynn's associates who were pressing the two facets of the net proceeds claim continued as if the "brush bill" remained in force. Efforts to collect the bonds received most of Peter's attention, but McKee and Blunt, working with the former senator from Arkansas, Alexander McDonald, successfully kept the balance of the award pending before Congress. Furthermore, they acquiesced in Pitchlynn's decision to let Albert Pike return to the Choctaw team. On January 5, 1872, the Colonel promised Pike 20 per cent of everything secured from Congress above the $1.8 million. Also, Pitchlynn even signed a statement written by Pike stating that the attorney had not abandoned the Choctaws in 1854 and that he ought to receive 5 per cent of all money paid on the Choctaw claim. In April, 1872, Pike prepared a memorial for Pitchlynn's signature asking Congress to restore the deduction improperly made by the Senate in 1860 and to allow interest on the whole claim.[36]

Immediately after the presentation of Pike's statement, Solicitor Banfield issued an interim report of the investigation authorized by the secretary of the treasury. Instead of confining himself to the matter of the bonds, Banfield reviewed the whole question of the Choctaws' right to the net proceeds of the sale of their tribal estate in Mississippi. He declared that in the treaty of 1830 the United States had never envisioned such a payment, for the Choctaws had been given valuable consideration for the cession. As examples of the compensation paid to the Indians he pointed to the various annuities, the guarantee

[35] Notice of a Meeting, March 30, 1874, and R. M. Jones, Goodland, to Pitchlynn, April 17, 1872, and April 24, 1872, Pitchlynn MSS, G.M.; Pitchlynn, Washington, to R. M. Jones, April 25, 1872, Section X, Robert M. Jones MSS, Indian Archives, O.H.S.

[36] Contract between Pike and Pitchlynn, January 5, 1872, Pitchlynn MSS, G.M.; compare 49 Cong., 2 sess., *Senate Report 1978*, 64, with Manuscript Statement, Folder 62–49, Pitchlynn MSS, G.M.; 42 Cong., 2 sess., *House Misc. Doc. 164*.

of self-government, and the allotment of reservations in Mississippi. Banfield argued that the Treaty of 1855 did not assent to the net proceeds claim but merely referred the question to the Senate of the United States. To be sure the Senate allowed the Choctaws the proceeds of the land sale, but the 1861 appropriation of $250,000 in cash and $250,000 in bonds was "manifestly not in accordance" with the law. The Treaty of 1855, Banfield pontificated, prohibited payment by Congress of any amount until the Choctaws adjudicated the individual claims of the tribe and then only to the amount of the adjudication. Furthermore, what sum was not apportioned to individuals must be held in trust for the tribe by the United States. He concluded that since no claims had ever been adjudicated by tribal authorities no federal appropriation was called for.[37]

To Pitchlynn it appeared that the solicitor general had disregarded all past investigations, determinations, and treaties in the construction of his report and had cast reflection upon the validity of the claim. He had Pike prepare a seventeen-page reply to Banfield's four-page declaration. Addressing himself primarily to the righteousness of the Choctaw demand, Pike reminded the Solicitor that the Treaty of 1855 had given the job of judging the merits of the claim to the Senate, not the Treasury department. After a thorough investigation, the chosen tribunal had ruled that the Choctaws were not strictly entitled to the net proceeds but that justice demanded they receive them nonetheless. The Senate decision was final, Pike argued, and since it could not now be impeached, Congress should appropriate the balance of the allowance. "We well enough know how absolutely conclusive such an award would be if in favor of a state or railroad corporation," he declared.[38]

[37] 42 Cong., 2 sess., *Sen. Exec. Doc.* 87; 42 Cong., 3 sess., *House Exec. Doc. 10.*

[38] Pitchlynn, "Letter to George S. Boutwell," Washington, 1872, Folder 72–83, Pitchlynn MSS, G.M.

The interim report issued by the Solicitor suggested the nature of his investigation. The inquiry had made no pretense to objectivity whatsoever. Secretary of the Treasury Boutwell had retained Nathanial Paige, a Washington claims agent, to supply information that would enable the federal government to deny the delivery of the bonds, promising to pay contingently 10 per cent of all Choctaw funds retained by the Treasury. He also involved Edward B. Grayson, who as clerk of the Indian Office had helped establish the Choctaw claim in 1859 and who was once employed to prosecute it before Congress by Sampson Folsom; Grayson opposed the net proceeds after Pitchlynn had refused him a 1 per cent interest in the total award. Paige and Grayson searched the government files until they discovered the 1852 receipt given by Thompson McKenney when he secured the final scrip payment to the claimants under the fourteenth article of the treaty of 1830. The document supposedly exempted the United States from additional claims against it by the Choctaws.[39]

Such a receipt was all Banfield needed to complete his investigation. His final report issued on November 14, 1872, declared that by virtue of the release given in 1852 the United States had no further obligations under the treaty of 1830. More specifically, the federal government was not bound to pay to the Choctaws the profit from the sale of their tribal estate in Mississippi. The argument was incredible, but it furnished sufficient pretext for Boutwell to refuse to deliver the bonds as directed by the 1871 congressional resolution. Congress took cognizance of the decision and, confused by the revelation, agreed on February 14, 1873, that the $250,000 should remain in the Treasury pending further investigation.[40]

The loss of the bonds constituted an important episode in

[39] 42 Cong., 3 sess., *House Exec. Doc. 69*; 42 Cong., 3 sess., *House Report 98*, 71–73; 42 Cong., 3 sess., *Congressional Globe*, February 4, 1873, p. 1082.
[40] *Ibid.*

the history of the net proceeds claim, and for that matter all Indian claims. It was a major personal blow to Pitchlynn's financial expectations, and it reflected the honest fear of some government officials that money awarded to Indians would end up in the hands of attorneys and speculators. The denial of the bonds also showed how high-handed, unobjective, and corrupt some federal officers could be when dealing with the rights and aspirations of Indian tribes. Powerless despite the justice of their position, tribal representatives resorted to bribing influential officials and to depending on agents to press their demands upon the government. If the special assistance brought recognition of their claims, then whatever accrued to them had to be shared with others. To divide a monetary award with speculators was unfortunate, but circumstances in Washington, like those at the Treasury, necessitated it. Pitchlynn and his colleagues had lost the $250,000 in bonds, but they were obviously playing the game according to the established rules.

CHAPTER VIII

The Final Years

As the Choctaw representative in Washington during the post-war period, Pitchlynn devoted himself to matters other than the net proceeds claim. Of principal concern to him were the Civil War reconstruction policies of the federal government designed to "rehabilitate" the tribe because of its former attachment to the Confederacy. In general these schemes sought to destroy Choctaw culture and society and to integrate the Choctaws and other tribes into American society. Pitchlynn opposed these proposals with vigor.

One of the many problems of the era concerned the tribal boundary with Arkansas. The Treaty of 1866 re-established the border as a north–south line that began on the Arkansas River one hundred paces east of old Fort Smith and terminated at Red River. From the survey of 1857 the Choctaws knew that the accepted boundary did not follow a true north–south line and thereby deprived them of considerably more than 100,000 acres of land. In April, 1867, Pitchlynn contracted with James W. Denver, former member of Congress, commissioner of Indian affairs, governor of Kansas and western explorer, to demand either an adjustment of the line or reasonable payment for the land lost. He promised Denver 30 per cent of any sum collected in settlement of the claim, of which the attorney agreed to rebate one-sixth to Pitchlynn.[1]

The Johnson administration favorably considered Denver's petitions in 1867 to resurvey the line, but funds for the project were not appropriated by Congress until March, 1875. The contract for the survey was awarded to Henry McKee, Pitchlynn's colleague in the net proceeds claim. McKee re-marked the boundary in the spring and summer of 1877 and confirmed the inaccuracy of the original survey, calculating at the same time that the acknowledged border deprived the Choctaws of 136,204.02 acres of land. Notwithstanding this revelation, the matter lay dormant despite the Colonel's best efforts until March, 1881, when Congress authorized the Choctaws to institute a suit against the United States in the court of claims. Denver represented the tribe in the litigation relating to the eastern boundary and ultimately secured a judgment of over $68,000, or fifty cents for each of the disputed acres. That the Choctaws received even this modest award was the result of Pitchlynn's interest and initiative.[2]

A more controversial aspect of the reconstruction years related to the survey and allotment of tribal lands. The Treaty of 1866 contained optional provisions calculated to induce the Choctaws and Chickasaws to accept lands in severalty, pro-

[1] Contract between James W. Denver and Peter Pitchlynn, Washington, April 17, 1867, Pitchlynn MSS, G.M.

[2] Pitchlynn and Israel Folsom, Washington, to O. H. Browning, April 24, 1867, A. G. Taylor, Commissioner of Indian Affairs, to U. T. Otto, June 29, 1867, Pitchlynn, Washington, to J. D. Cox, August 31, 1870, and William Cody, Commissioner of Indian Affairs, to Cox, September 6, 1870, Eastern Boundary, Indian Division, Records of the Secretary of Interior, N.A.; 40 Cong., 2 sess., *House Exec. Doc. 133*; Pitchlynn, "Report," Washington, 1870, H10.59, Hargrett Pamphlet Collection, G.M.; Field Notes of the Boundary Survey between Arkansas and the Choctaw Nation, Henry E. McKee, Surveyor, April to June, 1877, Box 3, Choctaw Misc. Doc., Western History Collection, U.O.L.; *Supreme Court Reports*, Vol. CXIX.

visions that Pitchlynn and Winchester Colbert supported in a published address of the same year. The Chickasaw legislature promptly voted for allotment, but the Choctaws postponed the question until it could be referred to the people. At the council in October, 1867, Chief Allen Wright urged that the tribe take its lands in severalty, a view that E. S. Mitchell, Pitchlynn's representative, also supported. But the Colonel had changed his mind, concluding that allotment would increase the white man's temptation to settle on Indian lands and ultimately destroy Choctaw independence. The full bloods of the tribe held the same view and on July 4 and 5, 1870, overwhelmingly voted against the proposition to "sectionize." In this instance, and as he often did in the postwar years, Pitchlynn aligned himself with the full bloods. Since this segment of the tribe was more numerous and could provide greater support in the tribal council for the Colonel's bid to represent the Choctaws in Washington, such a position was politically expedient.[3]

Three years after the Chickasaws had agreed to survey their nation, the federal government suddenly decided to act upon that authority. Blaming Douglas Cooper, Pitchlynn protested the belated decision by maintaining that since the tribes held equal title to the land the consent of the Choctaws was also necessary. The protest did not defeat the survey; yet it did prevent the immediate allotment of the Chickasaw lands. Secretary of the Interior Columbus Delano ruled in 1872 that ownership in severalty was impossible without the consent of the Choctaws. Thus, unlike some other prominent mixedbloods, particularly Elias C. Boudinot of the Cherokees, Pitchlynn did not support survey and allotment of tribal lands, though he may have lent his name to such proposals in 1866. Various factors contributed to the Colonel's opposition to allotment, a position he maintained vigorously the rest of his

[3] E. S. Mitchell, Boggy Depot, to Pitchlynn, February 13, 1870, and Letter draft to Friend, Washington, March 9, 1870, Pitchlynn MSS, G.M.; Debo, *Rise and Fall*, 212.

life: the influence of Albert Pike, the belief that it would destroy the Choctaws rather than improve them, the knowledge
that it was a position popular among the full bloods, and his
rejection of anything Cooper favored.[4]

The establishment of territorial government for the Indians
so closely paralleled the drive for allotment that the two questions can hardly be considered separately. And Pitchlynn ap-
proached the two matters almost identically. Beginning in 1868
he rejected all legislation that would have consolidated and
organized the Indian tribes into an Indian Territory as but
another aspect of "manifest destiny . . . the plea of those who
fear not God and covet their neighbors' goods."[5] For that
matter, in nearly every year of the 1870's Pitchlynn either personally submitted or added his name to memorials that reminded
Congress of those treaty rights which guaranteed the tribes
perpetual control of their own destinies.[6] That Congress enacted no territorial legislation during Pitchlynn's lifetime tes-
tifies to his and his colleagues' effectiveness.

Pressure for land allotment and territorial government all
stemmed, the Colonel believed, from the railroads. In the
Treaty of 1866 the Choctaws agreed to the construction of one
north–south and one east–west line across tribal lands. On July
25, 1866, even before the Senate had ratified the treaty, Con-

[4] Pitchlynn, Washington, to Secretary Cox, August 3, 1870, and Charles
E. Mix and Company, Washington, to Cox, August 3, 1870, Box 37h, Letters
Received, Private Sources, Indian Division, Records of the Secretary of In-
terior, N.A.; J. D. Cox, Secretary of Interior, to Sir, August 29, 1870, 17651,
Choctaw Nation–Federal Relations, Indian Archives, O.H.S.; Debo, *Rise
and Fall*, 213.

[5] Pitchlynn et al., to William Windom, House of Representatives, July 2,
1868, Pitchlynn MSS, G.M.; 41 Cong., 2 sess., *Sen. Misc. Doc. 143*.

[6] "Protest of the Cherokee, Creek, and Choctaw Nations," Washington,
January, 1872, 42A–H10, Records of the United States Senate, N.A.; 42 Cong.,
2 sess., *Sen. Misc. Doc. 53*; 43 Cong., 1 sess., *House Misc. Doc. 87*; Pitchlynn
et al., "Protest of the Indian Delegation," Washington, February 10, 1875, in
Phillips Collection, U.O.L.; 45 Cong., 2 sess., *Sen. Misc. Doc. 82*; 46 Cong.,
1 sess., *House Misc. Doc. 13*; 46 Cong., 2 sess., *Sen. Misc. Doc. 41*.

gress authorized that the first of three specified Kansas-char-
tered railroads to reach Indian Territory from the north would
receive a free grant of right of way and a conditional allotment
of five alternate sections on each side of the track. The provi-
sional grant, however, depended on the extinguishment of
Indian title "by treaty or otherwise" and the released lands'
becoming a part of the public domain of the United States.
The Union Pacific, Southern Branch—later known as the Missouri, Kansas, and Texas—reached the southern boundary of
Kansas first and therefore was awarded the right of way to
build further south across Indian Territory to Red River. But
because the tribes retained title to their lands, the lucrative
grant, in addition to the right of way, was withheld. If the Indian domain was ever relinquished to the United States, though,
the alternate sections would presumably accrue to the railroad.
No wonder the "Katy" and other railroad companies, especially
after Congress assumed direction of Indian affairs without
benefit of treaties in 1871, pressed for any measure that would
weaken tribal land titles and political autonomy.[7]

The railroad question also placed Pitchlynn at odds with
Cooper and Wright who saw the railway as a progressive step
and speculative possibility. In a special session of the council
in March, 1870, they secured charters for the Choctaw and
Chickasaw Central Railway Company and the Choctaw and
Chickasaw Thirty-fifth Parallel Railway Company and, to
make the move palatable to Pitchlynn, named him as one of
the incorporators. The Nation would buy part of the stock in
these east-west lines and pay for it by selling alternate sections
of land along the right of way. The Colonel, however, believed
that railroads "were much to be dreaded," and after the Choctaws and the secretary of the interior refused to confirm the
charters, his forces at the October session of the council re-

---

[7] Debo, *Rise and Fall*, 117; Pitchlynn et al., "Memorial," Washington, June,
1872, HR 43A–F12.3, Records of the House of Representatives, N.A.

voked the articles of incorporation. Wright and Cooper never forgave the Colonel for what they regarded as an act of vengeance.[8]

Pitchlynn's opposition to the railroads stemmed in part from his general conservatism in the postwar period. But more specifically he believed that the corporations were the genesis of all evil. They wanted grants of tribal lands to pay for track construction, and to get them they supported not only allotment and territorial government but any scheme designed to alter the legal status of the American Indian. For example, the railways insisted that the Indians had become citizens with the Fourteenth Amendment to the U.S. constitution, and that as citizens they should have delegates in Congress. This seemingly magnanimous interpretation would have made the Indian subject to the laws of the United States, destroying his independence. Pitchlynn quickly pointed out this veiled purpose and the source of the scheme.[9]

Problems more germane to reconstruction were those concerning the former slaves. The Treaty of 1866 gave the Choctaws and Chickasaws the alternative of either adopting the freedmen into their respective tribes and receiving $300,000 for the Leased District or having the former slaves removed by the government at the end of two years and the money used for their benefit. The pamphlet Pitchlynn signed in 1866 encouraged the adoption of the Negroes, but most Choctaws favored the removal of the freedmen to another location, a feeling officially confirmed by the council in November, 1867.

---

[8] Acts and Resolutions, 1870–75, Volumes from the Choctaw Nation 291, Indian Archives, O.H.S.; Pitchlynn, Washington, to Israel Folsom, March 6, 1870, Pitchlynn MSS, G.M.; *Report of the Commissioner of Indian Affairs, 1870*, 292; An Act to repeal the Charters, October, 1870, 19459, Choctaw Nation–Railroads, Indian Archives, O.H.S.

[9] Pitchlynn, "Argument before the Judiciary Committee," Washington, 1870, 41A–E9, Records of the United States Senate, N.A., 45 Cong., 2 sess., *Sen. Misc. Doc. 8*; 45 Cong., 2 sess., *House Misc. Doc. 32*.

The tribe wanted the freedmen removed, but it also wanted the $300,000 compensation for the Leased District. Partially in pursuit of this contradictory goal, the Choctaws sent Sampson Folsom to Washington in early 1868. After Folsom arrived, Pitchlynn impressed upon him the fact that insistence on Negro removal would not endear the tribe to the radical Republicans and might damage chances of obtaining the net proceeds from Congress. When Folsom agreed not to press the matter, the Colonel was even more amenable to including him in the profits of the net proceeds claim. But the lack of action meant that the two-year deadline would pass without removal or adoption or disbursement of the $300,000. The unsettled situation was due in no small measure to Pitchlynn's consuming interest in the net proceeds claim.[10]

The Choctaw freedmen soon tired of their ambiguous position. Inspired by white men such as Valentine Dell, editor of the Fort Smith *New Era*, and Colonel D. C. Finn, an Arkansas carpetbagger, in 1870 they asked Congress to grant them all the rights and privileges of the Indian citizens. Acting in his role as tribal delegate Pitchlynn responded to these petitions quickly and vigorously. He argued that the Treaty of 1866 bestowed United States citizenship upon the freedmen who remained after the two years and had not been adopted by the tribe. As the former slaves were all citizens of the United States, it stood to reason they could not be members of the Choctaw Nation. Only when the freedmen relinquished their American citizenship could they receive the benefits of tribal society.[11]

Nevertheless, in 1874 the Interior Department urged Congress to direct the Choctaws and Chickasaws to adopt their former slaves and to bestow upon them the rights of citizenship,

[10] Report of the National Attorney, Chahta Tamaha, September 30, 1869, Vol. I, Acts of the Choctaw Nation, Western History Collection, U.O.L.

[11] 41 Cong., 2 sess., *Sen. Misc. Doc. 106*; Pitchlynn, "Report," Washington, 1870, H10.59, Hargrett Pamphlet Collection, G.M.; Pitchlynn, Washington, to William Bryant, February 2, 1872, Pitchlynn MSS, G.M.

an equal share of the tribal annuities, and a 160-acre tract of the Indian domain. In support of his suggestion, the secretary of the interior wrote:

> If you look at the manner in which the Chickasaw and Choctaw Nations acquired their property, and if you consider that the improvements made thereon have been made by the labor of the African people, you will see that there is not any injustice in giving to these persons of African descent equal rights in all respects with the Choctaw and Chickasaw people.[12]

Though this was an unobjective assessment, the House of Representatives passed the proposed bill, but the Senate adjourned without acting on the legislation. After Pitchlynn's death, the Choctaws finally adopted their former slaves in May, 1883, giving each of them 40 acres of land and all the rights and privileges of citizenship except for participation in annuities, somewhat less than the federal government had once demanded. The Colonel's steadfast opposition to Negro equality within the tribe and zealous protection of Indian prerogatives had made the inevitable somewhat more palatable.[13]

Associated with the question of the freedmen was the matter of compensation for the Leased District. By terms of the Treaty of 1866 the Choctaws and Chickasaws relinquished any title to the six million acres of the Leased District for $300,000, or five cents an acre, to be delivered upon adoption of the former slaves. Yet the tribe never received the money from the United States, nor was it used for the freedmen since they refused to remove. Clearly the government had evaded an obligation either to the Negroes or to the Choctaws. Pitchlynn energetically demanded restitution from Congress, arguing that since

[12] 43 Cong., 1 sess., *House Misc. Doc. 294.*

[13] 43 Cong., 1 sess., *Congressional Record*, May 27, 1874, pp. 4296–98; Remonstrance of Pitchlynn, William Roebuck, and McKee King, Washington, April 27, 1874, 43A–H10.1, Records of the United States Senate, N.A.; Acts of the Choctaw Nation, May 21, 1883, Western History Collection, U.O.L.

the government had not paid any consideration no sale had occurred and the Leased District still belonged to the Choctaws. The status of the district remained in dispute throughout the remainder of Pitchlynn's life. With the solution of the freedmen question after his death, the Choctaws received $50,000 in 1885 to quitclaim their title, additional sums in 1892, and sued for more in the twentieth century. But whatever accrued to them resulted from the Colonel's seminal efforts.[14]

Frequently during the postwar years, various matters arose in Washington which were important to the welfare of all tribes. Pitchlynn usually studied these questions and assumed a position in harmony with his role as Choctaw delegate. For example, he joined with other Indian delegates in opposing the transfer of the Bureau of Indian Affairs from the Department of the Interior to the War Department. Together they also objected to a United States district court in Indian Territory with a jurisdiction not limited wholly to criminal matters. Similarly, when Judge Isaac Parker in 1878 tried James E. Reynolds, a white Choctaw citizen, for murdering a fellow citizen on tribal soil, Pitchlynn united with others in denying Parker's jurisdiction. The Indians maintained that Reynolds should have been turned over to the Choctaw Nation for trial. On other occasions, the Colonel objected to the federal government's ceding the old Fort Smith military reserve to the city of Fort Smith without compensation to the Choctaw family residing on the site; and beginning in 1868 he objected to the United States practice of taxing Indian tobacco factories.[15]

[14] Pitchlynn, Washington, to the Hon. J. P. C. Shanks, February 5, 1872, Pitchlynn MSS, G.M.; Debo, *Rise and Fall*, 105–106, 198, 202.

[15] Indian Delegates to N. G. Taylor, Commissioner of Indian Affairs, December 28, 1868, 40A–H9, and Indian Delegates, "Protest," Washington, March 27, 1876, 44A–H9, Records of the United States Senate, N.A.; 45 Cong., 2 sess., *House Misc. Doc. 33*; Indian Delegates, "Memorial of the Indian Delegates," Washington, n.d., and Indian Delegates, "Ex Parte James E. Reynolds," Washington, February 6, 1878, Phillips Collection, U.O.L.; Statement to the House of Representatives, Washington, April 3, 1872, Pitchlynn MSS, G.M.;

Most of Pitchlynn's protests were exercises in futility in the long run, but they do suggest the nature of his duties as tribal delegate. Vigilant of the Indian prerogatives, he set himself foursquare against any measure that threatened either the common ownership of tribal lands or Choctaw autonomy. He seldom prepared his own petitions, but he saw the threat and provided the leadership necessary to counter it. Yet his honest opposition was frequently self-serving, and in printed annual reports he kept the chief and the national council informed of every battle he fought in behalf of the tribe. The causes he espoused were popular with most Choctaws, especially the full bloods, and gained him many friends in the Nation at the very time he needed tribal support in his contest to control the prosecution of the net proceeds claim. Such opportunism had earlier prompted one missionary to term Pitchlynn "supremely selfish, without principle and without patriotism," and another to call him a "broken down politician."[16] Certainly he merited some of the criticism, but in the main it was criticism of the era in which he lived; exploitation and manipulation were very much a part of mid-nineteenth-century America. Still, what little sovereignty the Indians retained was due in large measure to Pitchlynn's zealous efforts.

The Colonel's major interest as Choctaw delegate, though, was always the net proceeds claim. The malicious and unobjective reports of the solicitor of the treasury, documents for which Cooper took unabashed personal credit, had seriously jeopardized the status of the claim. To overcome this disaster it was important that a vigorous defense of the Colonel's lifework

---

Pitchlynn, Washington, to E. S. Parker, June 29, 1869, N.A., O.I.A., Choctaw Agency, Letters Received, Microcopy 234, Roll 179; A. T. Skallum, Attorney General, to President Grant, December 28, 1872, N.A., O.I.A., Choctaw Agency, Letters Received, Microcopy 234, Roll 180.

[16] Alexander Reid, Spencer, to Walter Lowrie, January 9, 1854, Box 12, Vol. I, American Indian Correspondence MSS, Presbyterian Historical Society; Henry C. Benson, *Life Among the Choctaw Indians*, 103.

be made. Pitchlynn now turned to the talented pen of Albert Pike. In January, 1873, Pike composed a memorial which argued that the 1859 award of the Senate was as final as the *Alabama* verdict at Geneva, a judgment granting the United States compensation for unneutral acts by Britain during the Civil War. Solicitor Banfield had made no new discovery or presented any questions that had not been settled long ago, and now was not "the time for the general resurrection of the dead." Pike's defense plus the able briefs prepared by John Luce, who had rejoined the Choctaw team in 1872, somewhat mitigated the ill effects of the Solicitor's findings and encouraged the Senate committee on Indian affairs to report again in January, 1873, in favor of delivering the $250,000 in bonds. Furthermore, the following month the committee's counterpart in the House recommended payment of the bonds and funding of the balance of the award. All in all it was an amazing recovery, one for which Pike predictably took the credit, though Pitchlynn gave it to Luce. In any event, neither legislative body took further action.[17]

More important to the claim was an investigation conducted by the House committee on Indian affairs under the direction of its chairman, John P. C. Shanks, a Republican from Indiana. Authorized on January 8, 1872, to examine and report on various aspects of Indian affairs relating principally to the Choctaws, Chickasaws, and Cherokees, the committee conducted hearings in Washington and Indian Territory. On March 3, 1873, it submitted a report, written largely by Shanks, that claimed to reveal wholesale fraud. Specifically, the report stated that John H. B. Latrobe, Douglas Cooper, John T. Cochrane, and James G. Blunt were guilty of "base ingratitude, pro-

[17] Pitchlynn, "Response of the Choctaw Nation," Washington, 1873, Folder 74–68, and Pitchlynn's History of the Net Proceeds, Washington, July 28, 1880, Pitchlynn MSS, G.M.; 42 Cong., 3 sess., *House Misc. Doc. 46*; 42 Cong., 3 sess., *Senate Report 318*; 42 Cong., 3 sess., *House Report 80*; *McPherson v. Pike*, September, 1872, in Pike MSS, Scottish Rite Library.

fessional treachery, and cold-blooded calculations for robbery." It concluded that, but for the "dishonest" interference of Latrobe, Cooper, John D. McPherson, and Allen Wright, the government would have long ago delivered the $250,000 in bonds to the Choctaws. The document revealed the perfidy of Grayson and Paige, who had inspired the Solicitor's second report, and it declared that Cooper was "both the serpent and brains of the dishonorable combinations to defraud" the Choctaws of their corn money. It concluded that the Latrobe contract constituted fraud and that the Baltimore attorney was "befouled with professional prostitution." Altogether, the Shanks Report was a 793-page exposé.[18]

The response to the document was dramatic. As early as August, 1872, when the thrust of the committee's investigation leaked out, Latrobe denied any wrongdoing in letters to Baltimore newspapers and insisted that instead of defrauding he had preserved the Choctaws.[19] After the release of the report in the spring of 1873, Latrobe published "An Address to the Choctaws and Chickasaws" reasserting his innocence and claiming that he had secured nearly two million dollars in back annuities for the tribe.[20] Douglas Cooper responded in a similar vein. In a fifty-page "Reply to the Charges made by J. P. C. Shanks," he sought to discredit the committee document and reply to the charges that had brought his disbarment from practicing as a claims agent before the Office of Indian Affairs. Cooper argued that Shanks had written the report after Congress adjourned and that the tribe had received full benefit of the corn money. Furthermore, he and Latrobe had saved the

[18] 42 Cong., 3 sess., *House Report 98*, 16, 69, 81, 119.

[19] Baltimore *Gazette*, July 29, 1872, p. 1, and August 5, 1872, pp. 1 and 2; Baltimore *American and Commercial Advertiser*, July 29, 1872, p. 1, and August 2, 1872, pp. 2 and 4.

[20] Latrobe, "An Address to the Choctaw and Chickasaw Nations," Baltimore, June 19, 1873, Box 42h, Letters Received, Private Sources, Indian Division, Records of the Secretary of Interior, N.A.

Choctaws from the loss of back annuities after the Fort Smith council under a contract granted by tribal delegates clothed with plenary powers. He sought to vindicate Allen Wright for his participation in the $100,000 attorney fee in 1866 and to discredit Pitchlynn's role, maintaining that "a corrupt ring" used the Colonel, a "poor imbecile old man."[21]

Cooper's attack stung Pitchlynn into a spirited defense published in two pamphlets: "Reply to a Libellous Pamphlet" and "A Letter from Tushkahomma." The Colonel accused the former general of having betrayed his trust as an Indian agent, of having "spoiled" the corn money in 1861, and of having taken attorney fees while serving as a government employee. He declared that Cooper, Wright, and Latrobe had resorted to blackmail to secure a part of the attorney fee for the net proceeds claim and that if it were not for the "Cooperites" the Choctaws would have already received the Senate award. "Tushkahomma" provided a catechism for Choctaw children: "Question: Who are the first men ever debarred from practicing before the Indian Bureau? Answer: D. H. Cooper and J. H. B. Latrobe. Question: What are they debarred for? Answer: Because they defrauded the Choctaw and Chickasaw people out of great sums of money. Question: Who defrauded the Choctaws out of $100,000? Answer: Cooper, Latrobe, Allen Wright, and Company." Albert Pike probably wrote both pamphlets, and they had a telling effect on Cooper's influence within the tribe.[22]

[21] John P. C. Shanks, Washington, to Secretary Delano, April 23, 1873, and Cooper, Washington, to Delano, July 7, 1873, N.A., O.I.A., Choctaw Agency, Letters Received, Microcopy 234, Roll 180; E. P. Smith, Commissioner of Indian Affairs, to the Secretary of Interior, July 5, 1873, Box 34, Letters Received, Office of Indian Affairs, Indian Division, Records of the Secretary of Interior, N.A.; Cooper, "Reply to Charges made by J. P. C. Shanks," Washington, August, 1873, Folder 73–108, Pitchlynn MSS, G.M.

[22] Pitchlynn, "Reply to a Libellous Pamphlet," Washington, 1873, and [Pitchlynn], "A Letter from Tushkahomma to the Choctaw Nation," August, 1873, Pike MSS, Scottish Rite Library.

The former agent replied to Pitchlynn in another pamphlet. He emphasized the Colonel's association with an unnamed but well known "Indian ring" and accused Shanks of "mental constipation." He charged Pitchlynn with having received a part of the corn money and maintained that he had saved the Colonel from a "lunatic asylum" in 1868. But, generally, Cooper painted the Choctaw delegate as a dupe who unwittingly shielded scoundrels and disseminated falsehood.[23]

Cooper's disclaimers notwithstanding, the Shanks Report strengthened Pitchlynn's hand both in Washington and in the Nation. Apparently the chairman designed the document to do just that, for he seldom criticized the Colonel, who always spoke of Shanks as his "good friend." Furthermore, the Indiana Republican relied upon Pitchlynn's confidant, George Wright, to oversee the printing of the document. However, this does not mean that Shanks's Report "constitutes vituperative and exaggerated statements that cannot be taken as correct and true evidence against those that it would condemn." Shanks included the interviews basic to his conclusions, and this primary evidence alone seems to reveal massive amounts of fraud. In most cases those condemned by the report appear to have convicted themselves.[24]

To Pitchlynn the report provided a favorable climate in which to make a concerted appeal to Congress to fund the balance of the net proceeds claim and to release the $250,000 in bonds. However, his ability to co-ordinate the efforts and satisfy the demands of those associated with the various facets of the Choctaw claim made it difficult to take advantage of the situation. In January, 1873, he had rewarded George Wright

---

[23] Cooper, "Address and Memorial," Boggy Depot, October, 1873, Folder 73-108, Pitchlynn MSS, G.M.

[24] J. P. C. Shanks to G. W. Wright, May 10, 1873, and M. S. Temple, Greenfield, to Pitchlynn, October 18, 1873, *ibid.*; Muriel H. Wright, "General Douglas H. Cooper, CSA," *The Chronicles of Oklahoma*, Vol. XXXII (Summer, 1954), 183.

for his services with a contract limited to two months that called for a contingent fee of everything collected above $1,800,000 and all the interest on the bonds. Of course, Pitchlynn had earlier signed a similar agreement with Albert Pike, who upon hearing of the new arrangement threatened to "expose the whole thing."[25] Henry McKee, James Blunt, and John Luce worked almost independently to have the "uncontested" $1,800,000 funded. To that end they involved numerous men of influence, including John H. Rice, the secretary-treasurer of the Natural Gas and Iron Company of Chicago, and Alexander McDonald and D. F. Rice, both former Republican senators from Arkansas. John McPherson even pretended to power as well.[26]

Despite the many sides of the team, in December, 1873, it still made a forceful presentation to the Forty-third Congress. Pitchlynn submitted a twenty-three-page "Brief and Appeal" prepared by Pike. The pamphlet declared Pike's favorite themes that the 1859 award of the Senate was final, that the $600,000 deductions made by the Indian affairs committee in 1860 had been improper and should be restored, and that interest ought to be paid on the whole claim. The argumentation was sound and impressive to lawyers, drawing as it did upon Domat and Lord Coke, but it seemed pretentious to the congressmen.[27] The lobby, particularly George Wright, proved more adept and in April, 1874, won an extremely favorable report from the House committee on appropriations. The document recognized the right of the Choctaws to the total $2,900,000 Senate

[25] Contract between Pitchlynn and Wright, Washington, January 28, 1873, and Pike, Washington, to Pitchlynn, February 12, 1873, *ibid.*

[26] Blunt, Chicago, to Pitchlynn, November 21, 1873, McKee, St. Louis, to Pitchlynn, December 9, 1873, and Luce, Little Rock, to Pitchlynn, November, 1873, *ibid.*; McPherson, Washington, to J. S. Black and J. H. B. Latrobe, February 14, 1874, Vol. LX, Black MSS, Library of Congress.

[27] Compare Pitchlynn, "Brief and Appeal," Washington, December, 1873, XH-10, Hargrett Pamphlet Collection, G.M., with Folder 71-100, Pitchlynn MSS, G.M.; 43 Cong., 1 sess., *House Misc. Doc. 89.*

award plus interest and confirmed the authority of Peter Pitch-lynn to receive the unpaid bonds. Furthermore, during the same month the House committee on Indian affairs followed with a document equally favorable to the Choctaws. Consid-ering the status of the claim eighteen months earlier, Pitchlynn was greatly encouraged by this new congressional support, support he attributed to the timely revelations of Indian fraud made by John Shanks in 1873.[28]

In the meantime, those same revelations had tended to strengthen the Colonel's hand in Indian Territory. The Shanks Report seriously damaged Cooper's reputation among the Choctaws, thereby presenting an opportunity for Pitchlynn to obtain a clear-cut endorsement of his credentials to represent the tribe in Washington. He wanted M. S. Temple to repre-sent him at the October session of the council in 1873, but the Tennessean declined to make the trip, excusing himself on the basis of family commitments and on the grounds that such a visit would be fruitless without "insurance" money. "It will require more than a mere interchange of views and opinions of public policy," he wrote. "So many pledges and promises have been made and so many leading men are now interested that more compliments will not make a success."[29] So Pitchlynn relied upon John Luce and Campbell LeFlore, a son of Green-wood who practiced law at Fort Smith, to secure the legisla-tion desired.

Henry McKee supplied Luce and LeFlore with a draft of the measure to be adopted by the council. The document pro-vided that one half of the total sum appropriated to satisfy the

[28] 43 Cong., 1 sess., *House Report 391*; Statement of Peter Pitchlynn, Wash-ington, to Committee on Appropriation, March 20, 1874, HR 43A–F3.3, Rec-ords of the United States House of Representatives, N.A.; 43 Cong., 1 sess., *House Report 599*; Peter Pitchlynn, "Memorial," Washington, May 16, 1874, XH–10, Hargrett Pamphlet Collection, G.M.

[29] M. S. Temple, Greenfield, Tenn., to Pitchlynn, September 1, 1873, Pitchlyn MSS, G.M.

net proceeds be sent directly to the Nation to pay individual claims against the United States. The other half would be paid to the Colonel in Washington and used to compensate the delegates and the attorneys holding the Cochrane contract. The proposal did not entirely satisfy Pitchlynn, who, anxious to capitalize on the tarnished reputation of Cooper, wanted to control and disperse all the money Congress might appropriate. Luce, however, knowing that council approval would come only with great diplomacy and relaxation of opposition, sought to dissuade Pitchlynn from his power play. He wrote the Colonel that such a request might provoke the Choctaw legislature into abrogating all contracts dealing with the net proceeds claim, Latrobe's, Cochrane's and Pitchlynn's. Furthermore, he questioned the morality of it since half of the money had always been destined to satisfy individual demands upon the government. Consequently, Luce ignored the tribal delegate's ambitions and presented the McKee bill as drafted, securing its adoption on October 30, 1873.[30]

Luce, McKee, and Blunt all insisted that the act represented a victory for the Colonel, who still remained unconvinced.[31] The McKee bill referred by name to the Cochrane contract, an instrument that Pitchlynn had replaced with others but one in which his adversaries claimed an interest. For that reason Cooper, John McPherson, and even Albert Pike considered the measure a vindication of their authority. This greatly distressed Peter, who had foreseen this possibility when McKee drafted the original model. To destroy any semblance of a Cooperite victory, on his own initiative he sent out a proposed

[30] Luce, Fort Smith, to Pitchlynn, October 11, 1873, *ibid.*; Acts of the Council 1870–76, Volumes from the Choctaw Nation 312, Indian Archives, O.H.S.

[31] Luce, Fort Smith, to Pitchlynn, November 15, 1873, McKee, Fort Smith, to Pitchlynn, November 13, 1873, Blunt, Chicago, to Pitchlynn, November 21, 1873, and Pitchlynn, Washington, to Loring Folsom, January 17, 1874, Pitchlynn MSS, G.M.

measure annulling all attorney contracts with Loring Folsom, who had made a trip to see his father-in-law in Washington. Loring prevailed upon Chief Bryant to call a special session of the council in February, 1874, presented the desired legislation, and after the usual promises secured its adoption. At first blush Pitchlynn would seem to have spited himself, but the move rendered his opponents powerless and left him seemingly in complete control of the Choctaw claim, unhampered by the pretensions of any party.[32]

Peter knew, however, that power in the tribal council was a transient position. To give his victory real substance he needed the support of powerful friends who would constantly protect his interests at home. To that end, on January 14, 1874, Pitchlynn agreed to pay $10,000 to Thomas Lanigan, a Fort Smith businessman who had advanced money and rendered valuable services to the Choctaw delegate, and $20,000 to James Thompson, the tribal treasurer who would receive any appropriation made by Congress.[33] And on February 18, 1874, the Colonel contracted to pay $20,000 to Jackson McCurtain, a prominent Choctaw who would later serve as chief, to sustain the authority of the old delegation.[34] At the same time he reassured David Harkins that he intended to honor the contract with his father, George Harkins, and share equally the delegates' 20 per cent fee.[35] The promises, of course, were contingent upon the success of the claim, but no wonder M. S. Temple said he heard "of contracts every day of my life."[36]

[32] Pitchlynn, Washington, to Loring Folsom, January 22, 1874, and Pitchlynn's History of the Net Proceeds, Washington, July 28, 1880, *ibid.*; Acts of the Council, 1870–76, Volumes from the Choctaw Nation 312, Indian Archives, O.H.S.

[33] Contract with Thomas Lanigan, Washington, January 14, 1874, and Contract with James Thompson, Washington, January 14, 1874, Folder Un–83, Pitchlynn MSS, G.M.

[34] Contract with Jackson McCurtain, Washington, February 18, 1874, *ibid.*

[35] Harkins, South Canadian, to Pitchlynn, August 21, 1874, *ibid.*

[36] Temple, Armstrong Academy, to Pitchlynn, October 27, 1872, *ibid.*

By late spring of 1874 Pitchlynn had strengthened his position at home and was on the threshold of success in Washington. With the extremely favorable committee reports, it seemed only a matter of time until Congress would fund the net proceeds claim. To facilitate the passage of the measure in the House, Pike urged Lucius Q. C. Lamar of Mississippi to support the measure "with all your might," and George Wright asked Judge Black to take the matter up with six key Democratic members.[37] But the hopes of the Choctaws based upon the committee reports and this leg work did not materialize. In June, 1874, the House approved a motion of James Garfield of Ohio to refer the matter of who should determine how much of the award belonged to the individual members of the tribe again to the secretary of the treasury.[38] Obviously, Congress was still concerned about the ultimate division of the money.

In a hearing held by the secretary in late summer of 1874, Luce appeared in behalf of the Choctaws. His presentation became the basis of the report the treasurer issued on December 23, 1874. The secretary found that the balance of the individual claims exceeded the whole amount due the Choctaws under the Senate award, which indicated that all money appropriated could theoretically be paid to individual members of the tribe.[39] This prospect quieted the fears of many congressional opponents and paved the way for Congressman Abram Comingo of Missouri to move an amendment to the Indian appropriation bill the following January. Comingo asked that Peter Pitchlynn and Peter Folsom, the Choctaw delegates, be paid the $2,900,000 claim plus 5 per cent interest, less the $250,000

[37] Albert Pike, Alexandria, to L. Q. C. Lamar, June 11, 1874, Pike MSS, Manuscript Collection, Perkins Library, Duke University; Wright, Washington, to J. S. Black, April 13, 1874, Vol. LXI, Black MSS, Library of Congress.

[38] Harry J. Brown and Frederick D. William, eds., *The Diary of James A. Garfield*, II, 336, 337; Pitchlynn, "Report," Washington, 1874, H10.99, Hargrett Pamphlet Collection, G.M.

[39] 43 Cong., 2 sess., *House Exec. Doc. 47.*

appropriated in 1861.[40] In other words, Pitchlynn and Folsom would receive the whole of the Senate award in Washington, a proposition that threw the Colonel into near ecstasy. His life ambition was now to be realized.

But Congress disappointed Pitchlynn once again. Supported by Shanks, Comingo, and Garfield, the claim made its strongest showing ever and passed the committee of the whole. Recommitted for additional consideration, on February 19, amid the hysterical opposition of G. L. Fort of Illinois and G. W. Scofield of Pennsylvania, it was eventually defeated by a vote of 89–136. His hopes dashed, Pitchlynn attributed the rebuff to the 170 freshman congressmen who were unacquainted with the claim, the disagreement about the amount really due the Choctaws, and the reckless promises made by George Wright. The defeat forced the team to reassess the traditional method of prosecuting the net proceeds.[41]

Simultaneously Pitchlynn faced a serious challenge at home. He had no more than defeated Cooper when the Choctaws, in the fall of 1874, elected as chief Coleman Cole, a full blood noted for his large pumpkins and coolness toward both Pitchlynn and Cooper. Obviously, the tribe had tired of the Pitchlynn-Cooper conflict and had been impressed by Cole's promise to obtain an appropriation for the net proceeds from the government quickly. During the four years that Cole served as chief, he besieged Congress and Washington officials, from President U. S. Grant on down, with letters and memorials attacking the Choctaws who prosecuted the claim. Pitchlynn and his friends, he said, worked against the tribe "day and night" and stood at the door of Congress "humbugging and howling around," stretching forth their hands for money that

[40] 43 Cong., 2 sess., *Congressional Record*, January 19 and 20, 1875, pp. 591–97, 610–17, February 9, 1875, pp. 1084–93; Pitchlynn, "Report," Washington, 1874, H10.99, Hargrett Pamphlet Collection, G.M.; Pitchlynn's History of the Net Proceeds, Washington, July 28, 1880, Pitchlynn MSS, G.M.
[41] *Ibid.*

did not belong to them. Accusations of this nature seriously hampered Pitchlynn's effectiveness in Washington and possibly contributed to the disappointing congressional vote in 1875.[42]

On another occasion, Cole assured President Grant that he did not blame the government for refusing to pay the net proceeds to "Pitchlynn and his clan." Now that he was chief, however, the money could be remitted directly to individual claimants and the remainder invested for educational purposes. With a touching faith that the President would accommodate his wish, he established a special court to adjudicate the different individual claims. Further, Cole even considered employing Albert Pike as tribal attorney, a thought that brought the former general hurrying to the Nation for the summer and fall of 1875. But when Pike refused to disavow Pitchlynn, Cole dropped the idea.[43]

The Colonel met Cole's attacks as he had met Cooper's. Beginning in October, 1874, he attended every regular session of the Choctaw council at Armstrong Academy until 1880 to prevent any serious erosion of his influence and to retain the authority granted by the 1873 McKee bill. In 1874, because of his presence, the council memorialized Congress to fund the net proceeds and to emphasize that Pitchlynn and Peter Folsom had been granted powers never revoked. Surely this endorsement encouraged Congressman Comingo to support the right of the tribal delegates to receive the $2.9 million in the 1875 congressional debate. The Colonel won continued support of the council in 1875, during which he roomed with his Wash-

[42] Coleman Cole, Choctaw Nation, to United States Congress, January 20, 1875, 43A-H10.1, Records of the United States Senate, N.A.

[43] Cole to President Grant, November 27, 1875, N.A., O.I.A., Letters Received, Microcopy 234, Roll 182; Cole to United States Congress, April 19, 1877, C-39, Coleman Cole Collection, Western History Collection, U.O.L.; Albert Pike, Armstrong Academy, to Coleman Cole, October 16, 1875, Pitchlynn MSS, G.M.

ington friend, John Shanks, no longer in Congress. Shanks, in Indian Territory as an agent for the Choctaw freedmen, thought Armstrong Academy was rather provincial. "I have been here so long," he wrote "that I neither know the course nor direction to any other point in the world, but am well satisfied that it is some distance." In 1876, Pitchlynn succeeded in utterly defeating Cole's legislative program, though he could not prevent his re-election as chief.[44]

Curiously, Cole's decisive defeat in the council made him an object of compassion, for no one denied the nobility of his intentions—just the method of his operation. Even Pitchlynn's strongest supporters felt sorry for the old chief. Still, important elements within the tribe adamantly opposed Cole and initiated plans to impeach him. The Colonel's advisers recommended that he not endorse such a movement; it might make a martyr of the chief and foster a reaction to Pitchlynn's direction of the net proceeds. Though the Choctaw delegate relished the plight of his antagonist, he recognized the wisdom of this advice and kept out of the fight. In October, 1877, the council refused to convict Cole on the charges brought against him, but a year later he was defeated by Isaac Garvin in his bid for re-election. Though Garvin was a strong supporter, Pitchlynn continued his visits to the council in 1878 and 1879 simply to maintain contacts and to prevent any alteration of his credentials. Because of these annual trips the Choctaws never repudiated the authority granted to the tribal delegate in 1853 and frequently sustained it, although they never dramatically increased it.[45]

44 Acts of the Council, 1870–76, Volumes from the Choctaw Nation 312, Indian Archives, O.H.S.; John P. C. Shanks, Armstrong Academy, to G. W. Wright, November, 1875, Folder 75–81, Pitchlynn MSS, G.M.; Pitchlynn, Washington, to President U. S. Grant, January 8, 1876, N.A., O.I.A., Choctaw Agency, Letters Received, Microcopy 234, Roll 183.

45 Luce, Fort Smith, to H. E. McKee, September 17, 1877, and James Thompson, Chahta Tamaha, to Pitchlynn, October 16, 1879, Pitchlynn MSS,

The postwar crises which Pitchlynn faced both at Washington and at home brought out traits in his character not always present in the antebellum days. When he returned to Washington in 1865, the welfare of his family became central to his life. He displayed a tenderness for and interest in his children that outside activities had prevented in earlier days. On trips away from home, he favored his youngsters with affectionate letters and prudent advice. And to repent for earlier neglect, he took into his home his orphaned grandson, Edward Everette, and made arrangements to place Louise Harkins, another grandchild, in St. Elizabeth's Hospital in Washington, D.C.

Pitchlynn continued to identify with the fullblood Choctaws politically in the postwar period, but personally he seldom appeared in any guise other than that of a white man. As the detached Indian scholar, he aided in the Smithsonian Institution's publication of Cyrus Byington's *Choctaw Lexicon* and contributed to the history of the Choctaws and early Mississippi. Like socially prominent whites he made regular trips to the fashionable spas in the Virginia mountains to drink sulphur water and bathe in it. The visits were partially therapeutic; Pitchlynn suffered intensely with arthritis, a condition that forced him to use a cane and made writing difficult. But he enjoyed the area and the society so much that he dreamed of purchasing property there once he completed his business. During the 1870's the Colonel abandoned the Cumberland Presbyterian fellowship which was popular among the Choctaws to join the more formal Lutheran Church. Furthermore, his reliance upon God and the Bible increased. "If it were not for the Bible," he once wrote, "we would be savages, worse than the Comanches." Pitchlynn also frequently jotted down scrip-

G.M.; Report of the Committee, October 19, 1877, Vol. IV, Acts of the Choctaw Nation, Western History Collection, U.O.L.; Atoka *Independent*, October 26, 1877, p. 4.

tures and religious thoughts in memorandum books. "The eternal God is thy refuge and underneath is the everlasting arms," one entry noted, while another prayed, "Help me Savior or I die." When death came, Pitchlynn looked forward not to the Indian's happy hunting ground but to the Christian heaven.[46]

As in the prewar period, the 1860's and 1870's were years of financial embarrassment. The Choctaws paid few if any of the Colonel's expenses and his plantation ceased to return an income immediately following the war. To meet the costs of day-to-day living he constantly looked to friends for assistance. McKee "loaned" Pitchlynn money and referred him to people of means. For example, a former senator, Samuel C. Pomeroy of Kansas, on at least one occasion furnished $100 so that Peter would "be sustained and have patience to see the end of your claim against the government." McKee later rewarded Pomeroy with $10,000 for his timely aid.[47]

George Wright also helped Pitchlynn financially. In addition to personal loans, he secured $1,000 from Jay Cooke and Company, an advance Peter found difficult to repay and perhaps never repaid. From the same company, Wright proposed that the Colonel request a $10,000 loan in anticipation of monies expected from the net proceeds. In consideration for the advance Pitchlynn would promise that when Congress made its appropriation he would purchase from Cooke and Company $500,000 worth of Northern Pacific Railroad bonds, allow Cooke a 2.5 per cent commission to negotiate a sale for

[46] H. S. Halbert, Lowndes County, Mississippi, to Pitchlynn, July 19, 1878, S. Byington, Belpere, Ohio, to Pitchlynn, August 2, 1873, Certificate of Membership, April 10, 1867, Pitchlynn to Family, August 19, 1874, August 25, 1874, October 11, 1869, Notebook, n.d., Folder 77–42A, and "Morning and Night Watches," n.d., Pitchlynn MSS, G.M.

[47] Pomeroy, Muscoth, Kansas, to Pitchlynn, August 19, 1876, and Choctaw Delegates, "Statement of Disbursement of Twenty-Percent," Fort Smith, July 18, 1889, Folder 89–11, *ibid*.

the confiscated Choctaw bonds, and place on deposit with the company those monies that would eventually go to the individual Choctaws.[48] Pitchlynn did not adopt Wright's scheme, but he did accept several thousand dollars from J. W. Denver, over $1,200 from Ward A. Lamon, Black's law partner, and smaller sums from whoever was at hand. He also received some support from the estate of his father-in-law and, to provide for himself, even entertained thoughts of purchasing a franchise on a "perpetual, self-heating, ironing machine." When Pitchlynn died he was penniless and in debt.[49]

In the postwar years, only Pitchlynn and Peter Folsom survived to guard the interests of the delegation of 1853. Folsom seldom assisted the Colonel, who was inclined to disregard him anyway, and when members of Congress thought of the Choctaws they thought of the "old chief, Colonel Pitchlynn." He thus symbolized the net proceeds claim and provided a point around which others could rally. As the interest of others waned, the Colonel could only write, "my friends think we shall succeed this time." Occasionally, though, he too grew tired of the frustrations on the Potomac and yearned to get "back to the woods again."[50]

The congressional defeat in 1875 had impressed upon the Choctaw team that some approach other than seeking a direct appropriation was necessary if the tribe was ever to receive the

[48] Peter Pitchlynn, Washington, to Henry D. Cook, October 19, 1872, and Draft of a letter to J. Cooke and Company, Washington, May 26, 1873, *ibid*.

[49] Letter draft, n.d., Folder Un–109, Pitchlynn's History of the Net Proceeds, Washington, July 28, 1880, and T. T. Smothers, Washington, to Pitchlynn, January 18, 1877, *ibid.*; *Henry E. McKee, Appellant,* v. *Ward H. Lamon,* Supreme Court of the United States, October Term, 1894, in Rare Book Section, G.M.

[50] 46 Cong., 3 sess., *Congressional Record*, February 21, 1881, p. 1898; M. S. Temple, Greenfield, Tenn., to Pitchlynn, November 29, 1879, Pitchlynn MSS, G.M.; Pitchlynn, Washington, to Nephew, May 7, 1874, and October 31, 1877, General Correspondence, A–P, Rogers–Neill MSS, Western History Collection, U.O.L.

net proceeds. As early as 1868, McPherson had suggested that the Choctaws submit the claim to some court of law for adjudication, and after the rebuff of February, 1875, others concurred in this opinion. Throughout the spring and summer Pitchlynn and his associates prepared to ask Congress to refer the case to the United States Court of Claims. Pitchlynn signed a contract with John Luce designating him as the attorney of record before the court and promised him a 5 per cent contingent fee out of McKee's contract, 2 per cent of which Luce was to rebate to the Colonel. M. S. Temple and Pike combined their efforts with those of McKee and Luce, who still employed John J. Weed and F. P. Cuppy, two Washington attorneys hired in the early 1870's. Blunt had retired from the case, but McPherson still claimed some authority and George Wright continued to dream about a congressional appropriation for the whole of the net proceeds. McKee and Luce, though, provided the real direction for the team.[51]

At the first session of the Forty-fourth Congress in December, 1875, Luce prepared lengthy memorials for both the Senate and the House requesting that the claim be referred to the court. After the House referred the submitted document to the committee on Indian affairs, Luce and Weed drew up a model bill including the referral desired by the Choctaws and submitted it for criticism to the former senator from Wisconsin, Matthew H. Carpenter. Retained by McKee and Pitchlynn for a contingent fee of $50,000, Carpenter prepared the section which prescribed the ground rules of the court petition and then retired from the team, returning to the Senate. Luce submitted the draft of the desired legislation to W. W. Wilshire of Arkansas, chairman of the House committee, who con-

---

[51] Contracts between Luce and Pitchlynn, Washington, March 26, 1875, and April 14, 1875, and G. W. Wright, Washington, to Pitchlynn, August 6, 1875, Pitchlynn MSS, G.M.; McPherson, Washington, to Black, March 17, 1875, Vol. LXIII, Black MSS, Library of Congress.

sidered the model and favorably reported a similar measure in May, 1876.[52] But Congress took no other action.

During the second session additional efforts were made to pass the bill. In January, 1877, Congressman J. H. Sealy of Massachusetts attempted to suspend the rules and call up the proposal for House consideration. His motion, however, failed to gain the necessary two-thirds majority. The same body defeated a similar effort in March. In February, 1877, Pitchlynn met with Senator Powell Clayton of Arkansas and the chairman of the committee on Indian affairs, Senator William B. Allison of Iowa, requesting them to bring the Choctaw legislation to the attention of the Senate. The committee staff urged favorable action, but the Senate did not consider the measure. And again Congress adjourned without final consideration of the claim.[53]

Defeat did not prevent the Choctaw team from again presenting its case to the Forty-fifth Congress. In late October, 1877, Pitchlynn prevailed upon Charles E. Hooker of Mississippi to reintroduce the bill in the House as written in the previous Congress. The Colonel submitted another memorial, called on friends in Congress, and, after checking with McKee and Luce, decided that this was *the* session. Once more, after a two-day presentation by Luce and Pitchlynn, the House committee on Indian affairs reported in favor of referring the case to the court of claims. The Senate Indian affairs committee also held hearings during which Pitchlynn and Luce appeared to urge adoption of the bill pending in the House. Albert Pike made a presentation as well, but he argued somewhat differently. As the Senate award in 1859 had been final, he stated

[52] 44 Cong., 1 sess., *House Misc. Doc. 40*; 44 Cong., 1 sess., *Sen. Misc. Doc. 34*; 44 Cong., 1 sess., *House Report 499*.

[53] 44 Cong., 2 sess., *Congressional Record*, January 22, 1877, p. 812, and March 3, 1877, p. 2218; Pitchlynn, Washington, to Clayton, February 17, 1877, and Pitchlynn to Allison, February 13, 1877, 44A–H9, Records of the United States Senate, N.A.

that the court of claims ought to rule upon that finding rather than upon the claim per se. In other words, the court should not go behind the Senate determination to consider the worthiness of the case, a procedure McKee and Luce had earlier rejected upon Carpenter's advice. Despite the favorable report of the House and consideration of the Senate, the Forty-fifth Congress ended without final action, and once more Pitchlynn had not succeeded.[54]

The measures having languished in Congress, in late 1878 Pitchlynn appealed to President Rutherford B. Hayes for assistance in transferring the claim to the court. As was commonly done in such cases, the President simply referred the matter to the Bureau of Indian Affairs for evaluation. The commissioner eventually ruled in favor of the Choctaws and recommended that Congress take some appropriate action, though he personally believed that the Senate award was final.[55]

The favorable report of the administration provided a convenient approach to the Forty-sixth Congress which met in March, 1879. Representative Hooker reintroduced the bill as written in previous Congresses. And as it had before, the House committee reported the measure favorably in May, 1879, declaring that the "halls of Congress are obviously not the place to adjust the items of an account."[56] In the Senate, A. H. Garland of Arkansas introduced the appropriate legislation, but the committee on the judiciary to which it was referred made little progress toward a final determination.

The fact that additional action was not taken by either House

[54] Pitchlynn, Washington, to Nephew, October 31, 1877, General Correspondence, A–P, Rogers–Neill MSS, Western History Collection, U.O.L.; 45 Cong., 1 sess., *House Misc. Doc. 14*; 45 Cong., 2 sess., *House Report 251*; W. B. Allison, Washington, to Pitchlynn, December 5, 1878, Pitchlynn MSS, G.M.; 49 Cong., 2 sess., *Senate Report 1978*; Walter L. Brown, "Albert Pike" (unpublished Ph.D. dissertation, University of Texas, 1955), p. 850.

[55] 45 Cong., 3 sess., *House Exec. Doc. 34.*

[56] 46 Cong., 1 sess., *House Report 4.*

proved tragic, for on January 17, 1881, worn out by his duties as Choctaw delegate, Peter Pitchlynn died at his home in Washington. But, shortly after his death, Chief Jackson McCurtain begged for congressional action, noting that "Colonel Pitchlynn always said that sooner or later Congress would keep faith with us. In behalf of our people I ask you to make good his words."[57] When the measure came up for debate in the House on February 21, 1881, Congressman Hooker called forth the name of "old Colonel Pitchlynn" and urged adoption of the legislation. The House finally passed the bill by a vote of 174–55. On March 1, the Senate agreed to the House measure, but only after Garland had pointed to Pitchlynn's long and fruitless residence at the capital.[58] After nearly thirty years, the United States had authorized the Choctaws to take the first step in the final adjudication of the net proceeds. What Pitchlynn had failed to do in life he accomplished in death.

Represented by John Luce, John Weed, F. P. Cuppy, Samuel Shellabarger, and J. W. Denver, the Choctaws immediately began litigation. After five years of argumentation and 4,000 pages of printed material, on January 25, 1886, the court of claims ruled that the law giving the court jurisdiction had destroyed the sanctity of the Senate award. Consequently, after considering the claim in its entirety, it awarded the Choctaws only $658,120, of which $250,000 had already been paid.[59] Accustomed to disappointment, the Choctaw team appealed the decision to the United States Supreme Court, which speedily reversed the lower court ruling and declared that the award of the Senate was indeed final. It also granted the tribe compensation for the mismarked eastern boundary and for unpaid annuities, making the total judgment well over $3,000,000.[60]

[57] 46 Cong., 3 sess., *Sen. Misc. Doc. 32.*

[58] 46 Cong., 3 sess., *Congressional Record*, February 21, 1881, pp. 1898–1901, 2276.

[59] *Court of Claims Report*, Vol. XXI, January 25, 1886, p. 72.

[60] *Supreme Court Reports*, Vol. CXIX.

Congress appropriated the money in early 1889 after a lengthy investigation.[61] One half of the judgment went to the tribe to satisfy the individual claims and the other half to the attorneys and delegation of 1853. The total amount granted by the Choctaw council to the heirs of the old delegation was $638,944.

After a highly questionable disbursement that became the basis of protracted lawsuits, Pitchlynn's heirs received the sum of $107,311.29 as the Colonel's share, twice as much as the heirs of any of his colleagues. Henry McKee, who survived to control the 30 per cent awarded the attorneys, did not pay the 5 per cent rebate agreed upon in 1870, nor did he assume his share of general expenses. In fact, to avoid an accounting with the Pitchlynn heirs and other parties he left the United States for Europe.[62]

In some ways it was fitting that Peter Pitchlynn did not live to see the final adjudication of the net proceeds claim. To have done so would have altered the general theme of his life—frustration. This is not to say that there were no successes. He made no mean contribution as architect of the Choctaw educational system, as participant in constitutional conventions, as principal negotiator of tribal treaties, as chief during the Civil War, and as national delegate after 1865. He also successfully obtained a measure of religious peace. But even these accomplishments came in the face of continued frustration.

For Pitchlynn the truly normal state of affairs was disappointment. The hopes he had for his children never materialized. The pre-eminent political power he demanded within the Choctaw Nation seldom accrued to him. His financial aspirations, which included the net proceeds claim, were so unsuccessful that he died penniless and deeply in debt. But most im-

---

[61] 49 Cong., 2 sess., *Senate Report 1978*.

[62] LeFlore and McCurtain, "Statement of Disbursement of Twenty-Percent," Fort Smith, July 3, 1889, Folder 89–11, Pitchlynn MSS, G.M.

portant, Pitchlynn never attained the measure of personal acceptance he so desired from his Choctaw kinsmen or his white associates. The funeral arrangements made for him underscored this recurring frustration.

The old chief's body was taken to a local mortuary where it was prepared for burial and placed in a merino-lined walnut casket to which was attached an engraved name plate. On February 21, 1881, four days after his death, fourteen carriages took the desolate family to Washington's Masonic Temple where Albert Pike presided over the last rites. But instead of an appropriate burial following the services, destitution of the family made it necessary to place Pitchlynn's body in a public vault pending further arrangements. These tragic circumstances moved Peter Folsom, the surviving Choctaw delegate, to petition the government to authorize burial in the Congressional Cemetery. The required consent came in late April, and the body was finally laid to rest on the banks of the Anacostia River at a site not far from the grave of Pushmataha. In 1884, after many frustrating delays, the Choctaw council paid the funeral expenses, and some time later the family placed a seven-foot white marble stone above the burial place. The marker was inscribed with the phrase, "Christian Brave," an epitaph that had a false ring, however. Unlike other Indian braves, Pitchlynn had died as a white man and was buried in a white man's grave.[63]

Still, the inscription is significant. To label Pitchlynn a "brave," Christian or not, meant that some people continued to consider him very much an Indian even after years of residence in a non-Indian world. For the Colonel, who longed for equal status with his white colleagues, this anomalous position

[63] Peter Folsom, Washington, to Samuel J. Kirkwoods, Secretary of Interior, April 19, 1881, *ibid.*; Account of Anthony Buchly, Undertaker, with Peter Pitchlynn, Washington, January 21, 1881, 17518, Choctaw Nation—Estates, Indian Archives, O.H.S.

was terribly disheartening. On such occasions his mind recalled the West:

> O, take me to my Nation,
> And let me there remain;
> This other world is strange, strange—
> I wish for home again!
>
> The sunshine and the flowers,
> My mother's grave again,
> Give me my race and kindred—
> O take me home again!

But home would not have brought the personal acceptance Peter Pitchlynn sought either. He was an alien there, too, because of his mixed blood, his boundless ambition, and his adoption of peculiar social patterns. To be suspect by both his own people and his white friends was the ultimate frustration. That is his significance; that, too, is his tragedy.

Bibliography

Manuscript Collections

1. *Austin, Texas*

University of Texas Library, Manuscript Division
  Edward Hanrick Papers

2. *Columbus, Mississippi*

Lowndes County Court House
  Records of the Chancery Court

3. *Durham, North Carolina*

Duke University Library, Division of Manuscripts
  Albert Pike Papers

4. *Jackson, Mississippi*

Mississippi Department of Archives and History
  Claiborne Papers
  George S. Gaines Collection (Typescript)
  Governors' Papers
  Lowndes County (W. P. A. Typescript)
  Lowndes County Tax Records (Microfilm)
  Mississippi State Session Laws

John Pitchlynn Subject File
Peter Pitchlynn Subject File
Plymouth, Mississippi, Subject File

5. *Madison, Wisconsin*
University of Wisconsin Library, Manuscript Division
Draper Collection (Microfilm)

6. *Nashville, Tennessee*
Tennessee State Library and Archives
John S. Claybrooke Papers
Andrew Jackson Papers (Microfilm)
James Robertson Papers
Records of the University of Nashville (Microfilm)

7. *Norman, Oklahoma*
University of Oklahoma Library
a. Western History Collection
Acts of the Choctaw Nation
Choctaw Miscellaneous Papers
Coleman Cole Collection
J. W. Denver Papers
I. L. Garvin Collection
J. L. Hargett Collection
LeFlore Collection
J. F. McCurtain Papers
Peter P. Pitchlynn Collection
Rogers-Neill Collection
Allen Wright Collection
b. Phillips Collection
Pamphlet File

8. *Oklahoma City, Oklahoma*
Oklahoma Historical Society, Indian Archives
Choctaw Nation—Auditor
Choctaw Nation—Census
Choctaw Nation—Estates

Choctaw Nation—Federal Relations
Choctaw Nation—Miscellaneous
Choctaw Nation—National Council
Choctaw Nation—National Secretary
Choctaw Nation—Principal Chiefs
Choctaw Nation—Railroads
Choctaw Nation—Treasurer
Grant Foreman Collection
Indian-Pioneer Papers
Section X—Cherokee, Federal Relations
Section X—Robert M. Jones Papers
Section X—Sue McBeth Papers
Section X—Reserve on Peter Pitchlynn
Volumes from the Choctaw Nation

9. *Philadelphia, Pennsylvania*
Historical Society of Pennsylvania
    Gratz Collection
Presbyterian Historical Society
    American Indian Correspondence

10. *San Marino, California*
Henry E. Huntington Library and Art Gallery
    Jeremiah Sullivan Black Papers

11. *Tulsa, Oklahoma*
Gilcrease Institute of American History and Art
    John M. Armstrong Papers
    Choctaw Papers
    John T. Cochrane Papers
    Grant Foreman Collection
    Hargrett Pamphlet Collection
    Peter Pitchlynn Papers
    Rare Book Collection

12. *Tuscaloosa, Alabama*
University of Alabama Library, Manuscript Division
    John McKee Papers

13. *Washington, D.C.*

Library of Congress
  Jeremiah Sullivan Black Papers
  John Coffee Papers
  Richard M. Johnson Papers
  John McKee Papers
  George W. Wright Papers
National Archives
  a. Records of the Department of Interior
    Division of Finance, Index to Appropriation Ledgers
    Indian Division, Letters Received, Private Sources
    Indian Division, Letters Received, Office of Indian Affairs
    Papers Relating to Claims
      Eastern Boundary of the Choctaws
      Trust Funds of the Choctaws
  b. Records of the Office of Indian Affairs
    Choctaw Agency, Letters Received (Microcopy 234)
    Choctaw Agency West, Letters Received (Microcopy 234)
    Choctaw Emigration, Letters Received (Microcopy 234)
    Choctaw Reserves, Letters Received (Microcopy 234)
    Letters Sent (Microcopy 21)
    Records of the Commissary General of Subsistence, Choctaw
      Emigration
    Schools, Letters Received (Microcopy 234)
  c. Records of the House of Representatives
  d. Records of the United States Senate
Supreme Court of the District of Columbia
  Old Marriage Records
Scottish Rite Library
  Albert Pike Papers

Government Documents

1. *Congressional*

Congressional Globe, 1854–1872.
Congressional Record, 1873–1881.
House Executive Documents:
  26th Cong., 2nd sess., No. 109

27th Cong., 2nd sess., No. 231
29th Cong., 1st sess., No. 189
36th Cong., 1st sess., No. 82
40th Cong., 2nd sess., No. 133
40th Cong., 2nd sess., No. 138
40th Cong., 2nd sess., No. 204
41st Cong., 3rd sess., No. 25
42nd Cong., 3rd sess., No. 10
42nd Cong., 3rd sess., No. 69
43rd Cong., 2nd sess., No. 42
43rd Cong., 2nd sess., No. 47
45th Cong., 3rd sess., No. 34
House Miscellaneous Documents:
22nd Cong., 1st sess., No. 194
30th Cong., 2nd sess., No. 35
41st Cong., 2nd sess., No. 21
41st Cong., 3rd sess., No. 37
42nd Cong., 2nd sess., No. 164
42nd Cong., 3rd sess., No. 46
42nd Cong., 3rd sess., No. 94
43rd Cong., 1st sess., No. 87
43rd Cong., 1st sess., No. 88
43rd Cong., 1st sess., No. 89
43rd Cong., 1st sess., No. 294
44th Cong., 1st sess., No. 40
44th Cong., 2nd sess., No. 41
45th Cong., 1st sess., No. 14
45th Cong., 2nd sess., No. 32
45th Cong., 2nd sess., No. 33
46th Cong., 1st sess., No. 13
House Reports:
40th Cong., 2nd sess., No. 77
41st Cong., 3rd sess., No. 41
42nd Cong., 3rd sess., No. 80
42nd Cong., 3rd sess., No. 98
43rd Cong., 1st sess., No. 391
43rd Cong., 1st sess., No. 599

43rd Cong., 2nd sess., No. 151
44th Cong., 1st sess., No. 499
45th Cong., 2nd sess., No. 251
46th Cong., 1st sess., No. 4
46th Cong., 2nd sess., No. 755
Senate Executive Documents:
19th Cong., 2nd sess., No. 21
24th Cong., 1st sess., No. 23
28th Cong., 1st sess., No. 168
28th Cong., 2nd sess., No. 86
42nd Cong., 2nd sess., No. 87
45th Cong., 2nd sess., No. 32
Senate Miscellaneous Documents:
18th Cong., 2nd sess., No. 35
23rd Cong., 1st sess., No. 512
24th Cong., 1st sess., No. 23
34th Cong., 1st sess., No. 31
41st Cong., 2nd sess., No. 90
41st Cong., 2nd sess., No. 106
41st Cong., 2nd sess., No. 143
41st Cong., 3rd sess., No. 65
42nd Cong., 2nd sess., No. 53
43rd Cong., 1st sess., No. 121
43rd Cong., 2nd sess., No. 78
44th Cong., 1st sess., No. 34
44th Cong., 2nd sess., No. 34
45th Cong., 2nd sess., No. 8
45th Cong., 2nd sess., No. 59
45th Cong., 2nd sess., No. 82
46th Cong., 2nd sess., No. 41
46th Cong., 3rd sess., No. 32
Senate Reports:
24th Cong., 1st sess., No. 265
35th Cong., 2nd sess., No. 374
35th Cong., 2nd sess., No. 574
36th Cong., 1st sess., No. 283
42nd Cong., 3rd sess., No. 318

45th Cong., 2nd sess., No. 251
49th Cong., 2nd sess., No. 1978

2. *Other*

American State Papers: Indian Affairs. Class 2, Vol. II, 1832.
Annual Report of the Board of Regents of the Smithsonian Institution, 1885. 2 vols. Washington, D.C., Government Printing Office, 1886.
Annual Report of the Commissioner of Indian Affairs, 1829–1881.
Court of Claims Reports, Vol. XXI and LIX.
Folsom, Joseph P., ed. *Constitution and Laws of the Choctaw Nation.* New York, William P. Lyon and Sons, 1869.
Kappler, Charles J. *Indian Affairs: Laws and Treaties.* Vol. II. Washington, D.C., Government Printing Office, 1904.
Meyer, W. E. "Indian Trails of the Southeast." *42nd Annual Report of the Bureau of American Ethnology.* Washington, D.C., Government Printing Office, 1928.
Supreme Court Reports. Vol. CXIX and CCLVI.
War of Rebellion: Compilation of the Official Records of the Union and Confederate Armies. First Series XLVII. Washington, D.C., Government Printing Office, 1880–1901.
United States Statutes at Large. Vol. VII.

Newspapers

Arkansas Gazette (Little Rock)
Arkansas Intelligencer (Van Buren)
Atoka (I.T.) *Independent*
Baltimore American and Commercial Advertiser
Baltimore Gazette
Cherokee Advocate (Tahlequah, I.T.)
Choctaw Intelligencer (Doaksville, I.T.)
Choctaw Telegraph (Doaksville, I.T.)
Clarksville (Tex.) *Standard*
Fort Smith (Ark.) *New Era*
Indian Journal (Eufaula, I.T.)
Indian Journal (Muskogee, I.T.)

McAlester (I.T.) *Star-Vindicator*
Missionary Herald
New Boggy (I.T.) *Vindicator*
New York Tribune
Niles' Weekly Register (Baltimore)
Oklahoma Star (Caddo, I.T.)
Washington (Ark.) *Telegraph*

Articles

Conlan, Czarina C. "Necrology, Peter P. Pitchlynn." *The Chronicles of Oklahoma*, Vol. VI (June, 1928), 215–24.

"Dancing Rabbit Creek Treaty." *Historical and Patriotic Series,* No. 10 (1928), 1–25.

DeRosier, Arthur H., Jr. "Andrew Jackson and Negotiations for the Removal of the Choctaw Indians." *The Historian*, Vol. XXIX (May, 1967), 343–62.

———. "Negotiations for the Removal of the Choctaws: U.S. Policies of 1820 and 1830." *The Chronicles of Oklahoma*, Vol. XXXVIII (Spring, 1960), 85–100.

Edwards, John. "My Escape in 1861." *The Chronicles of Oklahoma*, Vol. XLIII (Spring, 1965), 60–89.

Foreman, Carolyn Thomas. "Charity Hall, An Early Chickasaw School." *The Chronicles of Oklahoma*, Vol. XI (September, 1933), 912–26.

———. "The Choctaw Academy." *The Chronicles of Oklahoma*, Vol. VI (December, 1928), 452–80.

———. "The Choctaw Academy." *The Chronicles of Oklahoma*, Vol. X (March, 1932), 76–114.

———. "Education Among the Chickasaw Indians." *The Chronicles of Oklahoma*, Vol. XV (June, 1937), 139–65.

———, ed. "Journal of a Tour in the Indian Country." *The Chronicles of Oklahoma*, Vol. X (June, 1932), 217–56.

Goetzmann, William R. "The Mountain Man as Jacksonian Man." *The American Quarterly*, Vol. XV (Fall, 1963), 402–15.

Hudson, Peter James. "A Story of Choctaw Chiefs." *The Chronicles of Oklahoma*, Vol. XVII (June, 1939), 192–211.

———. "Recollections." *The Chronicles of Oklahoma*, Vol. X (December, 1932), 501–19.

Lanman, Charles. "Peter Pitchlynn, Chief of the Choctaws." *The Atlantic Monthly* (April, 1870), 486–99.

McDermott, John Francis. "Isaac McCoy's Second Exploring Trip in 1828." *The Kansas Historical Quarterly*, Vol. XIII (August, 1945), 400–62.

Meserve, John Bartlett. "Chief George Hudson and Chief Samuel Garland." *The Chronicles of Oklahoma*, Vol. XX (March, 1942), 9–17.

———. "The McCurtains." *The Chronicles of Oklahoma*, Vol. XIII (September, 1935), 297–312.

"Notes and Documents." *The Chronicles of Oklahoma*, Vol. XXII (Summer, 1944), 210–20.

"Peter Perkins Pitchlynn." *The New Age*, Vol. LXVIII (June, 1940), 355–56.

Plaisance, Aloysius. "The Choctaw Trading House, 1803–1822." *The Alabama Historical Quarterly*, Vol. XVI (Fall and Winter, 1954), 393–423.

Shirk, George H. "The Confederate Postal System in the Indian Territory." *The Chronicles of Oklahoma*, Vol. XLI (Summer, 1963), 160–218.

West, Ruth Tenison. "Pushmataha's Travels." *The Chronicles of Oklahoma*, Vol. XXXVII (Summer, 1959), 162–74.

Wright, Muriel H. and Peter J. Hudson. "Brief Outline of the Choctaw and Chickasaw Nations in the Indian Territory, 1820–1860." *The Chronicles of Oklahoma*, Vol. VII (December, 1929), 386–413.

Wright, Muriel H. "General Douglas H. Cooper, C.S.A." *The Chronicles of Oklahoma*, Vol. XXXII (Summer, 1954), 142–84.

———. "Review of *The Rise and Fall of the Choctaw Republic* by Angie Debo." *The Chronicles of Oklahoma*, Vol. XIII (March, 1935), 108–20.

———. "The Removal of the Choctaws to the Indian Territory, 1830–1833." *The Chronicles of Oklahoma*, Vol. VI (June, 1928), 103–28.

Books

Abel, Annie Heloise. *The American Indian as Slaveholder and Secessionist.* 3 vols. Cleveland, The Arthur H. Clark Co., 1915.

Abernethy, Thomas Perkins. *From Frontier to Plantation in Tennessee.* Chapel Hill, University of North Carolina Press, 1932.

Bassett, John Spencer, ed. *Correspondence of Andrew Jackson.* 7 vols. Washington, D.C., Carnegie Institution, 1926.

Benson, Henry C. *Life Among the Choctaw Indians.* Cincinnati, L. Swormstedt and A. Poe, 1860.

Boyd, William A. *Boyd's Washington and Georgetown Directory.* Washington, D.C., Taylor and Maury, 1860.

Brigance, William Norwood. *Jeremiah Sullivan Black: A Defender of the Constitution and the Ten Commandments.* Philadelphia, University of Pennsylvania Press, 1934.

Brown, Harry James, and Frederick D. Williams, eds. *The Diary of James A. Garfield.* 2 vols. Lansing, Michigan State University Press, 1967.

Catlin, George. *Letters and Notes on the Manners, Customs and Conditions of the North American Indians.* 2nd ed. 2 vols. London, George Catlin Publisher, 1842.

Claiborne, J. F. H. *Life and Times of General Sam Dale, the Mississippi Partisan.* New York, Harper and Brothers, 1860.

———. *Mississippi, as a Province, Territory and State.* Reprint. Baton Rouge, Louisiana State University Press, 1964.

Conversations on the Choctaw Mission. 2 vols. Boston, Massachusetts Sabbath School Union, 1830.

Cotterill, R. S. *The Southern Indians: The Story of the Civilized Tribes Before Removal.* Norman, University of Oklahoma Press, 1954.

Cushman, H. B. *History of the Choctaw, Chickasaw, and Natchez Indians.* Reprint. Stillwater, Redland Press, 1961.

Debo, Angie. *The Rise and Fall of the Choctaw Republic.* 2nd ed. Norman, University of Oklahoma Press, 1961.

DeRosier, Arthur H., Jr. *The Removal of the Choctaw Indians.* Knoxville, University of Tennessee Press, 1970.

Dickens, Charles. *American Notes*. Greenwich, Conn., Fawcett Publications, Inc., 1961.

Farnham, Thomas J. *Travels in the Great Western Prairies*. In *Early Western Travels, 1748–1846*, edited by Reuben Gold Thwaites. Cleveland, The Arthur H. Clark Co., 1906.

Foreman, Grant. *Advancing the Frontier, 1830–1860*. Norman, University of Oklahoma Press, 1933.

———. *The Five Civilized Tribes*. Norman, University of Oklahoma Press, 1934.

———. *Indian Removal: The Emigration of the Five Civilized Tribes of Indians*. Norman, University of Oklahoma Press, 1932.

Gregg, Josiah. *Commerce of the Prairies*, edited by Max L. Moorhead. Norman, University of Oklahoma Press, 1954.

Hargrett, Lester. *A Bibliography of the Constitutions and Laws of the American Indians*. Cambridge, Harvard University Press, 1947.

Harmon, George Dewey. *Sixty Years of Indian Affairs*. Chapel Hill, University of North Carolina Press, 1941.

History of Tennessee. Nashville, Goodspeed Publishing Co., 1887.

Hodge, Frederick W., ed. *Handbook of American Indians North of Mexico*. 2 vols. Washington, D.C., Government Printing Office, 1910.

Hofstadter, Richard. *American Political Tradition*. New York, Vintage Books, ca. 1948.

Holmes, Jack D. L. *Gayoso: The Life of a Spanish Governor in the Mississippi Valley, 1789–1799*. Baton Rouge, Louisiana Historical Society, 1965.

Hurley, Patrick J., ed. *Choctaw Briefs and Papers*. [N.p.], 1916.

Johnson, Roy M., ed. *Oklahoma History South of the Canadian*. 3 vols. Chicago, S. J. Clarke Co., 1925.

Lewis, Anna. *Chief Pushmataha*. New York, Exposition Press, 1959.

Lipscomb, W. L. *A History of Columbus, Mississippi During the 19th Century*. Birmingham, Press of Dispatch Printing Co., 1909.

Marshall, Ann J. *The Autobiography of Mrs. A. J. Marshall*. Pine Bluff, Adams-Wilson Printing Co., 1897.

McCoy, Isaac. *History of Baptist Indian Missions.* Washington, D.C., William M. Morrison, 1840.

McKenney, Thomas L. *Memoirs, Official and Personal.* Two volumes in one. New York, Paine and Burgess, 1846.

McMurray, J. F. *Choctaw Nation v. the United States.* 2 vols. McAlester, News-Capital, [n.d.].

Meyer, Leland Winfield. *The Life and Times of Colonel Richard M. Johnson of Kentucky.* New York, Columbia University Press, 1932.

Morse, Jedidiah. *A Report to the Secretary of War of the United States, on Indian Affairs.* New Haven, Converse, 1822.

Owen, Roger C. et al., eds. *The North American Indians: A Sourcebook.* New York, The Macmillan Co., 1967.

Pickett, Albert James. *History of Alabama.* 2 vols. Charleston, Walker and James, 1851.

Pierson, George Wilson. *Tocqueville in America.* Garden City, Doubleday and Company, 1959.

Riley, Franklin L., ed. *Publications of the Mississippi Historical Society.* 8 vols. Oxford, Mississippi Historical Society, 1904.

Rowland, Dunbar, ed. *Jefferson Davis, Constitutionalist: His Letters, Papers and Speeches.* 10 vols. Jackson, Mississippi Department of Archives and History, 1923.

——, ed. *Official Letter Books of W. C. C. Claiborne, 1801–1816.* 6 vols. Jackson, Mississippi Department of Archives and History, 1917.

Semmes, John E. *John H. B. Latrobe and His Times, 1803–1891.* Baltimore, The Norman, Remington Co., ca. 1917.

Swanton, John R. *Source Material for the Social and Ceremonial Life of the Choctaw Indians* in *Bureau of American Ethnology, Bulletin 103.* Washington, D.C., Government Printing Office, 1931.

Thoburn, Joseph B. and Muriel H. Wright. *Oklahoma, A History of the State and Its People.* 3 vols. New York, Lewis Historical Publishing Company, 1929.

Wright, Muriel H. *A Guide to the Indian Tribes of Oklahoma.* Norman, University of Oklahoma Press, 1951.

Young, Mary Elizabeth. *Redskins, Ruffleshirts, and Rednecks: Indian Allotments in Alabama and Mississippi, 1830–1860.* Norman, University of Oklahoma Press, 1961.

Unpublished Sources

Brown, Walter L. "Albert Pike." Unpublished Ph.D. dissertation, University of Texas, 1955.

Index

45–52; defeated as district chief, 55; personal qualities and appearance of, 56, 63, 89, 90–94, 124, 203–204; as superintendent of Choctaw Academy, 57–61; first service as tribal delegate, 61–62, 67–69; meets Charles Dickens, 63; educational architect, 64–67; speculator in removal claims, 70–80; represents orphan claimants, 73–76; investments of, 80–81; inept management of educational funds, 81–83; superintendent of tribal schools, 81–82; agricultural activities of, 83–85, 95; as a husband and father, 85–88, 134; appointed to delegation of 1853, 97; contract with Pike, 98; rebates to, 98, 102, 106–109, 116, 132, 151–55, 182, 206, 210; Cochrane contract with, 102–103; and Arkansas-Choctaw boundary dispute, 110, 181–82; and Senate recognition of net proceeds, 111–14; and the Doaksville constitution, 115–16; and initial funding of net proceeds claim, 117–21; and partial payment of net proceeds, 122–24; collects net proceeds fee, 128–34; as a Civil War civilian, 134–35; loyalty to the United States, 135; elected as chief, 136; chieftaincy of (domestic affairs), 136–39, 148–49; chieftaincy of (diplomatic), 139–45; surrender of, 141; at Fort Smith conference, 143–45; contract with Black, 157–66; opposes Latrobe, Cooper, and delegation of 1866, 160–66; net proceeds claim pre-eminent to, 163–65; co-operates with Cooper, 166ff.; contracts with George W. Wright, 168, 194–95; seeks release of bonds, 169–80; contracts with McKee and Blunt, 170; seeks confirmation of authority, 174–76; will of, 174; another contract with Pike, 177; opposes survey and allotment, 182–84; opposes territorial government, 184; opposes railroads, 184–86; views on the freedmen, 186–89; and

the Leased District, 188–89; responds to Banfield's adverse report, 190–92; assisted by Shanks' report, 191–96; net proceeds authority affirmed, 196–98; insurance contracts of, 198; challenged by Cole, 200–202; near bankruptcy of, 204–205; symbol of net proceeds claim, 205ff.; contract with Luce, 206; death of, 209; legacy of, 210–12; funeral of, 211; *see also* net proceeds claim

Pitchlynn, Peter Perkins, Jr. (son of Peter Pitchlynn): 85, 86, 87, 88, 94

Pitchlynn, Rhoda (daughter of Peter Pitchlynn): 86, 87, 88, 90, 91

Pitchlynn, Rhoda (sister of Peter Pitchlynn): 6

Pitchlynn, Rhoda (the first Mrs. John Pitchlynn): 6

Pitchlynn, Rhoda (the first Mrs. Peter Pitchlynn): 22, 85–86

Pitchlynn, Sampson (son of Peter Pitchlynn): 94

Pitchlynn, Silas (brother of Peter Pitchlynn): 6

Pitchlynn, Sophia (daughter of Peter Pitchlynn): 94

Pitchlynn, Sophia (the second Mrs. John Pitchlynn and the mother of Peter Pitchlynn): 6, 19, 79

Pitchlynn, Thomas (brother of Peter Pitchlynn): 6, 89, 106

Pitchlynn, Tommy (son of Peter Pitchlynn): 94, 134

Plains Indian tribes: 100, 103, 139, 143

Plymouth Bluff, Miss.: 7, 19, 51

Polk, James K.: 68, 75

Polygamy: 22

Pomeroy, Samuel C.: 204

Post of Arkansas: 43

Presbyterian Board of Foreign Missions: 65–66

Princeton University: 67

Prophet, the: 33

Pugh, George E.: 121

Pushmataha: 10, 11, 14, 17, 25, 62, 211

Pushmataha District: 44

of which *Peter Pitchlynn: Chief of the Choctaws* is Volume 117, was inaugurated in 1932 by the University of Oklahoma Press, and has as its purpose the reconstruction of American Indian civilization by presenting aboriginal, historical, and contemporary Indian life. The following list is complete as of the date of publication of this volume.

1. *Forgotten Frontiers:* A Study of the Spanish Indian Policy of Don Juan Bautista de Anza, Governor of New Mexico, 1777–1787. Translated and edited by Alfred Barnaby Thomas.
2. Grant Foreman. *Indian Removal:* The Emigration of the Five Civilized Tribes of Indians.
3. John Joseph Mathews. *Wah'Kon-Tah:* The Osage and the White Man's Road.
4. Grant Foreman. *Advancing the Frontier, 1830–1860.*
5. John H. Seger. *Early Days Among the Cheyenne and Arapahoe Indians.* Edited by Stanley Vestal. Out of print.
6. Angie Debo. *The Rise and Fall of the Choctaw Republic.*
7. Stanley Vestal. *New Sources of Indian History, 1850–1891:* A Miscellany. Out of print.
8. Grant Foreman. *The Five Civilized Tribes.*
9. *After Coronado:* Spanish Exploration Northeast of New Mexico, 1696–1727. Translated and edited by Alfred Barnaby Thomas.
10. Frank G. Speck. *Naskapi:* The Savage Hunters of the Labrador Peninsula. Out of print.
11. Elaine Goodale Eastman. *Pratt:* The Red Man's Moses. Out of print.
12. Althea Bass. *Cherokee Messenger:* A Life of Samuel Austin Worcester.
13. Thomas Wildcat Alford. *Civilization.* As told to Florence Drake. Out of print.
14. Grant Foreman. *Indians and Pioneers:* The Story of the American Southwest Before 1830.
15. George E. Hyde. *Red Cloud's Folk:* A History of the Oglala Sioux Indians.
16. Grant Foreman. *Sequoyah.*
17. Morris L. Wardell. *A Political History of the Cherokee Nation, 1838–1907.* Out of print.
18. John Walton Caughey. *McGillivray of the Creeks.*
19. Edward Everett Dale and Gaston Litton. *Cherokee Cavaliers:* Forty Years of Cherokee History as Told in the Correspondence of the Ridge-Watie-Boudinot Family.
20. Ralph Henry Gabriel. *Elias Boudinot, Cherokee, and His America.* Out of print.
21. Karl N. Llewellyn and E. Adamson Hoebel. *The Cheyenne Way:* Conflict and Case Law in Primitive Jurisprudence.
22. Angie Debo. *The Road to Disappearance.*

The paper on which this book is printed bears the watermark of the University of Oklahoma Press and has an effective life of at least three hundred years.

UNIVERSITY OF OKLAHOMA PRESS

NORMAN